West Virginia

A Guide to Backcountry Travel & Adventure

D1444079

West Virginia

A Guide to Backcountry Travel & Adventure

James Bannon

out there press
post office box 1173 • asheville, north carolina 28802

West Virginia:
A Guide to Backcountry Travel & Adventure

Library of Congress Catalog Card Number: 97–69894
ISBN   0–9648584–4–4

Maps drawn by: James Bannon

Cover photograph and design: James Bannon
Author photo: Morrison Giffen

Out There Press
P.O. Box 1173
Asheville, NC 28802
out_there@earthlink.com

Manufactured in the United States of America

10 9 8 7 6 5 4 3 2 1

This book is dedicated to all the individuals & organizations who work to preserve the natural habitats of West Virginia

The ridge of mountains next beyond the Blue ridge, called by us the North mountain, is of the greatest extent; for which reason they were named by the Indians the Endless mountains.

—Thomas Jefferson

Contents

Maps

Map Legend

.... Trail

.... Gated Road

.... Developed Campground

.... Primitive Campground

.... Backcountry Camping Area

.... Group Campground

.... Shelter

.... Boat Ramp

.... Interstate

.... U.S. Highway

.... State Highway

.... County Road

.... Forest Service Road

.... Ranger Station/Park Office

.... Other Building

.... State Border

.... Forest/Park Boundary

Acknowledgments

The author wishes to thank all the people who answered questions, provided information, made suggestions and recommendations, and generally assisted in the research-gathering stage of this book. Most were simply doing their jobs and didn't even realize that they were contributing to a guidebook to the West Virginia outdoors. In particular I would like to thank the employees of the Monongahela National Forest, George Washington National Forest, Jefferson National Forest, National Park Service, and the Division of Natural Resources. Without their work and dedication to the natural areas of West Virginia this book would not have been possible.

Thanks to Gene Kistler of Blue Ridge Outdoors in Fayetteville for heroically keeping the book on schedule by overnighting us the USGS topo map printed on the cover.

Thanks to Morrison Giffen for his input and efforts on this book and at Out There Press.

Thanks too to all the outdoor stores and booksellers who have been willing to take a chance on an unknown author and publishing company over the past two years, and who continue to support our efforts. They are far too numerous to name, but without them none of this would have been possible.

Personal thanks to Mary and J.D. for letting me use their home as a base camp on several of my research trips into northern West Virginia.

And last, but not least, thanks to my mother for her continuing support and encouragement. She has rescued me from dire straits more times than I care to remember.

Series Preface

Out There Press was started in 1994 with a single idea: to create guidebooks for outdoor travel and adventure that are as comprehensive and easy-to-use as possible. While there were plenty of other outdoor guides already available, we found that most focused on either a single region or a single activity. If you're like us, though, you're a generalist rather than a specialist when it comes to the outdoors. One weekend you might backpack deep into mountainous backcountry with a fly rod and reel in search of brook trout in remote headwater creeks. The next you might decide to kayak across a sound and set up camp on a deserted barrier island. The one after that...well, you get the point.

Each book in the *Guide to Backcountry Travel & Adventure* series covers an entire state, end to end, up and down. If there's a significant parcel of land where you can hike, camp, mountain bike, paddle, or fish, it's included. And all the information you need to decide where to go and how to get there is included too. Important facts like precise directions, location of trailheads, boat launches, and campground opening and closing dates. What we leave out of each guide may be as important as what we put in, too. It seems to us that "adventure" travel ought to be primarily about discovery and the unpredictable. About *not* knowing what's around every corner, down every river, or up every trail. Put simply, these guides are tools to get you there, not highly descriptive, colorful travelogues meant to bring the outdoor experience into your living room.

As you use this guide, keep in mind that things change. All the information included was accurate as of the time the book went to press. And while odds are very good that the lake we suggest for a paddling trip will still be there as you read this, the trail that once skirted its shoreline or the campground that overlooked it may have been rerouted or closed. Which brings us to a final request: if on your travels you notice that some of the information in the book is inaccurate, please drop us a line and let us know. One other thing: all our books are written by avid outdoor enthusiasts, who spend months in the backcountry pursuing their passions and gathering information so we can publish the most accurate guides possible. See ya out there.

Asheville
1997

Abbreviations

4WD	four wheel drive
AT	*Appalachian Trail*
CCC	Civilian Conservation Corps
CO	county route
E	east
ft	foot/feet
FS	Forest Service
hr	hour
jct	junction
I	interstate
L	left
mi	mile(s)
mtn	mountain
N	north
NF	national forest
NHP	national historical park
NR	national river
NRA	national recreation area
R	right
RD	ranger district
RV	recreational vehicle
rec	recreation
RS	ranger station
S	south
SA	Scenic Area
SF	state forest
SP	state park
SR	secondary road
USFS	United States Forest Service
USGS	United States Geological Survey
W	west
WMA	Wildlife Management Area

Introduction

Nicknamed the "Mountain State," West Virginia is a land of ridges and valleys, of mountain folds and narrow hollows. Even in the Ohio River Valley, where the forces of geology have had a less dramatic impact than elsewhere in the state, a flat horizon or long stretch of straight highway is just about impossible to come by. And the mountains and coal fields of the southwestern corner are so rugged that ridges and valleys seem to define entire worlds. The earth here is wrinkled, and the state's geography has kept it relatively rural and relatively isolated. For backcountry enthusiasts and adventure travelers, this translates into a state that is becoming rapidly known as the East's outdoor playground. The state's four distinct seasons mean year-round outdoor recreation and an exhilarating variety of activities to pursue. You can hike or backpack for days or weeks on the vast trail network; mountain bike on rail-trails and backcountry single-track that have earned the state a reputation as the fat tire mecca of the East; fly fish for trout on cool mountain creeks amidst stunning natural beauty; kayak or canoe on whitewater rivers that churn through magnificent gorges; rock climb on the 900-foot spires of Seneca Rocks; or in winter cross-country ski on hundreds of miles or roads, railroad grades, and trails. In short, you could spend a year in the West Virginia backcountry and only begin to understand its riches.

Located near the geographic center of the "East," West Virginia is both a small state and a large one. In terms of area, it ranks 41st, covering just over 24,000 square miles. But draw a line from its eastern tip to its western edge, or from the top of the northern panhandle to the bottom of the state, and it covers 275 and 240 miles, respectively. Another contradictory aspect of the state is its location. Does it belong to the East? The eastern panhandle borders Maryland and is just an hour outside of Washington, DC. Midwest? The Ohio River forms most of its western border. North? West Virginia separated from Virginia in 1863 over the issue of slavery and other differences it had with the ruling powers of the tidewater region. South? Its capitol is south of Washington, DC and only slightly north of Richmond. In fact, there is a little of all these regions in the character of West Virginia.

For West Virginia, geography has been destiny in other ways too. The vast forests and rich coal deposits were central to the state's early economy and continue to play a significant role. More advanced economic development came slowly, impeded by the difficulty in carving transportation routes out of the mountainous terrain. Even though the Allegheny Mountains are technically limited to West Virginia's eastern half, all corners of the state help it earn its nickname. The state's western half is characterized by the major valley of the Ohio River and the rivers, stream, and creeks that drain into it, but even here the land folds and buckles in a seemingly endless series of undulations. While this has been a hurdle for industry to struggle to cross, for fans of undeveloped backcountry it has been a boon. Most of West Virginia remains wonderfully rural, and it's still possible to drive for hours without encountering a single mall, fast food restaurant, or other instance of standard American commerce. In fact, in most regions of West Virginia, the distinction between backcountry and civilization, between city and country, is just a little more blurred than it is elsewhere in the East.

Climate & Weather

All of West Virginia lies in the North American temperate zone, although climate varies considerably across the state. The four seasons are distinct and all are roughly equal in length. Temperatures are warmest in the Ohio River Valley, where summertime highs reach into the mid-80°s and wintertime lows rarely drop below 20°. Annual snowfall accumulations are in the 1–2 foot range. As you move east into the mountains temperatures drop considerably, particularly in winter and at the highest elevations. Here temperatures can average 10° cooler or more on a day-to-day basis. Annual snowfall measures more than 10 ft in many locations. Precipitation is relatively consistent across the state and throughout the year; May, June, and July are the wettest months. Local topography, however, can translate into extreme differences in precipitation due to the "shadow effect," where the western slope of a mountain usually receives considerably more rain and snow than the eastern slope. Weather at the highest elevations is less stable than elsewhere in the state, with sudden storms, strong winds, and unpredictable temperature changes all common.

For backcountry travelers, the four distinct seasons translate into constant variety. Summers are pleasantly cool in the mountains, but can be hot and sticky at the lower elevations. During fall the crisp air and brilliant autumn foliage bring people to the mountains in droves. In winter cold temperatures and heavy snowfall means skiing and the extra care and equipment needed to avoid hypothermia when in the backcountry. While spring comes late to the mountains, the brilliant blooms of wildflowers, rhododendron, and laurel make it a popular time to be outdoors.

The Backcountry

Almost 1.5 million acres of publicly owned land are included in this book. Most of these are administered by federal, state, and local governments, although a few of the areas are privately owned. Although management objectives differ in the various jurisdictions, outdoor recreation plays a significant role in all of the areas featured. Among these areas are national park service lands, national forests, state forests, state parks, state wildlife management areas, and US Army Corps of Engineers lakes.

National Forests

In acreage and facilities, the national forests account for the largest percentage of public lands open to outdoor recreation in West Virginia. Although sections of the Jefferson National Forest and George Washington National Forest extend into the state from Virginia, the vast majority of land belongs to the Monongahela National Forest, which encompasses 909,084 acres in the Allegheny Mountains. The forest is divided into six different ranger districts, which are managed to serve a variety of (often competing) objectives. The most controversial of these in recent years has been commercial logging, which taxpayers subsidize to the tune of millions of dollars annually. Outdoor recreation, on the other hand, is the fastest growing use of the forests, with millions of visitors coming each year to enjoy the trails, roads, rivers, and natural beauty. Wildlife management is another objective, and in fall and winter hunting is the most popular outdoor activity on the Monongahela NF. Special designations such as wilderness or primitive backcountry generally restrict use of the forest to non-motorized low-impact travel. Slightly less than 10% of the Monongahela NF has been set aside as a designated wilderness.

All of the NF areas included in this guide offer outstanding opportunities for backcountry recreation. Individual locations range from developed recreation areas with facilities such a swimming beaches on small lakes, bath houses, and picnic areas, to designated wildernesses where the only signs of human presence are the primitive hiking trails. For additional information contact the Forest Supervisor, Monongahela National Forest, 200 Sycamore

St, Elkins, WV 26241, 304/636-1800; Forest Supervisor, George Washington National Forest, 101 N Main St, Harrisonburg, VA 22801, 540/564-8300; or Forest Supervisor, Jefferson National Forest, 5162 Valley Pointe Parkway, Roanoke, VA 24019, 540/265-6054.

National Parks

Three of the areas included in this guide are overseen by the National Park Service—Harpers Ferry National Historic Park, New River Gorge National River, and Gauley River National Recreation Area. Although the areas are all different, each is part of the nation's historical and natural heritage. Harpers Ferry NHP preserves the town at the confluence of the Potomac and Shenandoah Rivers that was the site notorious abolitionist John Brown's raid. The area's natural beauty has been drawing comments from visitors dating back at least to Jefferson. Even more impressive are the gorges that the New and Gauley Rivers flow through. Outdoor recreation is the primary focus at both, which have gained fame in recent years as two of the best white-water rivers in the East. Information about all NPS parks is available on line at www.nps.org

State Parks

West Virginia has thirty-eight state parks in all, spread throughout the state. Since most are smaller than the NF or NPS areas—they range in size from 4 acres to just over than 10,000—they're managed for outdoor recreation on a more modest scale.. Not all are suitable for the outdoor activities included in this book, and therefore not all have been included. Although backcountry recreation is a focus at the majority of the parks, the level of development and range of facilities varies considerably from park to park. At some, full-scale resort facilities such as golf courses, tennis courts, and lodges are found. Others are largely primitive natural areas with few facilities at all. Two are rail-trails, long, skinny parks that are simply a trail where once there was a railroad corridor. All parks feature at least some level of development. Most have campgrounds; picnic areas and swimming pools are also common. The parks are ideally suited to families or to those wishing to explore a backcountry area that's easily accessible and doesn't require as much preparation or independence as an excursion on the national forests. Park hours are from 6 am to 10 pm. Alcohol is not allowed at most and pets must be kept on a leash. For more information on West Virginia's state parks, contact the West Virginia Division of Natural Resources, Parks & Recreation, State

Capitol Complex, Charleston, WV 25305-0662; 800/CALL WVA; wvweb.com/www.

The Allegheny Trail

The 300-mile *Allegheny Trail* is the longest trail in West Virginia. It was modeled after the *Appalachian Trail*, which is on WV soil for only a short distance in the Harpers Ferry area. Following a route from Pennsylvania to Virginia, the *Allegheny Trail* passes through some of the most remote backcountry and spectacular natural scenery in West Virginia's mountain region. It was constructed by volunteers and is managed by the West Virginia Scenic Trails Association. Since its route runs through so many of the areas covered in this guide, no separate section is devoted to the trail alone. If you want to follow long sections, or even the entire length, using this book, start by looking it up in the index. Another option is to purchase the *Hiking Guide to the Allegheny Trail* for $8, a comprehensive guide that includes descriptions, maps, and all access points. It's published by the West Virginia Scenic Trails Association, P.O. Box 4042, Charleston, WV 25364.

Wildlife Management Areas

Almost 50 wildlife management areas are scattered across the state, most in areas not covered by national forest. Their primary purpose is to preserve tracts where wildlife, and game animals in particular, have viable habitats. Most recreational use at the WMAs comes from hunters on strictly managed seasonal game hunts. A few of these areas offer hikers, backpackers, paddlers and anglers opportunities for outdoor travel that they may have overlooked. Since hunting only takes place in fall and winter, for much of the year these areas are virtually deserted. Conditions on the preserves are primitive, with few amenities and none of the developed recreation facilities found in the parks and national forests. Even signed hiking trails are few. This primitive state offers hikers the challenge of traveling through backcountry without the customary advantages of clearly marked trails. For information about the WMAs contact the WV Division of Natural Resources, Wildlife Resources Section, 1900 Kanawha Boulevard, East, Charleston, WV 25305; 304/558-2771.

State Forests

West Virginia's nine state forests are scattered throughout the state. They range in size from 5,130 to 12,713 acres. The forests are managed for timber extraction, resource conservation, education, study, and recreation. Similar to the state parks but with more acreage, less development, and fewer visitors, the state forests offer outstanding opportunities for primitive backcountry travel. Most have substantial trail networks open to hikers, mountain bikers, and cross-country skiers. In addition to designated trails, miles of forestry roads add to the hiking and riding potential. Other options for outdoor recreation include camping, canoeing, kayaking, fishing, and rock climbing. For information contact the West Virginia Division of Natural Resources, Parks & Recreation, State Capitol Complex, Charleston, WV 25305-0662; 800/CALL WVA; wvweb.com/www

Other Natural Areas

Aside from the public landholdings described above, several private resort areas offer backcountry travel extensive enough to merit inclusion in this book. Since these areas are privately owned, visiting them is considerably different from visiting the public areas. In most instances a fee is required (although that is becoming increasingly likely on the public lands as well). More importantly, strict regulations are usually enforced regarding what activities are permitted in the areas. Also, since these are commercial resort areas, the backcountry experience they offer is somewhat less pristine than it is on many of the national forest or state forest areas.

Backcountry Travel

At first glance, backcountry travel doesn't seem like it should require any specialized knowledge. At its most basic it's no more than walking in the woods, along the beach, or through some other natural habitat. While there is an element of truth to that, it's also true that every year dozens of adventurers get themselves into situations from which they have to be rescued by others. These operations risk lives and cost considerable amounts of money. In addition to these well-publicized misadventures, there are the more mundane mishaps that endanger outdoor enthusiasts and the natural world they value. Although each of the five activities featured in this book requires at least some specialized knowledge and preparation unique to it, what follows is a basic outline of helpful information and potential hazards common to all backcountry pursuits.

How much preparation you need to do before setting out on your trip and how much you need to bring in the way of supplies will of course depend on a number of factors, including time of year, location, length of trip, and planned activities. Short, summertime hikes require little more than the clothes on your back and a water bottle. Longer trips and even short wintertime trips require more involved preparation and additional supplies. The items in the first list below should be included on all but very short hikes on well-marked, heavily-traveled trails. Items from both lists should be included on any trip that involves at least one night spent in the backcountry.

The 10 Essentials

Topographic Map	Compass
Warm Clothing	Adequate Food
Flashlight	Fire Starter & Matches
First Aid Kit	Water
Knife	Whistle

10 More Essentials

Insect Repellent	Sunscreen
Sunglasses	Rain Gear
Hat with brim	Hiking Boots
Camera	50–100-ft Nylon Cord
Backpack or Daypack	Tent or Other Shelter

Clothing

During the past quarter-century, a revolution in outdoor clothing has occurred with the invention of waterproof-breathable materials such as Gore-Tex and synthetic fabrics that wick moisture away from the skin. Utilizing these technologies, clothing is now made for the most extreme climatic conditions, from the sub-zero temperatures of the poles and the planet's highest peaks to the hot, humid soup of the tropical rain forests. Fortunately, West Virginia's climate is pleasantly in between from these two extremes. For much of the year, in fact, temperatures are moderate enough that specialized clothing isn't really necessary, except for rain gear, which should always be carried on any trip of more than an hour or two. During the colder months, however, more attention to dress is required.

In outfitting yourself for backcountry travel, there are two points to keep in mind: 1) comfortable footwear is the single most important piece of equipment; and 2) Clothing should keep you comfortable and dry under the worst weather conditions you're likely to encounter. This means carrying raingear on almost every outing. In the mountains especially, storms can seem to come out of nowhere, materializing from blue skies in a matter of hours. The large majority of backcountry tragedies involve hypothermia, the condition that results when the body's core temperature drops below a critical level. Wet clothes, fatigue, and cool or cold temperatures are usually the main culprits. In general, avoid wearing cotton, except during the hottest months. Cotton retains moisture and is extremely slow to dry, which means that if you're wearing jeans and a sweatshirt and get caught out in a rainstorm, you can expect to stay wet until you can change clothes. In winter, wearing the right clothes can mean the difference between misery (not to mention frostbite) and comfort. An appendix at the back of this book lists all of the outdoor stores in the state. They can help you outfit yourself so that your next outing will be an enjoyable one.

Water

It's no longer safe to assume that water taken from rivers, lakes and streams is safe to drink. Regardless of how crystal clear the water of a cool mountain creek may look, odds are good that it contains bacteria and viruses. Giardia, a microscopic organism, has become the number one culprit in illnesses resulting from drinking untreated water. If you're going to drink surface water, you'll need to treat it first. There are currently three main methods of treatment. The oldest, and probably safest, is to boil the water for several minutes (some sources recommend 10 minutes). This is the method usually recommended by park and forest rangers. Another method, increasingly popular with backpackers, is to filter the water through a portable water filter. Many different models are available; most cost between $50 and $150 and weigh less than 20 ounces. If you choose this method, be sure to buy a filter that eliminates organisms as small as 0.5 microns. One that also eliminates bacteria is preferable to one that doesn't. The third method is to treat the water with iodine tablets. The tablets impart a taste to the water that many find unpleasant. This is probably the least effective method, particularly if the water is very cold.

Hypothermia

Hypothermia is the condition that results when the body's core temperature drops below normal. If untreated, it is fatal. Symptoms include disorientation, lack of coordination, slurred speech, shivering and fatigue. To treat a victim, change him into warm, dry clothes, give him warm drinks, and put him in a sleeping bag. Building a fire can also help, as can using your own body temperature to raise his or hers. In most cases of hypothermia, a combination of cold temperatures and wet clothes are responsible. The best way to prevent the condition is to be prepared. Bring clothes that will keep you dry and warm during the worst weather you might encounter.

Snakes and Insects

Two species of poisonous snakes inhabit West Virginia—the timber rattlesnake and the copperhead. There is little reason to fear these snakes, as they are nonaggressive unless provoked. The greatest danger is in stepping on one or placing a careless hand on one without realizing it. When hiking in snake territory, always be aware of where you're putting your hands and feet. A snakebite kit, available at most outdoor stores, should be part of your first-aid kit.

Although insects are considerably less dangerous than snakes, they can turn an otherwise pleasant trip into a maddening ritual of swatting, itching, and cursing. Mosquitoes and flies are the most numerous and bothersome, particularly near standing water and in large open areas at the highest elevations. A good repellent should always be included in your pack between the months of May and October.

Bears

The black bear is West Virginia's state animal. Their range is primarily limited to the mountains, where there are sufficient forested lands to provide them with the room they need to roam. Their numbers are relatively small and the odds of seeing one of these shy creatures are fairly low in most areas. Evidence of them, however, is quite abundant, particularly in wilderness and backcountry areas where they make a habit of chewing trail signs. Black bears are not naturally aggressive toward humans, and they should not be feared. The few recorded instances of black bear attacks on people have almost always been the result of the bear having been acclimatized to people from food or garbage, a camper sleeping with food in his or her tent, or a bear being threatened. If you're camping in bear country, be sure to store all food in a manner so that bears (or other animals) cannot get at it. If no food storage container is available, suspend the food between the limbs of two trees at least 10 ft off the ground and 5 ft from the nearest tree branch. Do not under any circumstances sleep with food in your tent.

Getting Lost

If you become lost while in the backcountry, the most important thing to do is to avoid panicking. Wherever you are, stop. Relax for a minute or two. Try to remember how you got where you are. If you're on a trail, backtrack and look for familiar landmarks. If it's getting dark or you're injured or exhausted, don't move. The universal distress signal is three of anything—shouts, whistles, flashes of light (a mirror works for this). If you've left or lost the trail, follow a creek or drainage downstream. Eventually it will lead to a road or trail. The best way to avoid getting lost is always to carry a topo map and compass and to know how to use them. Also, be sure to leave plans of your trip with a friend or relative. Give them specific locations so they'll know where to send rescuers if you don't return on time.

Hunting

Hunting is one of the most popular outdoor activities in West Virginia. White-tailed deer, wild turkey, ruffed grouse, black bear, and small mammals are all hunted in the state. Hunting seasons vary among species and from region to region, but generally the larger game species can be hunted with guns for short periods in fall and winter. Hunting is permitted on most of the areas covered in this book. If you're going to travel in an area where hunting is permitted in fall or winter, be sure to wear at least one article of blaze orange clothing. Deer gun season varies by region, but it's advised that you avoid backcountry travel during these periods—unless of course you're a hunter. For information on hunting licenses and seasons contact the West Virginia Division of Natural Resources, Wildlife Resources Section, 1900 Kanawha Blvd, East, Charleston, WV 25305; 304/558-2771.

The No-Trace Ethic

The no-trace ethic is neatly summarized in the oft-quoted phrase, "Leave only footprints, take only photographs." Where once the untraveled portions of the country were true wildernesses, unvisited regions where the principal dangers were to the traveler, today the situation is reversed. When we speak of wilderness now, we mean a designated area protected by law from development and set aside for natural resource protection and backcountry recreation. The greatest dangers are to the wilderness, not to those who visit. Far from the mysteries and dangers that the word wilderness conjures, these places too often show abundant signs of human presence. Littering is of course inexcusable anywhere. But other, less obtrusive signs of human impact can also diminish the quality of a trip into the backcountry—and of the backcountry itself.

Campfires are first among these unsightly blemishes. Although the appeal of an open fire is undeniable, so too is its impact. Fire rings and the tramped-down, scarred earth that inevitably spreads around them remind us that we are not in the wilds, but are merely following in the footsteps of many others. Burning firewood deprives the soil and forest floor of important nutrients. Whenever possible, a portable camp stove is preferable. It may lack the visceral, romantic appeal of an open fire, but it preserves resources that are unfortunately jeopardized by our numbers. If you do build a campfire, keep it small and contained within an already existing fire ring. If no fire ring exists, build your fire on soil cleared of vegetation; a fire ring is not necessary. When you break camp, make sure the fire is extinguished; scatter the fire ring and any remaining wood and return the surrounding area to a natural state.

In choosing a campsite, it's best to select a site that already exists, but has not deteriorated into an obviously overused state. Minimize impact in making camp. Do not alter the site by digging trenches or creating log benches. When you break camp, return the area to a natural state by scattering leaves, twigs and other forest debris over the area.

To dispose of human waste, dig a hole six inches deep at least 100 feet from trails, campsites and water sources. After use, fill the hole in with soil and lightly tramp it down. Toilet paper should be burned or packed out.

Anything you bring with you into the backcountry should be packed out. When hiking, avoid using shortcuts on switchbacks.

Using this Book

This guidebook has two main purposes: 1) To catalog and describe all of the major backcountry areas in West Virginia open to the public for recreation; and 2) To provide all the information you need to decide where to go, to get there once you do decide, and to know what to expect when you arrive. The book is divided into various backcountry areas covered in three main sections—The Potomac Highlands & Eastern Panhandle, The Greenbrier & New River Valleys, and The Ohio River Valley. Within each section the areas are arranged geographically, from north to south and from east to west, with a few minor exceptions. This layout is intended to make it easy to locate an area geographically and to enable you to plan trips where you visit more than one area.

Each listing begins with a description of the backcountry area. Information such as size, location, major natural features, outdoor recreation potential, and open dates is included here. The main purpose of these descriptions, however, is to convey a general sense of the area—whether it's isolated, roadless wilderness; an easily accessible park frequently crowded on weekends; a busy recreational lake; or a remote barrier island where water is scarce and mosquitoes abundant. Also included is the nearest town or city and the direction in which it lies.

A number of the areas have accompanying maps. These maps are intended to give a very general overview of an area. They are for illustration purposes only and should not be used for navigation or backcountry travel.

contact: Each entry includes the address and phone number of the administrative office that manages the area. This is your best source for additional information. If you have questions about local conditions or are uncertain about opening dates or times, this is the number to call. For all areas where there's a main listing followed by sublistings (i.e. national park areas and national forest ranger districts) the address and phone number are listed just once, under the main heading.

getting there: Directions to each area are from either a nearby town or city or from a major highway. All directions given in the book were checked first hand, not simply estimated from maps. Because odometer readings vary, you should start looking for turns several tenths of a mile before where they're indicated. In general there are five major types of roads in WV: interstate, US highway, WV highway, county route, and forest road.

A good road map is necessary to locate the starting point of the directions. You can buy one at any service station or get one free by calling the Division of Tourism at 800/CALL WVA. If you're going to be doing a lot of traveling in the remoter regions of West Virginia, DeLorme's *West Virginia Atlas & Gazetteer* is an excellent investment; It's a 64-page atlas with large-scale maps that are particularly useful for finding and navigating back roads. You can buy it in most outdoor stores and better bookstores.

topography: This section is intended to give you a rough idea of the type of terrain you can expect to encounter. Major geographical features—rivers, lakes, mountains, forest cover—are described, and high and low elevations are given. Trail users will find this section useful in determining the general profile and level of difficulty to expect on the trails. **maps:** A good topographic map should be considered essential equipment for backcountry travel. More specifically, this book is designed to be used with a map and compass. Maps listed under this heading are only those that have a large enough scale to be useable as topo maps for backcountry navigation. There are 3 major types of topo maps that cover the backcountry areas described in this book: The 7.5-minute series published by the United States Geologic Survey, district maps and wilderness or recreation area maps published by the USFS, and maps published by private companies that cover the state's reservoirs. USGS topo maps are listed for every area covered in the book. For areas where other maps are available, those are also listed. The list of outdoor stores at the back of this book indicates which stores sell the USGS topo maps. They are also available by mail from the USGS, Distribution Branch, Box 25286, Denver Federal Center, Denver, CO 80225.

starting out: The primary purpose of this section is to indicate what you can or must do, once at an area, before heading out into the backcountry. Facilities such as rest rooms, water, pay phones, etc. that are located in the area are always mentioned here. Also included is any on-site source of information, such as a ranger station, visitor center, or park office. If you need to obtain a permit or pay a fee, that's indicated as well.

The last paragraph of the section lists some of the more important restrictions, such as rules against alcohol use and pet regulations. Don't assume that because something isn't included here it's allowed. Complete lists of restrictions are available from the various administrative contacts.

activities: This guidebook describes West Virginia's backcountry in terms of seven major outdoor activities: mountain biking, hiking, camping, canoeing & kayaking, fishing, cross-country skiing, and rock climbing. The activities are listed in a rough sort of order, starting with the one that is the most popular at a given area and working in descending order. Although many areas are suitable for other outdoor activities, such as horseback riding,, nature study, and photography, only those seven are listed under this heading. If one or more of the other activities is a significant attraction, it's typically mentioned as part of the main description or under *starting out.*

hiking: There are almost 2,000 miles of maintained hiking trails in West Virginia. The highest concentration of trails and those that are most popular are located in the state's mountain region, particularly on the Monongahela National Forest. The state's longest trail is the *Allegheny Trail*, which crosses its namesake mountains from Pennsylvania to Virginia. An increasingly popular type of trail is the converted rail-trail. These follow abandoned railroad corridors for distances of anywhere from a mile or two to more than seventy.

Descriptions under this heading are intended to give an overview of hiking opportunities and conditions at each of the areas. Mention of individual trails is of secondary importance. An attempt has been made to indicate total trail mileage, conditions, allowed uses (other than hiking), location of trailheads, level of difficulty and any improvements, particularly bridges across rivers or streams. Mileages have been taken from administrative sources and cross-checked with maps and first-hand observation. In many instances they've been rounded to the nearest mile. With a good topo map and a compass, this section should provide you with all the information you need to take to the trails.

mountain biking: In recent years, West Virginia has gained a national and international reputation as a mountain biking destination. Indeed, one biking magazine named it the fourth best place to ride *in the world*. The large majority of trails in West Virginia are open to mountain bikers. The greatest concentration of trails is on the national forests, where only the trails in the designated wildernesses and a few special trails are closed to bikes. One of the great benefits of riding in West Virginia is the genuine cross-section of trail types and conditions available for riding. Spend enough time and you'll find everything from wide, easy rail-trails to technical single-tracks so remote, rocky, and steep that negotiating them pushes riding to its limits.

Information in this section can usually be used in conjunction with information included under *hiking*, where the most extensive trail information is often given. If mountain biking precedes hiking in an area, however, the same trail information—total mileage, location of trailheads, difficulty level, trail types, and high lights—has been included.

camping: Camping facilities have been divided into three main categories: developed campgrounds (usually referred to here as car campgrounds), primitive campgrounds that are accessible to vehicles but have facilities limited usually to pit toilets and/or hand water pumps, and backcountry camping. Dates for campground openings and closings should be considered estimates, as they vary from year to year depending on the weather, and in some areas, Congressional funding. Fees were accurate as of the fall of 1997.

kayaking/canoeing: Opportunities for paddling in West Virginia fall under two broad categories: flat water on enclosed bodies of water and whitewater rivers. The main intent of this section is to make you aware of the general conditions you can expect to encounter on a body of water and to indicate where access points are.

West Virginia is home to some of the biggest, wildest whitewater runs in the United States. Paddlers travel from all over the East and beyond to test their mettle against renowned rivers such as the Gauley, the Cheat, and the New. Although there are sections of flatwater on these rivers as well, the state's mountainous topography favors whitewater runs. Whitewater classifications, where given, are somewhat subjective, but are based on first-hand experience, general agreement among the paddling community, and official sources. The standard ratings system of class I–VI is used.

Information in this section includes put-ins and take-outs, class of whitewater, general river profile, and runnable seasons. It should not be read as a primer on paddling techniques. If you are inexperienced or uncertain about whether conditions on a particular body of water are within your capabilities, please avoid the water or seek instruction or advice from a qualified whitewater instructor. Many rivers are affected by upstream dam releases or heavy rains than can turn mild whitewater into life-threatening rapids. Always call administrative sources to check water conditions. Every year canoeists and kayakers become stranded or are seriously injured or killed because they put themselves in dangerous situations. The inevitable rescues cost money, risk lives, and give the sport of paddling a bad name.

Whitewater rafting has become a major business in West Virginia and the way most visitors get to experience the state's rivers. As a guide to independent backcountry travel and adventure, this book does not include whitewater rafting as a separate activity. A number of the outfitters listed in the appendix, however, are the state's major whitewater rafting companies.

fishing: Fishing in West Virginia can be broken down into two main categories. In the mountains brook, rainbow, and brown trout are the primary species of game fish. They inhabit the region's cool, clear creeks that provide the pure habitat they need to survive. There are approximately 1,200 miles of rivers that support populations of trout. Half of these are on the Monongahela National Forest. Anglers will find both native trout waters and hatchery supported waters.

The second major category of fishing is for warmwater species. Warmwater fish such as bass, muskellunge, tiger musky, walleye, crappie, bluegill and catfish can be found throughout most regions of the state. Smallmouth bass are a favorite game fish in some of the larger rivers of the mountains. Largemouth, white, and striped bass are frequently caught on the large lakes near the middle of the state, as are the other major game species mentioned above. The rivers and streams of the Ohio River Valley provide the other major angling destination for warmwater fish.

This section is intended primarily to list most of the major game species found in a particular body of water; to describe the most appropriate angling methods, whether from a boat, shoreline, or by wading; and to describe access. Information for trout waters is more specific, and includes stream characteristics and special regulations.

A fishing license is required to fish West Virginia's lakes, rivers, and streams. You can get one from an authorized seller at bait and tackle stores, a county clerk's office, or from the West Virginia Department of Natural Resources, Wildlife Resources Section, 1900 Kanawha Blvd, East, Charleston, WV 25305; 304/558-2771. When you get your license you'll be given a complete list of regulations, size limits, and creel limits.

rock climbing: Although only a few of the area's covered in this book feature rock climbing as an activity, they are some of the best-known and most challenging rock faces on the East Coast. Both the New River Gorge and Seneca Rocks have hundreds of routes that offer challenges to climbers of all skill levels. Information included in this section includes where the routes are, how many there are in a particular area, difficulty levels of rated climbs, and access to routes.

cross-country skiing: All regions of West Virginia receive at least moderate snowfall in winter. In the mountains, however, annual snowfall is heavy and snow is often on the ground from November to March. Accumulations of as much as ten feet occur at the higher elevations. This means that for four months out of the year the hiking and biking trails are converted to nordic ski tracks. These include specially groomed trails, roads, railroad grades, and ungroomed backcountry trails. Since most information about the trails is given under either *hiking* or *mountain biking*, this section should be read as a supplement to what's included under those.

lodging: A select number of country inns, lodges, B & Bs, and cabins have been included in this guide. They have been chosen for their rustic atmosphere, attractiveness, and proximity to the backcountry areas featured. A single place is included for most of the backcountry areas featured, although some smaller areas are without a lodging listing. Since this is first and foremost a guide to areas of undeveloped backcountry, no attempt was made to provide an exhaustive list of lodging options. The book's arrangement by geography should help you to choose between several lodging options for a general region.

The Potomac Highlands
& Eastern Panhandle

Potomac Highlands & Eastern Panhandle Regional Key Map

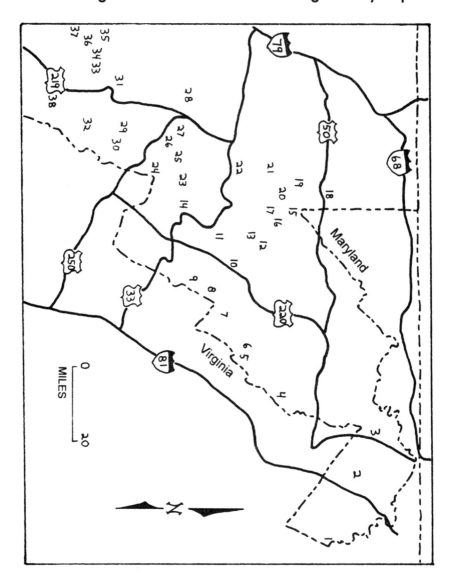

Potomac Highlands & Eastern Panhandle Areas

1. Harpers Ferry NHP
2. Sleepy Creek WMA
3. Cacapon Resort SP
4. Hawk Recreation Area
5. Wolf Gap Area
6. Trout Pond Rec Area
7. Lost River SP
8. Camp Run Rec Area
9. Brandywine Rec Area
10. Smoke Hole Area
11. Seneca Rocks Area
12. Dolly Sods Wilderness
13. Flatrock Plains/Roaring Plains Area
14. Spruce Knob Area
15. Blackwater Falls SP
16. Timberline Resort
17. Canaan Valley Resort SP
18. Cathedral SP
19. Horseshoe Rec Area
20. Canaan Mountain Area
21. Otter Creek Wilderness
22. Bickle Knob Area
23. Laurel Fork Wilderness
24. Island Rec Area
25. West Fork Rail Trail
26. Gaudineer Scenic Area
27. Cheat Mountain Area
28. Kumbrabow SF
29. Snowshoe Resort
30. Seneca SF
31. Tea Creek/Slatyfork Area
32. Middle Mountain Area
33. Cranberry Wilderness
34. Cranberry Backcountry
35. Lower Cranberry River Area
36. Summit Lake Area
37. Cranberry Tri-Rivers Trail
38. Watoga SP

Weather & Climate Readings in Pocahontas County

Month	Avg High F°	Avg Low F°	Precipitation (Inches)	Snowfall (Inches)
Jan	38	13	3.4	18.1
Feb	43	16	3.4	15.6
Mar	53	24	4.1	11.7
Apr	63	31	3.9	3.1
May	72	40	4.8	0
Jun	79	49	4.2	0
Jul	82	54	4.9	0
Aug	81	53	4.6	0
Sep	75	46	3.6	0
Oct	64	34	3.8	0.7
Nov	53	26	4.0	6.3
Dec	43	18	4.3	12.8

Introduction

The Eastern Panhandle and Potomac Highlands cover West Virginia's northeastern quadrant. It is an area defined by long mountain ridges, narrow valleys, lofty summits, and rivers that rise as minor headwater streams high on mountain slopes before powering through the major valleys on a course to either the Atlantic Ocean or Ohio River. Although this area comprises less than a third of West Virginia's total area, if contains more than half of all public lands in the state and consequently offers the largest tracts of undeveloped backcountry and the best opportunities for outdoor recreation and wilderness travel.

In the Eastern Panhandle, where the Potomac forms the border with Maryland and the land to the south of it rolls to the horizon in modest undulations, the mountains are slight and intermittent. Here just a few long ridges rise up like spines from the spread of surrounding farmland. Seen from the air or viewed on a map, an almost geometric precision becomes apparent: row after row of mountain ridge is lined up in a parallel series, all oriented northeast to southwest. The pattern is consistent throughout the Appalachian Mountains, which stretch from Maine to Alabama.

West of the panhandle the broad valleys shrink to long, narrow slots and the mountains become the dominant geographical feature. Farmland is replaced by mountain slopes blanketed in dense broadleaf and conifer forests. The Blue Ridge gives way to the Alleghenies and elevations reach 4,861 feet on Spruce Knob, the state's highest point. West of the Allegheny Front the valleys essentially vanish, and the mountain peaks rise from an elevated plateau with elevations that are mostly above 3,000 ft.

For much of the past two centuries the main natural resource to come out of these mountains has been timber. At one time or another, virtually every acre of land was logged, putting considerable stress on local ecosystems. Today almost a million acres are incorporated in the Monongahela National Forest. While commercial logging still continues, the scale is considerably smaller than in decades past and other forest uses such as wildlife habitat protection and outdoor recreation are part of the forest's management plan.

The forests encountered in this part of the state represent three different ecosystems, depending on factors such as elevation and climate. On the tops of mountains and in areas with the coolest climate, the boreal forest is dominant. In West Virginia, the red spruce is the key indicator species. Examples of this forest type can be found on Spruce Knob, in the Cranberry Wilderness, and in the

Gaudineer Scenic Area, among other places. At slightly lower elevations and common throughout the region is the northern deciduous forest. Look for sugar maple, yellow birch, Eastern hemlock, and American beech to identify this forest community. The northern hardwood forest is responsible for the spectacular autumn foliage in the West Virginia mountains. At the lower elevations is the ubiquitous oak-hickory forest, common throughout the central and southern Appalachians. Wildlife that you might encounter in these forests includes white-tailed deer, which is common throughout the state, black bear, snowshoe hare, beaver, mink, fisher, groundhog, wild turkey, and ruffed grouse, to name just a handful.

Opportunities for outdoor recreation in the region are abundant and diverse. The vast expanses of forested mountain terrain and the extensive trail networks that wind through them invite backcountry trips of a day, a weekend, or longer. Hiking and backpacking are both popular, with the designated wildernesses among the favorite destinations. Avid mountain bikers need no introduction to this part of West Virginia. Areas such as Canaan Valley, Snowshoe, Slatyfork, and the Cranberry Backcountry have reputations that extend well beyond the state's borders. All trails on the national forests, except for those in the wilderness areas, are open to bikes. In winter many of these same trails become ideal nordic ski tracks. With annual snowfall that exceeds 150 inches in some places, cross-country skiing is becoming a favorite way of exploring the backcountry during the winter months. And extreme sports enthusiasts flock to the Alleghenies for the climbing at Seneca Rocks and the dozen or so kayak/canoe/raft runs that rank at the top of any short list of the East Coast's wildest whitewater.

Perhaps the best aspect of spending time in the outdoors in this corner of West Virginia is the climate. Summer in the mountains is cool and pleasant, making it the most comfortable season for a visit. Spring and Fall offer the greatest variety and choice. Temperatures can be chilly on mountain peaks and on the Allegheny Plateau, but at lower elevations are usually pleasantly crisp. Winter is cold and snowy, time to strap on the skis and snowshoes. At all times of year keep in mind that mountain weather can be extreme and unpredictable. Sudden storms are not uncommon, and snow has occurred during every month of the year in some places.

Harpers Ferry National Historical Park

Located at the eastern edge of the state and just over an hour from Washington, D.C., Harpers Ferry is the most popular tourist destination in West Virginia. Although the natural setting at the confluence of the Potomac and Shenandoah Rivers is spectacular—particularly in autumn, when the hills and bluffs explode in a colorful display—and caused Thomas Jefferson to declare the sight "worthy of a voyage across the Atlantic", it is the town's central role in American history that draws most visitors. Although the abolitionist John Brown's name is more inextricably linked to the city than any other, the list of visitors to the area in the late 18th and early 19th century reads like a who's who of the nation's first 100 years. George Washington, Thomas Jefferson, Merriweather Lewis, Robert E. Lee, and Abraham Lincoln all feature in the city's history in one way or another.

The centerpiece of the park, which spreads beyond the city limits into Maryland and Virginia, is the historic district known as Lower Town. Beyond the marvelously preserved buildings and cobblestone streets, however, backcountry enthusiasts will find the rushing waters of the Shenandoah and Potomac and the rocky bluffs that overlook them much as they were when the region was still a wilderness. The park provides a perfect setting for a visit that combines a glimpse into America's past with outdoor recreation. The *Appalachian Trail* passes right through town, and a couple of other hiking trails allow further exploration of the town's wooded environs. Whitewater enthusiasts know the stretch of the Shenandoah above its confluence with the Potomac as one of the most scenic short runs in the state. And anglers can wade these waters, casting for smallmouth and largemouth bass.

Services and facilities are available in Harper's Ferry.

contact: Superintendent, Harper's Ferry NHP, PO Box 65, Harper's Ferry, WV 25425; 304/535-6371; www.nps.gov/hafe.

getting there: The visitor center is located on US-340 1.5 mi W of the bridge across the Shenandoah River. Trail and river access is also from a parking area on Shenandoah St: just W of the bridge turn R and go 0.1 mi.

topography: The park sits at the confluence of the Shenandoah and Potomac Rivers. Steep bluffs rise from the rivers on all sides, creating much of the dramatic setting. Outside of the town itself, a forest of hardwoods and conifers covers much of the park. Elevations are between 240 ft on the water and 1,448 ft at Maryland Heights. **maps:** USGS Harpers Ferry.

starting out: All visits to the NHP should begin at the visitor center, where a $5 admission fee is charged (unless you're arriving via foot on the *AT*). Inside you can pick up maps and brochures about the park. Rest rooms and water are there too. Hours are 8 AM to 7 PM daily.

activities: Hiking, Canoeing/Kayaking, Fishing, Camping.

hiking: Although there are also several short trails, the main hiking attraction in the NHP is the *Appalachian Trail,* which passes right through the heart of the historic district, briefly forgoing forest footpaths for well worn cobblestones and crooked steps. Near the trail's midpoint between Georgia and Maine, Harpers Ferry is home to the Appalachian Trail Conference (located on the corner of Jackson and Washington Streets), the organization that oversees and maintains America's most famous and beloved trail. From the N, the *AT* enters both the NHP and WV on a bridge across the Potomac River. From there it winds briefly through the historic buildings of Lower Town before entering the forested bluffs that overlook the Shenandoah River. The views from this part of the trail are excellent, particularly from Jefferson's Rock. The trail briefly rejoins civilization to cross the Shenandoah on a bridge before turning S and following the state line with VA for about 18 mi to just N of Snickers Gap in Jefferson Co. The trail sports the familiar white bar blazes, and a million footsteps keep the trail clearly defined and easy to follow. Hiking is mostly easy to moderate along this stretch. Access is either from Lower Town of from the parking area just W of the bridge described under *getting there.*

The other main trail in the park is the 1.5-mi *Loudon Heights Trail.* A spur trail that connects to the *AT,* it leads through serene woodlands to a scenic overlook above the confluence of the rivers. Hiking is moderate. Access is from the *AT,* where it joins the WV/VA state line and turns SW. A free map with topo contours is available at the visitor center.

For additional information about the *AT* contact the Appalachian Trail Conference, PO Box 807, Harpers Ferry, WV 25425-0807; 304/535-6331.

canoeing/kayaking: The park is located at the upstream confluence of 2 of the most storied rivers in early American history, the Potomac and Shenandoah. Not only do the rivers come together to frame the historic town, but West Virginia, Virginia, and Maryland meet as well. Since both rivers leave WV at Harpers Ferry, the park serves as the last take-out for paddle trips that begin upstream on either river. (The Potomac is entirely in Maryland, so it isn't covered here).

The 7-mi stretch of the Shenandoah from below the dam in Millville to just above the confluence with the Potomac is one of the most scenic and fun short whitewater runs in WV. The wide river drops down over a long series of ledges beneath cliffs, bluffs, and heavily forested mountainsides. The difficulty of the run depends on the water level, with rapids in the class I-II range during normal and low water, but rising to class IV+ when the water is up. The put-in is located on CO-27 in Millville. Take-out is river L just past the US-340 bridge (park at the area described above under *getting there*). Or if you'd rather paddle past the park and float a mile of the Potomac, take out at the Potomac Wayside on the VA side of the US-340 bridge (the one that crosses into MD, *not* WV) 1 mi below the confluence of the 2 rivers.

fishing: Fishing in the area is on the Shenandoah River, which has populations of largemouth and smallmouth bass. Although the river flows through some beautiful primitive countryside above the park, anglers should keep in mind that the primary purpose of the NHP itself is historical. The best access is from the parking area on Shenandoah St, which is a little upstream from the often congested Lower Town area. From there it's just a short walk to the river. Wading is the best method for fishing the river, though conditions of course vary with the water level.

camping: There are no developed campgrounds in the NHP and backcountry camping is not permitted within park boundaries. If you're determined to backpack, your best bet is to hike on the *AT* either N or S of the park. Since the park is relatively small, it's a short hike in either direction to suitable camping areas.

Sleepy Creek Wildlife Management Area

This large wilderness area (almost 23,000 acres) encompasses a pair of the long, narrow mountain ridges that rise from the broad valleys of the eastern panhandle. The ridges of Sleepy Creek Mountain and Third Hill Mountain are forested with hardwoods and conifers, providing an extensive refuge for wildlife in a region of the state that is primarily agricultural. Although most visitors to the WMA are hunters—white-tailed deer, wild turkey, and ruffed grouse are abundant—and anglers, other backcountry enthusiasts will not be disappointed. At the center of the WMA is Sleepy Creek Lake, a 205-acre impoundment that is serene and stunning when autumn turns the surrounding mountain slopes yellow, orange, and red. Hikers will find a large trail network on blazed trails and primitive roadways, anchored by a 20-mile stretch of the *Big Blue Trail*. Mountain bikes are well suited to exploring the WMA's roads, both gated and open to vehicles. For overnight stays, a (very) primitive car campground is spread out over 4 different areas. Located about 90 minutes from Washington, D.C., Sleepy Creek WMA offers the largest tract of backcountry amidst the scenic farms and small towns of the eastern panhandle.

Martinsburg (E) and Berkeley Springs (W) are the closest towns.

contact: Division of Natural Resources, 1 Depot St, Romney, WV 26757; 304/822-3551.

getting there: From the jct of WV-9 and CO-7 in Hedgesville, turn S onto CO-7 and go 6.8 mi to CO-7/9. Turn R and go 1.5 mi to the WMA entrance, where the pavement ends.

topography: Sleepy Creek Mtn and Third Hill Mountain are long NE–SW ridges that frame the WMA. Steepest terrain is on the W slope of the former. Between the mountains, the terrain is relatively mild, with rolling uplands and modest slopes. Elevations reach 1,884 ft, with a low point of 1,100 ft. Apart from wildlife plots and the campgrounds, the WMA is heavily wooded by a pine-oak forest. **maps:** USGS Stotlers Crossroads, Gerrardstown (the maps don't show the lake).

starting out: There are few developed facilities on the WMA, which is primarily a large backcountry area left in a primitive state. Hand water pumps and vault toilets are located in the campground. The manager's office is located near the entrance; you might be able to pick up a map and other info, but during non-hunting season it can be difficult to find anyone on the premises.

Visitors should be sure to wear blaze orange during hunting season.

activities: Canoeing/Kayaking, Fishing, Hiking, Mountain Biking, Camping.

canoeing/kayaking: 205-acre Sleepy Creek Lake offers a scenic setting for a short paddle, or, better yet, a combined float/fish trip. The lakeshore and surrounding mountains are blanketed with a dense forest, and the number of boats on the water at any one time can usually be counted on one hand. Primitive boat ramps are located in several places around the lake, and access from several of the camping areas is possible, allowing for overnight paddling trips. Only boats that are paddled or powered by electric motors are allowed on the lake.

fishing: Along with hunting, fishing is the reason most sportsmen visit Sleepy Creek WMA. The lake is managed for populations of largemouth bass, bluegill, and crappie. You can fish from the shoreline or from a boat; the latter is more popular and will allow you to cover more water.

hiking: The trails and hunter's roads of the WMA will appeal to hikers with a strong sense of adventure. With the exception of a 20-mi section of the *Big Blue Trail* that runs N–S through the WMA, the network of hiking trails and gated roads are unsigned and un-blazed. The main attraction of the trails is their remoteness, the chance for wilderness solitude, and the abundance of wildlife that inhabits the forests of the WMA. The *Big Blue Trail* is blazed with blue rectangles. The easiest access to the trail and to trails that intersect it is from the main WMA road that leads to the camping areas. Hiking on the trail is mostly moderate, with some long level stretches.

camping: 75 primitive campsites are spread out in 4 main areas on the lake's E side. Sites at each of the areas are similar; each has a grill, lantern post, and fire rings. Many of the sites offer lakeside camping. The sites are generally large and well spaced, and provide a good measure of privacy. The sites themselves are rather scraggly, however, and those wishing something like the carefully maintained campgrounds of the state parks and national forests may be disappointed. Vault toilets and hand water pumps are located at each of the camping areas. Sites cost $5/night. The fee station and entrance to the camping areas is 4.1 mi from the WMA manager's residence. The campground is open all year.

Camping outside of the designated areas is not allowed.

lodging: The Farmhouse on Tomahawk Run B & B (304/754-7350; www.travelwv.com) is nestled on 280 acres in the valley of its namesake creek. The compound includes the restored Civil War-period farmhouse and a carriage house. All together, five rooms with private baths are available. Rates are $75/night for the farmhouse, $100/night for exclusive use of the carriage house. The B & B's location between Martinsburg and Berkeley Springs makes it convenient to Harpers Ferry NHP and Cacapon Resort SP also.

Cacapon Resort State Park

Like its neighbor Sleepy Creek WMA to the east, this large park occupies a long narrow ridge that rises from the broad, level farm land that covers the majority of the eastern panhandle. Located in Morgan County south of Berkeley Springs, the park encompasses 6,115 acres, most of them on the summit and eastern flank of Cacapon Mountain. The park is one of those hybrids common in West Virginia—part resort, part backcountry recreation mecca. Among the resort amenities are a large lodge, an inn, three types of cabins, an 18-hole golf course designed by Robert Trent Jones, tennis courts, and a small lake where swimming and paddle-boating are popular pastimes. Fortunately, all these recreational facilities are confined to a relatively small area, leaving most of the park acreage remote and undeveloped. A large network of hiking trails and grassy roadbeds leads visitors along the forested mountain slopes, where the sounds of songbirds or a glimpse of white-tailed deer is more common than the thwack of golf balls being struck. In winter when there's sufficient snowfall, the golf course is transformed into a perfect cross-country skiing circuit.

Berkeley Springs (N) is the closest town.

contact: Superintendent, Cacapon Resort State Park, Route 1, Box 304, Berkeley Springs, WV 25411; 304/258-1022; wvweb.com/www /cacapon.html.

getting there: From Berkeley Springs, take US-522 S 9.3 mi to the park entrance, R.

topography: With elevations that range from 900 to 2,300 feet, Cacapon Mtn has the highest, steepest, and most rugged terrain in the region. Compared to the Alleghenies, however, the topography is relatively gentle. The natural forest cover is deciduous, but large areas have been cleared and landscaped to accommodate the resort amenities such as the golf course, lodge, and tennis courts. **maps:** USGS Great Cacapon, Ridge.

starting out: The large lodge serves as park HQ. Inside you can pick up trail maps and park brochures. With so many developed facilities in the park, locating water, rest rooms, or a pay phone is not a problem.

activities: Hiking, Cross-country Skiing, Fishing.

hiking: A 15-mi network of trails spreads out over the E slope of Cacapon Mountain between the lower park area in the valley and the summit. A grassy fire road follows the summit for most of the park's length, adding to the hiking possibilities. Highlights along the trails are the quiet woodland setting, vistas that extend for miles east across the broad valley to Sleepy Creek Mountain, and an abundance of wildlife. The trails intersect at numerous locations, making hikes of various lengths possible. Backtracking generally isn't necessary. Trailheads are signed, and the trails are blazed and easy to follow. Hiking is mostly moderate, with a few steep areas and some level stretches. Trail access is at several different locations, including the cabin area, main park road, and the Batt picnic area. This last trailhead is in closest proximity to the park's remotest regions.

cross-country skiing: Unlike many parks and forests that feature cross-country skiing, Cacapon's hiking trails don't do double duty as nordic tracks come winter. Instead skiers take to the 18-hole championship golf course. Skiing is permitted anywhere on the course except the tees and greens. The wide fairways and scenic vistas offer appealing conditions. With moderate terrain and no narrow forest tracks to negotiate, skiing is easy. Access is from the lodge or clubhouse. Snow is most common in Jan and Feb.

fishing: Hardcore backcountry anglers won't find much to pique their interest at Cacapon SP. Families looking to introduce the youngsters to fishing or other sports enthusiasts looking for a couple hours' diversion, however, shouldn't be disappointed. Fishing in the park is at the small recreational lake, which is stocked with both bass and trout. You can cast from the shore or rent a row boat and get out on the lake itself. Keep in mind that the sandy beach and swimming area are popular destinations on the lake, so you definitely won't have the place to yourself.

lodging: Overnight options in the park include a lodge, a small historic inn, and rustic cabins with various levels of amenities. The long, narrow lodge has 49 hotel-style rooms, a restaurant, and a large lounge with fireplace. Rates are $58/night for a double.

11 more rooms are available in the Old Inn, built in the 1930s and located not far from the more modern lodge. With its rough hewn log beams, stone chimneys, and chestnut and knotty pine walls, the inn recalls an earlier era. Rooms are available with or without private bath. Rates are $36/night. The inn is only open from Apr to Oct.

Cabins come in 3 different configurations—modern, standard, and economy. They're all secluded in wooded areas away from the main park activities. All cabin types have electricity and a bathroom with shower. Only the modern cabins are available year round. Rates for a 4-person cabin range from $55 to $85/night. Pets are not allowed in any of these facilities.

Lee Ranger District

George Washington National Forest

The majority of the landholdings that comprise the Lee Ranger District are located on Massanutten Mountain and west of the Shenandoah Valley in Virginia. Only slightly more than 50,000 acres are located in the mountains of Hardy and Hampshire counties in West Virginia. But these are the district's remotest lands, with forested slopes and valleys that are a haven to wildlife and a boon to backcountry travelers. Among the former are white-tailed deer, black bear, beaver, and wild turkey. Three recreation areas facilitate outdoor activities. Trout Pond, the most intensively developed, has a man-made lake for swimming, boating, and fishing; a car campground; and large picnic areas. Smaller, primitive campgrounds are found at the other two rec areas. For backcountry enthusiasts, a large trail network that connects the three different rec areas is accessible from each one. These are multi-use trails, open to hikers and mountain bikers. The district is a good choice for weekend trips, especially during the peak season when some of the better known areas are overcrowded.

Wardensville and Woodstock, VA are the closest towns.

contact: Lee Ranger District, US Forest Service, 109 Milineau Rd, Edinburg, VA 22824; 540/984-4101.

getting there: Main highway access to this part of the district is on WV-55 and WV-259. To reach the district RS: From I-81 in VA take exit 279. Turn E onto VA-185/SR-675 and go 0.2 mi to Windsor Knit Rd. Turn L and go 0.2 mi to Molineau Rd. Turn L and go 0.2 mi to the RS.

topography: The long ridge of Great North Mtn, aligned NE to SW, is the most prominent geographical feature. To the W is the broad valley of the Cacapon River. Mountain slopes are forested with northern hardwoods and conifers. Elevations are between 1,050 ft and 3,117 ft. **maps:** Listed below under the different areas.

starting out: Trail maps, trails lists, and brochures are available free at the district RS. For sale is a topo map of the entire district that shows most of the trails. USGS topo maps are for sale too.

activities: Hiking, Mountain Biking, Camping, Fishing.

hiking: Although the district boasts almost 300 mi of trails, only a small fraction of those are in WV. Each of the areas described below has its own trail network; each one is also anchored by a single long trail that follows the contour of the landmass in a NE-SW direction. Better yet for backpackers, the trails of the different areas can be connected to form long loops or one-way trips. Footpaths and old logging roads comprise the trails, with a few short sections on gravel roads open to vehicles. Hikers who spend any time in the backcountry will be treated to solitude, outstanding vistas, and encounters with the abundant wildlife. The trails are well marked and generally easy to follow. Hiking is mostly moderate.

mountain biking: All trails on the district are open to mountain bikes. Since most trails follow moderate contours and many of the trails are old road beds, they're well suited to fat-tire riding. Riders will find some primitive conditions as well, but nothing exceptionally difficult. The gravel roads that wind through the mountains add more possibilities. Traffic is usually quite light, and several long loops can be formed by combining roads and trails. There's access to the trails at each of the rec areas described below.

camping: Campers can choose between backpacking or bikepacking on the one hand, and a trio of car campgrounds, one at each of the rec areas described below, on the other. Only Trout Pond is fully developed; the others are small primitive camping areas intended as base camps for explorations of the backcountry.

fishing: There's a single stocked trout creek on the WV portion of the district, and the lake and pond at Trout Pond Rec Area are also stocked with trout.

lodging: The Inn at Lost River (304/897-6788) features a 19th century inn, a pair of cottages, and rustic cabins. All rooms in the inn and cottages have private baths. Rates are $75/night. The cabins can accommodate from 2 to 4 people. Each has a deck and fireplace or woodstove. Rates are $180/weekend. The inn is located W of the NF district on WV-259 near the community of Lost River.

Hawk Recreation Area

The Hawk Recreation Area is at the northern extremity of the Lee Ranger District. It consists of a primitive car campground and picnic area in a remote region of forested mountain slopes. Recreation is primarily on the *Big Blue Trail*, which passes directly through the rec area. It offers possibilities for hiking, backpacking, and mountain biking trips through relatively rugged terrain. A single trailside shelter provides a place to overnight, though tent camping is permitted throughout the area. The main attraction of the area is its remoteness and general quiet, even on summer weekends when other parts on the district are quite busy.

Wardensville (SW) is the closest town.

getting there: From WV-55 in Wardensville, drive E 4.2 mi to FR-502. Turn L onto the unpaved road and go 2.9 mi to FR-347. Turn L and go 0.7 mi to the campground, R.

topography: A NE-SW ridge defines the area's topography and designates the state line. Forest cover is heavy, with northern hardwoods predominant and scattered hemlocks and pines interspersed. Elevation in the campground is 1,400 ft; the ridge rises to the E and S to 2,424. **maps:** USGS Mountain Falls, Wardensville, Capon Springs.

starting out: The only facilities in this area are at the small campground, where there's a hand water pump and pit toilets.

activities: Hiking, Mountain Biking, Camping.

hiking: Hiking in the area is primarily on trails that form sections of the blue-blazed *Big Blue Trail*, which winds through the campground and follows the ridge of North Mtn on the WV/VA state line. There are 14 mi of trail in the area between the Hawk Campground and CO-5/1. From there trail connections can be made to the Wolf Gap and Trout Pond rec areas. The trails follow a combination of single-track and old roads. Highlights are the remote mountain setting and the chance to observe wildlife. Hiking is moderate. Trail use is light. Access to the trail is from the picnic area.

mountain biking: All trails in the area are open to mountain bikes. The *Big Blue Trail*, the main artery on the WV portion of the district, offers varying riding conditions. It follows rutted double-track roads, unpaved roads open to vehicles, old road beds, and even some single-track. Riding is moderate to strenuous.

camping: Primitive backcountry camping is permitted throughout the area on NF land. A shelter dedicated to Paul Gerhart is located on the *Big Blue Trail.*
The small primitive campground features 15 sites in an area that's heavily forested. Sites are only average in size, but the dense forest cover adds to the degree of privacy. Each of the sites has a picnic table, grill, and lantern post. There's a hand water pump and pit toilets in the campground. There's no fee to camp. A group campground is also located in the area. The campground is open from Apr 1 to Dec 31.

Wolf Gap Area

Like the Hawk Recreation Area to the north, this is a relatively remote backcountry area served by a small primitive recreation area with facilities for camping and picnicking. The campground is located on the Virginia/West Virginia border, which follows a line formed by a series of long, narrow ridges. Several hiking trails also trace this route, providing access to the backcountry and the area's main recreation. Hiking, mountain biking, and backpacking trips are all possible on the trails, and the views from several lookouts are exceptional. With connections to the *Big Blue Trail* and the Trout Pond Recreation Area, the Wolf Gap Campground makes a convenient base camp for an extended exploration of the area.

Woodstock, VA (E) and Wardensville (NE) are the closest towns.

getting there: From WV-55 in Wardensville, drive SW on CO-23/10 13.2 mi to the campground and trailheads.

topography: The eponymous gap is in Great North Mtn, a NE-SW ridge that forms part of the WV/VA state line. Forest cover is heavy, with northern deciduous trees forming most of the canopy. Elevations are between 2,250 ft in the campground and 3,293 ft on Mill Mtn to the NE. **maps:** USGS Wolf Gap.

starting out: The only facilities in this primitive area are at the campground, where there's a hand water pump and pit toilets.

activities: Hiking, Mountain Biking, Camping.

hiking: 2 trails—2.4-mi *Tibbet Knob Trail* and 6-mi *Mill Mountain Trail*—depart the campground in opposite directions. Both offer spectacular vistas, wildlife, and a remote mountain setting. By following either connections can be made with larger trail networks, including those of the Hawk Rec Area and Trout Pond Rec Area. This makes the area suitable for both day trips and weekend backpacking excursions. The trails follow a combination of narrow footpaths and old roads. Hiking is moderate to strenuous.

mountain biking: All of the trails and roads in the area are open to mountain bikes. Trail conditions vary, but generally the trails are ridable, though some effort is required. The trails follow both single-track and road beds. A couple of different loops can be put together

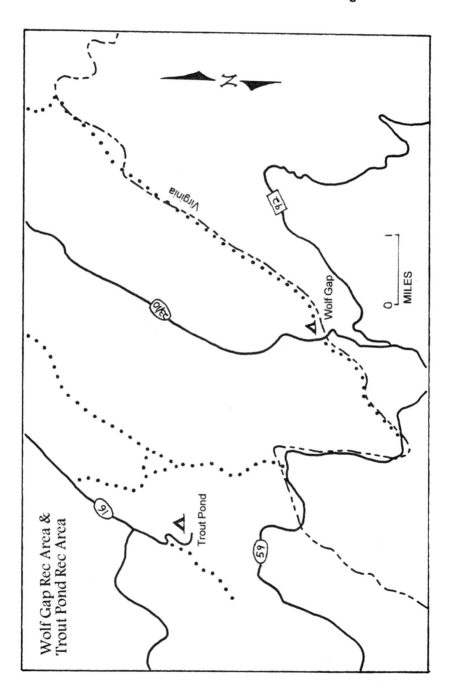

Wolf Gap Rec Area &
Trout Pond Rec Area

by riding a combination of forest roads and trails. Riding is moderate to strenuous.

camping: Primitive backcountry camping is permitted throughout the area on NF lands. Campsites are not difficult to find along the trails.

The 10 sites in the primitive car campground are shaded by a dense canopy of hardwoods. The sites are large and well spaced, ensuring a high measure of privacy. Each site has a tent pad, picnic table, grill, and lantern post. Facilities are limited to pit toilets and a hand water pump. There's no fee to camp. The campground is open year round.

Trout Pond Recreation Area

The only developed recreation area on the district in West Virginia, Trout Pond features a man-made lake for swimming, boating, and fishing; a full service campground; picnic areas; and network of multi-use trails. Also in the area is the 1.5-acre Trout Pond, West Virginia's one and only natural lake. It is formed by a natural sink hole; several others are in the area too. Although backcountry enthusiasts may find the atmosphere and general crowding at the swimming beach a little too reminiscent of resort-style areas, the excellent network of trails allows escape into the lush, forested mountainsides that cradle the lake. Day hikes, backpacking trips, and mountain biking rides are all possible here.

Wardensville (NE) and Woodstock, VA (E) are the closest towns.

getting there: From the jct of WV-55 and CO-259 in Baker, drive S on CO-259 7 mi to CO-16 (Mill Gap Thorn Bottom Rd). Turn L and go 4.5 mi to FR-500 and the entrance to the rec area, R. At 0.8 mi reach a gate, R and a parking area, L.

topography: The campground and lake sit in a narrow valley between mountain ridges. Forest cover of northern hardwoods and pines is heavy, with mountain laurel prominent in the understory. Elevation at the rec area is 1,300 ft; on Long Mtn (S of the campground) it reaches 3,266 ft. **maps:** USGS Wolf Gap.

starting out: The rec area has the most developed facilities on the WV side of the Lee RD. Around the lake are a bathhouse, water fountains, and modern rest rooms. A pay phone is located at the entrance to the campground. Parking costs $2/car, swimming costs $2/person.

activities: Hiking, Camping, Fishing, Mountain Biking.

hiking: 5 trails in and around the rec area cover a total distance of 12.4 mi. The longest of these, *Long Mountain Trail*, runs 7.8 mi from CO-59 S of the rec area to CO-23/10, from which connections are possible to the trail networks described above under the other 2 areas of the Lee RD. The other trails in this area are short, scenic paths in the vicinity of the lake. All of the trails connect, so they can be hiked in series or various combinations. Trails follow both narrow footpaths and old roads. Trailheads are signed, and the trails are blazed and easy to follow. Highlights are the rec area attractions and the backcountry flora and fauna. Hiking is easy to moderate. Trailheads are in the rec area and on CO-59.

camping: Primitive backcountry camping is permitted throughout the area, except where posted otherwise. In the rec area itself, camping outside of the campground is prohibited. The best opportunity for backpacking trips is along the *Long Mountain Trail.*

The 50-site car campground is fully developed, with hookups for RVs and bathhouses with hot water. The sites are shaded by a thick canopy of hardwoods, but the modestly sized sites are squeezed together, minimizing privacy. Each site has a picnic table, grill, and lantern post. Sites cost $16/night, $20 with hookup. Sites can be reserved by calling 800/280-CAMP. The campground is open May 6 to Dec 15.

fishing: 1.5-acre Trout Pond and 17-acre Rockcliff Lake are both stocked trout waters. Fishing on the pond is from the banks, which are semi-clear in places, but will give fly casters fits. Anglers can fish the lake from the shore or a boat. Large sections of the shoreline are open, but a boat will allow you to cover more water. Keep in mind that the lake's sandy beach is very popular with swimmers and sunbathers.

mountain biking: As elsewhere on the district, mountain bikes are permitted on all the trails in the Trout Pond Area. The short *Rockcliff Lake Trail* provides a nice circuit around the lake, but the best riding is on the longest trails—the *Trout Pond Trail* and *Long Mountain Trail*. Both trails are blazed and easy to follow. The combination of single-track and old roads offers riders a nice mix of challenging and relatively easy conditions. Longer loops can be formed by combining the trails and roads to the E around the Wolf Gap Area. The region's best scenery is there too.

Lost River State Park

This large remote park encompasses 3,712 acres of forested mountain terrain in Hardy County, not far from the border with Virginia. The park combines opportunities for backcountry exploration with recreation facilities such as a swimming pool, tennis courts, archery range, and large picnic area with rustic shelters, tables, and grills. An extensive trail network extends into most regions of the park, and is used by both hikers and equestrians. Away from the swimming and recreation area, an atmosphere of mountain calm pervades the heavily forested ridges and coves of the Lost River backcountry. The quiet isolation and scenic setting have made the area a summer destination for vacationers since the beginning of the 19th century, when "Light Horse Harry" Lee, father of Robert E. Lee, built a summer retreat here. The building—listed on the National Register of Historic Places—still stands, and is now run as a small museum. Although the park is big enough and far enough off the beaten path to ensure an uncrowded backcountry experience, if you plan to stay a while and are looking for more acreage, the George Washington National Forest is less than a half hour away. The rustic cabins at Lost River SP make an excellent base for explorations further afield.

Moorefield (NW) is the closest large town.

getting there: From the jct of WV-55 and CO-259 in Baker, drive S on CO-259 13.2 mi to Lost River State Park Rd (CO-12). Turn R and go 2.8 mi to the park entrance.

topography: The dominant geographic feature is a NE-SW ridge that rises to 3,111 ft in the park. Numerous small drainages drop down through the mountain's folds. Low point is 1,800 ft on Howard's Lick Run. A forest of northern hardwoods, hemlocks, and pines covers most of the park. **maps:** USGS Lost City, Lost River State Park.

starting out: You can pick up trail maps and park brochures at the main office. Water and rest rooms are located in the bath house beside the pool, restaurant, and rec area. A pay phone is outside the restaurant.

activities: Hiking.

hiking: A large trail network fans out from the main park road to cover most of the SW half of the park. Another single trail that ends at Miller's Rock crosses the park's NE half. Most of the trails are less than a mile, but jcts are frequent, and you can put together longer hikes by linking 2 or more trails. In all, the trails cover approximately 20 miles. Highlights along the trails are scenic mountain vistas, the serenity afforded by the lush hardwood and hemlock forest, and the park's historical features. Most trails follow dirt single-tracks that are blazed and easy to follow. Most of the trails are open to horseback riders. The trails are improved with footbridges across creeks. Trailheads are signed and spread out along the main park road. Hiking is easy to moderate. Trail use is light to moderate.

lodging: Overnight accommodations are available in the park's 24 cabins. The 9 deluxe cabins are heated and open year round. 15 log cabins are open from the last weekend in Apr to the end of Oct. All cabins have wood burning fireplaces, baths with showers, and modern kitchens. The cabins are isolated from park activity in a scenic wooded setting. Cabins vary in size, and can accommodate from 2 to 8 people. Nightly rates for 2 people range from $65 to $93. Multi-night or weekly stays are discounted. Pets are not allowed in the cabins.

Dry River Ranger District

George Washington National Forest

Nearly 50,000 acres of this district of the George Washington National Forest are located on the long, narrow summit and slopes of Shenandoah Mountain in West Virginia. With a northeast-southwest orientation, the ridge is consistent with the prevailing topography of this part of the Appalachians. The South Fork South Branch Potomac River, which drains the mountain's western slopes, follows a parallel course. The West Virginia portion of the district—most of it lies in Virginia—has been used mostly for timber extraction and resource protection, with little attention to recreational development. There are two small recreation areas; Brandywine Rec Area is the larger, with a small lake for swimming, a picnic area, and a developed campground. The Camp Run Rec Area is simply a small primitive campground tucked into a remote corner of the district. Backcountry travel will challenge the resourcefulness of hikers and mountain bikers. The number of maintained hiking trails is very small, but a larger network of logging roads, old roadbeds, and unmaintained trails awaits exploration.

Franklin (W) is the closest large town.

contact: Dry River Ranger District, US Forest Service, 112 North River Rd, Bridgewater, VA 22812; 540/828-2591.

getting there: The major highway access to the rec areas described below is on US-33. To reach the district RS: From I-81 take exit 240. Turn W onto VA-257 and go 3.3 mi to VA-42 in downtown Bridgewater. The district RS is located on North River Rd.

topography: The long summit ridge and slopes of Shenandoah Mtn dominate this part of the district. The major drainage is the S Fork S Branch Shenandoah River, which flows N to the W of NF lands. Forest cover is consistent throughout the area, with northern hardwoods and pines comprising most of the canopy. **maps:** See below under the different areas.

starting out: The district RS in Bridgewater, VA can supply you with brochures and other info about the district. A trail/recreation topo map of the district is for sale, as are USGS topos. Water and rest rooms are in the Brandywine Rec Area.

activities: Camping, Hiking, Mountain Biking.

camping: Backcountry camping is permitted throughout the district on NF land, though opportunities are limited due to the rather small trail network.

Both of the rec areas described below has a small campground. Brandywine is more developed, but Camp Run is open all year.

hiking/mountain biking: Opportunities for backcountry travel, whether on foot or by bike, are limited in this part of the district. The number of maintained trails can be counted on one hand, so longer trips have to be cobbled together by traveling a combination of trails and primitive forest roads. The latter are OK for mountain biking, but require a tolerance for less than ideal conditions.

Camp Run Recreation Area

Encompassing the northern edge of the West Virginia portion of the Dry River Ranger District, this is a remote area of forested mountain slopes and abundant wildlife. Recreational opportunities are limited and primitive. A small, often overlooked, campground provides a nice base camp for explorations of the area. Backcountry travel is on the small network of primitive forest roads and a single hiking trail. The area will appeal most to those looking to escape the madding crowds of the more popular rec areas or a destination where the phrase "roughing it" has real bite.

Brandywine (SW), Upper Tract (W), and Fulks Run, VA (SE) are the closest towns.

getting there: From the jct of US-33 and CO-21 in Brandywine, take US-33 W 3.4 mi to Sweedlin Valley Rd (CO-3). Turn R and go 9.7 mi to Camp Run Rd (CO-3/1). Turn R onto the gravel road and go 1.3 mi to the camping area, R.

topography: Camp Run flows through a gap between two summits of Shenandoah Mtn. Elevations reach 3,015 ft on Ant Knob. Terrain to the W of the campground is moderate; steep slopes rise in the other 3 directions. Forest cover is deciduous with a scattering of white pines. **maps:** USGS Fort Seybert.

starting out: Except for a pit toilet in the campground, there are no facilities at all in the area. The campground is nevertheless the focal point and logical starting place for explorations. Gravel roads and seeded, gated roadbeds lead into the backcountry.

activities: Camping, Mountain Biking, Hiking.

camping: Primitive backcountry camping is permitted throughout the area on NF lands. Opportunities for backpacking are limited,

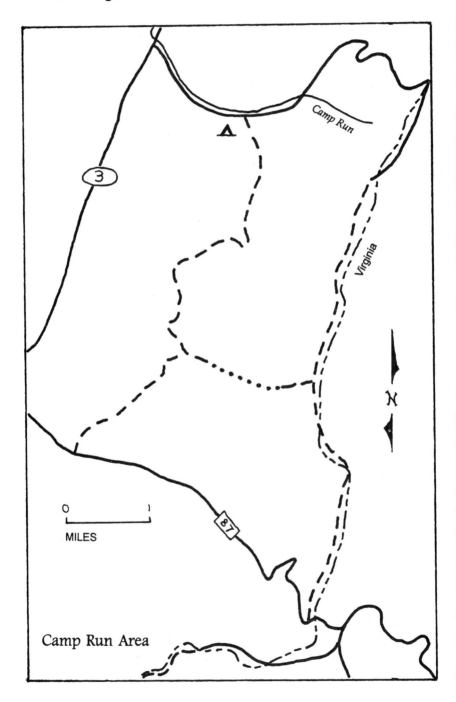

Camp Run Area

however, by the lack of an extensive trail network.

A small, primitive car campground has 9 sites spread out along a gravel spur. A canopy of hardwoods and white pines provides shade. The area is a bit scraggly, but offers car camping in a remote backcountry setting. Privacy at the sites isn't really a problem, as few people use the area. The only improvement is a pit toilet. There's no potable water source. Each site has a picnic table, grill, and lantern post. There's no fee to camp in the area. It's open year round.

mountain biking/hiking: Backcountry travel in the remote region S and SE of the campground is primarily on forest roads in various states of repair. The roads and a section of single-track trail combine to form a network of about 15 mi. In general the roads are rough, rugged, and primitive. They are best suited to hikers and bikers who don't mind less than perfect conditions. The rewards are remote isolation and the chance to see wildlife. Hiking or riding is moderate to strenuous. Access is from the campground, where you can start by hiking up the forest road.

Brandywine Recreation Area

The Brandywine Rec Area is located off US-33 just west of the Virginia state line in Pendleton County. It features a small man-made lake for swimming and sunbathing, and an attractive car campground. The entire area is very scenic, set in a landscaped valley amidst modest mountain slopes. A lakeside picnic area has shelters, tables, and grills. Backcountry travel is limited to a single maintained hiking trail and a larger network of primitive trails and roads. A day-use fee is charged for the swimming and picnicking areas.

Brandywine (W) is the closest town.

getting there: From the jct of US-33 and CO-21 in Brandywine, take US-33 E 2.7 mi to the rec area entrance, R.

topography: The lake and rec area sit on the lower W slope of Shenandoah Mtn. Conifers and Appalachian hardwoods comprise the forest, but some areas have been cleared and landscaped. Elevation at the lake and campground is 1,858 ft. S of there, Cowger Mtn reaches 2,830 ft. Terrain is steep at the higher elevations, but mild on the lower slopes. maps USGS Brandywine.

starting out: Water and modern rest rooms are located at the swimming area on the beach.

Boats with gas motors are not allowed on the lake. Alcohol is not permitted in the day-use area.

activities: Camping, Hiking.

camping: Primitive backcountry camping is permitted outside of the rec area on NF land. The lack of any real trail network, however, severely limits the possibilities for backpacking in the area.

Car campers can overnight at the attractive 30-site campground. The sites are large and well spaced in a heavily wooded part of the rec area; privacy is outstanding. Each site has a picnic table, grill, lantern post, and tent pad. If the sites happen to be full, you can pitch your tent in an overflow area at the back of the formal campground. This area is just a large grassy clearing with scattered fire rings and picnic tables. There are modern rest rooms, but no showers. Sites cost $10/night. If you're arriving late, keep in mind that the campground is gated from 10 PM to 6 AM. The campground is open May 15–Nov 30.

hiking: The only maintained hiking trail in the area is the 3.6-mi *Saw Mill Trail*. It follows a yellow-blazed routed on a combination road beds-single-track trail. Highlights are the creek, woodland setting, and wildlife. Hiking is moderate. The signed trailhead is in the last campground loop next to site #25. Other opportunities for hiking in the area are on the network of unmaintained trails and primitive roads. The district topo map is a good guide to these trails.

Potomac Ranger District

Monongahela National Forest

The Potomac Ranger District encompasses 146,241 acres of land in Randolph, Pendleton, Grant, and Tucker Counties. Within its boundaries are some of the most magnificent ecological communities and geologic formations encountered in West Virginia. Highlights are the 900-ft Seneca Rocks, the wind-scoured heath barrens of Dolly Sods, and Spruce Knob, the state's highest point. These natural wonders and the backcountry areas that have been established to protect them, draw visitors from across the state and beyond. Among the plant communities are forests of red spruce and northern hardwoods; plains of low-lying shrubs such as blueberry, huckleberry, laurel, and rhododendron; and grassy sods. Geological forces have shaped the region into dramatic landforms, including canyons, the Allegheny Front, and Seneca Rocks. The district takes its name from 2 branches of the Potomac River. The North Fork South Branch effectively splits the district in two. To its west is the precipitous eastern slope of the Allegheny Front and, beyond, the Allegheny Plateau. To its east is North Fork Mountain and the South Branch Potomac River.

Recreation on the district centers around all of these natural treasures. There are extensive trail networks to permit exploration of the seemingly misplaced northern plant communities; fly-fishing on rivers and streams; rock climbing on the Seneca Rocks. paddling trips on the two branches of the Potomac River; and a handful of campgrounds to permit the prolonged stays that are necessary to fully appreciate the marvels of this part of the state.

Petersburg (NE) is the only large town on the district.

contact: Potomac Ranger District, Monongahela National Forest, Route 3, Box 240, Petersburg, WV 26847; 304/257-4488.

getting there: Primary highway access to the district is on WV-28, which runs N-S along the N Fork S Branch Potomac River. US-220 parallels the district's E boundary • The district RS is on WV-28/55 3 mi W of downtown Petersburg. The Seneca Rocks Visitor Center is 18 mi W of the RS (on the same highway) and just N of the jct of WV-28/WV-55, US-33/WV-55, and US-33/WV-28. Really.

topography: NF holdings are primarily on the forested slopes, ridges, and plains of North Fork Mtn and the Allegheny Plateau. Vegetation at the highest elevations is characteristic of more northern latitudes. Heath barrens, bogs, sods, red spruce forests, and northern hardwood forests are all encountered. Elevations are between 900 ft in Petersburg and 4,861 ft on Spruce Knob. **maps:** See below under the individual areas.

starting out: You can pick up trail maps, brochures, or buy any of several NF maps at either the district RS or the Seneca Rocks Visitor Center. The district RS is open weekdays from 7:30 AM to 4:45 PM. The visitor center is open daily from 9 AM to 5:30 PM and is more geared toward visitors.

activities: Hiking, Canoeing/Kayaking, Fishing, Rock Climbing, Camping, Mountain Biking, Cross-country Skiing.

hiking: The district is one of the best destinations in the state for hiking and backpacking. The scenery and diverse natural habitats are unsurpassed anywhere else in the Allegheny Mountains. Highlights are the Dolly Sods area, Seneca Rocks, and Spruce Knob. The largest trail networks are in the magnificent highlands on the Allegheny Plateau and in the Seneca Creek backcountry below Spruce Knob. Backcountry excursions of a day, a weekend, or a week are possible in these areas. North Fork Mtn is served by a single long trail that follows its ridge line for 24 miles. Despite the loftiest elevations in WV and some of the steepest terrain, the trails tend to follow contours that offer easy to moderate hiking. Outside of the Dolly Sods Wilderness, the trails are all multi-use, open to mountain bikers and, in some cases, equestrians. Trails are blazed and improved with footbridges, except in the wilderness, where primitive conditions prevail.

canoeing/kayaking: Paddling on the district is on 2 branches of the Potomac River that follow similar routes through canyons and gorges that offer some of West Virginia's most dramatic scenery. The long summit ridge of North Fork Mountain divides the North Fork South Branch Potomac River and the South Branch Potomac River, which meet N of the mountain near Petersburg. Paddling conditions on the rivers are similar, with whitewater that reaches class III. Both are suitable to open-deck canoes.

fishing: Fly fishing for trout, both native and hatchery supported, is one of the most popular activities on the Potomac RD. The 2 branches of the Potomac River offer fishing on large water in a magnificent setting. More intimate conditions and backcountry solitude prevail on the smaller creeks that drain the Dolly Sods Wilderness and the Seneca Creek backcountry.

rock climbing: The 900-ft vertical cliffs of exposed Tuscarora sandstone that are the Seneca Rocks are a mecca for rock climbers. Climbers from all over the country make pilgrimages to test their skill on almost 400 individual routes that range in difficulty from 5.0 to 5.13.

camping: Backcountry camping is permitted throughout the district on NF lands. Except for the Seneca Rocks area, which has no trail network, all of the areas featured below offer excellent opportunities for extended backpacking expeditions.

There are 4 main developed campgrounds on the district, as well as a couple of very primitive areas with almost no facilities. Seneca Shadows, just down the road from Seneca Rocks, is the largest and most developed. Each of the other backcountry areas is served by a primitive car campground that is well situated to serve as a base camp. The season varies at the different campgrounds, but camping is generally available from early spring through autumn.

mountain biking: In a state that's world famous as a fat tire destination, the Potomac RD is less highly regarded than some of the other regions of the Monongahela RD. That's chiefly because one of the main trail networks—in Dolly Sods Wilderness—is closed to bikes. It's also because the Canaan Valley, just W of the district, may be the state's #1 destination. Nevertheless, there's some good riding to be had. No road in the Allegheny Mountains is more scenic than FR-75, which forms the E boundary of the Dolly Sods Wilderness. And the roads and trails of the Spruce Knob area offer awesome scenery, lots of mileage, and some challenging single-track. In fact, for long rides or multi-day trips, it's the best destination on the district.

cross-country skiing: The Potomac RD straddles the Allegheny Front, which has a very strong impact on local weather patterns. The broad plateau W of the front receives tons of snowfall every year; E of the front, not so much. Which means that come winter the roads and trails of the Dolly Sods area and Spruce Knob area are perfect for cross-country skiing. The only obstacle may be getting to the areas, since there's no snow removal on the roads that run through either.

lodging: Situated amidst 1,500 acres of backcountry in scenic Smoke Hole Gorge, the Smoke Hole Lodge (304/242-8377 [winter], 304/257-4774 [summer]) is ideal if you're looking for a truly rustic retreat. The log and stone lodge is only accessible via 4WD (they provide a shuttle), and has no electricity or phones. What power there is is supplied by gas, kerosene, and wood. The lodge has 5 bedrooms and 2 dorm-style rooms. A large deck, stone fireplaces, and communal dining area add to the sense of backcountry community. Rates start at $75/night and include transportation and 3 meals per day.

The North Fork Mountain Inn (304/257-1106) provides a more accessible option in the same general vicinity. The long front porch looks out over scenic mountain vistas, and the large wooden lodge blends nicely with the surrounding forest. Inside, stone fireplaces and country furnishings create a relaxed, rustic atmosphere. All six of the lodge's rooms have private baths; some have stone fireplaces and jacuzzis. 2 separate guest houses are also available. Rates start at $70/night.

Smoke Hole Area

Straddling the South Branch Potomac River as it flows north through rugged gorges and a scenic canyon, this is an area of immense natural beauty and tell-tale remnants of the pioneers who first settled it. Early explorers noticed that the mist rising from the canyon resembled smoke leaving a hole and gave the area its name. Steep forested mountain slopes, spectacular rock formations, and caves are the main geological features. The walls of the canyon rise as much as half a mile from the river, often in sheer cliffs. Because it's cut off from neighboring valleys, an atmosphere of remote isolation permeates the area. Visitors come to paddle or fish the river, hike or backpack in the backcountry, or overnight at the riverside campground. The two developed recreation areas, Smoke Hole and Big Bend, are unobtrusive and offer only limited facilities.
Petersburg (NE) and Franklin (SE) are the closest towns.

getting there: From Petersburg, take US-220 S 16.1 mi (just across the bridge over the S Branch) to Smoke Hole Rd (CO-2). Turn R and go 0.1 mi to a river access for boats, R. At 4.2 mi is the entrance to the Smoke Hole Picnic Area across a low bridge, R. At 5.4 mi the pavement ends. At 7.9 mi pass the Jess Judy Campground. And at 9.1 mi come to the end of the road and the Big Bend Rec Area. • From the jct of US-33 and US-220 in Franklin, take US-220 N 12.2 mi to CO-2 and follow directions above to access points and rec areas.

topography: Terrain here is rugged, steep, and spectacular, with elevations between 900 ft (Petersburg) and 3,776 ft (N Fork Mtn). Forest is predominantly deciduous, with scattered pines, hemlock, and red spruce. **maps:** USGS Upper Tract, Petersburg W, Mozer, Hopeville.

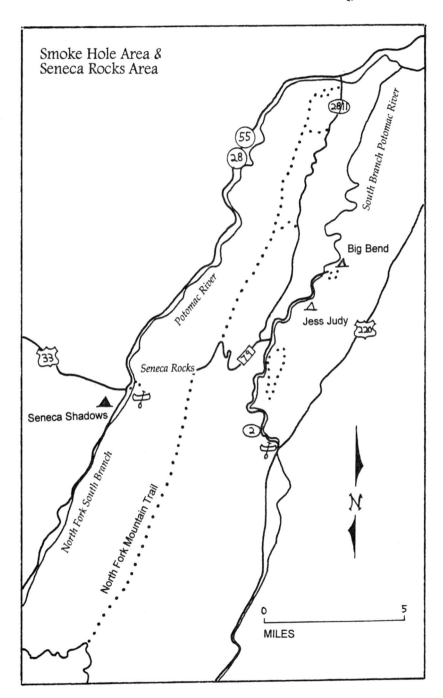

Smoke Hole Area &
Seneca Rocks Area

South Branch Potomac River

28/11

55

28

Big Bend

Potomac River

Jess Judy

220

79

33

Seneca Rocks

Seneca Shadows

North Fork South Branch

North Fork Mountain Trail

2

N

0   5

MILES

starting out: Facilities in this semi-remote backcountry area are limited. Water and pit toilets are available at Big Bend campground and Smoke Hole picnic area.

Pets must be leashed in the rec areas.

activities: Fishing, Kayaking/Canoeing, Hiking, Camping.

fishing: The South Branch Potomac River is big water that flows down a mild to average gradient over a very rocky bed. Cover is excellent on both banks, except where the vegetation has been removed to accommodate CO-2, the main access route. The road follows the river for 9 mi from the entrance to the area to the Big Bend Campground. Beyond there, the river flows another 16 mi through mostly pristine natural habitats before reaching Petersburg. The section of river beside CO-2 is most heavily fished. To help preserve the resource, special delayed harvest regulations have been put in effect on the river from Mar 1 to May 31. Anglers cast for trout, smallmouth, and largemouth bass in the river. Canoe/fish trips permit exploration of the river's remotest section, amidst stunning natural beauty.

kayaking/canoeing: The long run from the put-in at the US-220 bridge to the take-out in Petersburg is 25 miles. Short runs are possible along the first 9 mi, with access at the Smoke Hole Picnic Area (5 mi) or Big Bend Campground (9 mi). Or the whole length can be run as a long daytrip, or broken up with an overnight at the Big Bend Campground or in the backcountry beyond it. The campground can also be used as a put-in for a 16-mi run to Petersburg. Whitewater on the river is class I-III, which makes it suitable for open-deck canoes. Long pools and flat stretches are punctuated by series of rapids, which are most intense near the start of the run. From start to finish, the scenery is majestic. The run is seasonal; in summer the water drops too low. Water level can be checked at any of the put-ins or by driving along CO-2.

hiking: The 24-mi *North Fork Mountain Trail* provides the main hiking opportunity in the area. It follows the long eponymous ridge from US-33 (S) to CO-28/11 just off WV-28 (N). Since it's a one-way trail, backtracking or a vehicle shuttle is necessary. Highlights along the trail are the spectacular vistas, a remote mountain setting, and wildlife, particularly birds of prey that ride the updrafts overhead. The trail follows a narrow footpath that is often rocky and steep. It's blazed with blue diamonds. The N trailhead is signed, the

S one is not. Hiking is moderate to strenuous. To reach the N trailhead: from the Seneca Rocks visitor center on WV-28, drive N 14.8 mi to CO-28/11 (It's 3.9 mi further to the district RS). Turn R across a bridge and go 0.4 mi on the unpaved road to the trailhead and parking area, R. To reach the S trailhead: From the jct of US-33 and US-220, drive W on US-33 8.1 mi to the top of the mountain (distinguished by a radio antenna) and a small pulloff, R.

Other trails in the area are a pair of short loops, the 3.5-mi *South Branch Trail* and the 1-mi *Big Bend Loop Trail.* The former begins in the picnic area, the latter at the campground.

camping: Backcountry camping is permitted anywhere along the trails or river on NF property, except where posted. Roadside camping is not allowed outside of the campgrounds.

A developed car campground and a primitive overflow camping area are both located in the area. The Big Bend Campground has 46 sites arranged in 2 different areas, one of which is in a scenic setting right beside the river. The sites are large and well spaced, affording a nice degree of privacy. Each site has a picnic table, grill, and lantern post. There are pit toilets and a hand water pump in the campground. The sites cost $10/night. Doubles cost $18/night. Some sites can be reserved by calling 800/280-2267. The campground is open Mar 15–Dec 1.

On weekends when the Big Bend Campground is full, the Jess Judy Campground opens to accommodate the overflow. 1.2 mi S of Big Bend, the camping area is just a large grassy clearing beside the river in an attractive valley. Several fire rings are scattered across the area. There are portable toilets but no water in the campground. There's no fee to camp in the area.

Seneca Rocks Area

Sheer faces of naked rock rising 900 feet from the North Fork Valley, the Seneca Rocks are the most dramatic expression of West Virginia's mountainous geography. The rocks are Tuscarora sandstone, a sedimentary rock that is harder and tougher than the other rocks that formed this region of the Appalachian Mountains millions of years ago. As weather eroded the mountains over eons, the sandstone remained, until the stark formations that stand today were exposed. In addition to their photographic and dramatic appeal, the rocks offer one of the best climbing walls in the East. To date more than 375 routes have been put up. In the shadow of the rocks flows the beautiful North Fork South Branch Potomac River. As it moves north past the rocks it enters a canyon between North Fork Mountain and the Allegheny Front. The river is a favorite with both fly fishermen and whitewater enthusiasts. For visitors wanting to spend more than a day, there's a large developed campground just down the road.

The closest towns are Petersburg (NE) and Franklin (SE).

getting there: From the S: From the jct of US-33 and WV-28 in Judy Gap, drive N on US-33 10.5 mi to the jct of US-33, WV-28, and WV-55. Turn R onto WV-28/WV-55 and go 0.1 mi to the visitor center, R. The visitor center is 18 mi W of the district RS in Petersburg on WV-28/WV-55.

topography: For sheer drama, the Seneca Rocks offer the most spectacular topography in the state. From an elevation of 920 ft on the N Fork S Branch Potomac River, the sandstone rocks rise from the lower slopes of N Fork Mtn to 2,400 ft. The rocks themselves have a 900 ft vertical. Except for the exposed sandstone spires, a lush deciduous forest blankets the mountain slopes. **maps:** USGS Upper Tract, Hopeville.

starting out: The Seneca Rocks Visitor Center is the logical starting point for this region. Available inside for free are brochures and trail maps. For sale are USGS topos and other maps, as well as a wide selection of guide books. There are exhibits on local ecology and geology, as well as a 3-D model of the entire district. The visitor center is open daily from 9 AM to 5:30 PM.

activities: Rock Climbing, Canoeing/Kayaking, Fishing, Hiking, Camping.

rock climbing: There are 2 major climbing destinations in WV—the New River Gorge and Seneca Rocks. Look in the parking lot and you'll see license plates from all over the eastern half of the U.S. More than 375 routes have been put up, ranging in difficulty from 5.0 to 5.13. Access is via a short hiking trail that begins in the visitor center. Guide books that cover individual routes are available for sale there, as well as at the 2 outfitters located just up the road next to Harper's Store (see appendix for addresses and phone numbers).

canoeing/kayaking: The run from the put-in just upstream of the visitor center to Petersburg is a fun, 20-mi stretch of class I-III whitewater punctuated by some flat stretches. The river flows N through a steep canyon formed by the Allegheny Front and North Fork Mountain. The mountain scenery is outstanding, though marred somewhat by the presence of the highway right beside the river. As the river approaches Petersburg it leaves the canyon and enters milder terrain dotted with farms. The run is seasonal, since the water level is too low in summer. The level can be checked at the put-in. Put in either behind the visitor center or just up the road, where there's a large parking area. The take-out is at the US-220 bridge in Petersburg. A couple of other take-outs are located along WV-28/WV-55, including one 14.6 mi N of the visitor center and 0.2 mi S of the bridge across the river.

fishing: Like it's twin to the E, the N Fork S Branch Potomac River is a large body of water that flows through stunning mountain scenery. Its gradient is mild to average, and the rocks and boulders that determine its course produce some exceptional pools. Cover is good on the E bank, but the W bank is open in many places due to the highway that runs beside the river. The N Fork is a popular fly-fishing destination, with a fishery that supports populations of smallmouth bass and all 3 species of eastern trout. The river is stocked trout waters. Catch-and-release regulations are in effect behind the visitor center. Access is from behind the visitor center and then by wading.

hiking: Although the 24-mi *North Fork Mountain Trail* passes behind the rocks along the mountain's long summit ridge, no trail in the Seneca Rocks Area connects to it. The only hiking trail is the 1.3-mi *West Side Trail*, which runs from the visitor center to near the top of the sandstone spires. From the viewing deck on top, the trail affords outstanding views of the North Fork Valley, Allegheny Front, and of the Seneca Rocks themselves. The trail starts out on a wide gravel footpath that leads to a footbridge across the river. It then winds through a lush forest of hemlocks and hardwoods up the side of the mountain. Along the way are steps, benches, and interpretive panels describing the local ecology. Hiking is moderate. Trail use is very heavy.

camping: Primitive backcountry camping is permitted anywhere on NF land, except where posted. It is not allowed in the Seneca Rocks area near the visitor center. The *N Fork Mountain Trail* offers the best opportunity for backpacking trips (see the Smoke Hole Area above).

As its name suggests, Seneca Shadows campground is located in the shadows of the massive monoliths that loom over the area. The large developed campground has a variety of sites: walk-in tent sites, car sites with hook-up, and a group camping area.

The 40 walk-in tent sites are in a particularly attractive area in full view of the Seneca Rocks. These sites are in an open mowed and landscaped area that offers less privacy than the car sites. Each site has a picnic table and grill. Vault toilets and water are in the area. The sites cost $5/night.

The 38 car campsites include singles and doubles, some with hook-ups, some without. The sites are moderately sized, but are well spaced; privacy is outstanding. The heavy forest cover in this part of the campground only adds to the isolation at the sites. Each site has a picnic table, grill, and lantern post. Modern rest rooms with showers are centrally located. Sites cost $10/night ($12 with hookup); double sites cost $15. A group site with 5 tent pads costs $35/night. Some of the sites can be reserved by calling 800/280-2267. The entire campground is open Apr 15–Oct 31.

Dolly Sods Wilderness

Located on a high plateau atop the Allegheny Front, the Dolly Sods Wilderness preserves 10,215 acres of one of the more unusual natural environments in West Virginia. With a climate and flora and fauna characteristic of Canada and the northern states, Dolly Sods is an anomaly in the central Appalachian Mountains. It is a land of windswept heath barrens, grassy sods, sphagnum bogs, and wind-gnarled red spruce and yellow birch. At lower elevations are lush forests with thick understories of laurel and rhododendron. In the adjacent 2,000-acre Dolly Sods Scenic Area are the Bear Rocks, a field of massive boulders and rock formations at the very edge of the Allegheny Plateau. The panoramic vistas alone are worthy of a visit. The entire plateau is subject to wildly unpredictable weather. Temperatures are often 10°-15° cooler than in the valleys below. And storms can arise quickly and without warning. Storm gear and warm clothes are essential for backcountry trips.

Recreation in the wilderness is necessarily low-impact only. There are no roads and no developed facilities. A network of hiking trails is the only sign of human impact. Hiking and backpacking are the most popular activities. Red Creek is a stocked trout creek where backcountry fly fishing trips are possible. Car camping is

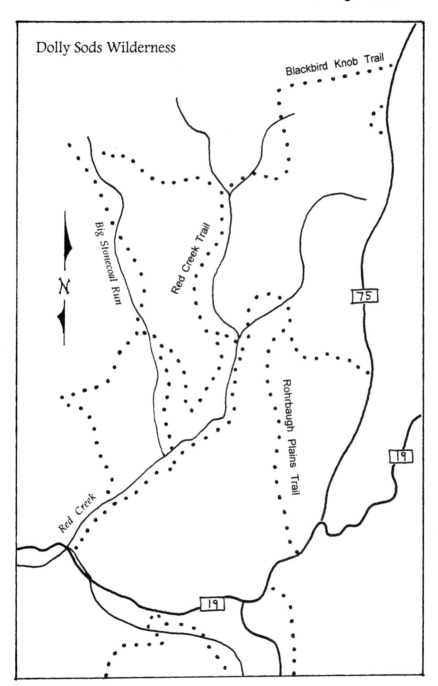

Dolly Sods Wilderness

possible at the edge of the wilderness in a small, primitive campground. And FR-75, which forms the wilderness' eastern boundary, is ideal for mountain biking or cross-country skiing.

Petersburg (E) is the closest town.

getting there: From the Seneca Rocks Visitor Center, drive N on WV-28/WV-55 11.7 mi to Jordan Run Rd (CO-28/7). Turn L and go 0.9 mi to unpaved FR-19. Turn L and go 6 mi to the jct with FR-75. Access to the wilderness is both R and L. R it's 5 mi to Red Creek Campground, 7.4 mi to Bear Rocks.

topography: The entire wilderness sits on a lofty plateau that falls off steeply and spectacularly to the N Fork Potomac River Valley. Elevations on the plateau are between 3,600 ft and 4,100 ft. **maps:** USGS Blackbird Knob, Blackwater Falls, Laneville, Hopeville.

starting out: The only facilities on the plateau are in the Rec Creek Campground. Water is available from a hand water pump there. FR-19, 75, and 70 are rough, steep gravel roads with no snow removal. FR-75 is closed Jan through Apr.

activities: Hiking, Camping, Cross-country Skiing, Fishing, Mountain Biking, Fishing.

hiking: 11 trails wind through the wilderness, covering a distance of almost 28 mi. The trails form a relatively compact network, with numerous intersections that makes it possible to hike some or all of the trails in series. Several different loops can be formed as well, though none of the individual trails is a loop. The main highlight along the trails, and reason enough to visit, are the area's unique flora and fauna. Trails are maintained in a primitive condition befitting a wilderness. There are no blazes, and creek crossings are unimproved, though trailheads and jcts are signed. Some of the trails are frequently muddy. Hiking ranges from easy to moderate on most trails, with just a few strenuous stretches. Trail use is moderate to heavy. Access to the trail network is from trailheads on FR-75 and FR-19.

camping: Primitive backcountry camping is one of the main appeals of the Dolly Sods Wilderness. It is permitted throughout the wilderness, except where posted, which includes within 300 ft of the roads. It is not permitted in the Dolly Sods Scenic Area. Outside the wilderness, primitive roadside camping is allowed along FR-75 and FR-19.

A small primitive car campground is located on the E edge of the wilderness. Red Creek campground has 12 sites, vault toilets, and a hand water pump. The sites are well spaced, and the ground vegetation adds to the degree of privacy, which is quite high. Each site has a picnic table, grill, and lantern post. The sites cost $8/night. The campground is on FR-75, 5 mi N of its jct with FR-19. It's open Apr 15–Oct 31.

cross-country skiing: The wilderness' location atop the Allegheny Plateau insures heavy annual snows. And since the unpaved forest roads that skirt the wilderness aren't cleared, they become ideal nordic ski tracks after snowstorms. This is particularly true of FR-75, which is level, arrow straight, and 7.5 mi long. It also offers spectacular views of both the wilderness and the valley and mountains to the E. The wilderness trails provide other skiing options. The trails best suited to cross-country skiing are those in the more open and level part of the wilderness, particularly near Bear Rocks. Although the peak season is from Nov to Mar, the region's severe weather often brings snowstorms earlier and later than that.

fishing: Red Creek flows S through the wilderness from end to end. Its headwaters are on the slope of Blackbird Knob, from where it flows 8 mi to the wilderness' S boundary. Across that distance the creek transforms from a low trickle to a large creek. It flows down a mild to average gradient through some of the most striking forest and mountain scenery in the state. Its bed is very rocky and cover is exceptional. Access is from the *Red Creek Trail*, which follows it for most of its length. The creek is stocked trout waters.

mountain biking: Although biking is not permitted on any of the trails in the wilderness, the scenic, seldom traveled forest roads that form half of its boundary are ideal for mountain bikes. FR-75, an arrow-straight dirt and gravel road with numerous scenic overlooks, is particularly apt. Riding is easy.

Flatrock Plains/Roaring Plains Area

Adjacent to the magnificent—and extremely popular—Dolly Sods Wilderness, this region of steep mountain slopes, heath barrens, and northern bogs occupies a part of the same plateau and offers a chance to explore similar habitats, but without the crowding that frequently minimizes the wilderness experience at Dolly Sods. The level uplands of Flatrock Plains and Roaring Plains are windswept barrens with flora and fauna more characteristic of Canada and the northern United States than of central Appalachia. Plant communities of heath, laurel, rhododendron, cranberry, and azalea are all encountered at the highest elevations. Red spruce and northern hardwood species dominate the forests that surround these barrens. Recreation is low-impact, backcountry travel. Hiking and backpacking trips are the best way to experience the area's rich and unusual ecology. Visitors should be prepared for extreme weather—temperatures considerably lower than in the surrounding valleys, strong winds, and frequent storms are all part of the outdoor experience here.

Petersburg (NE) is the closest town.

getting there: From the Seneca Rocks Visitor Center, drive N on WV-28/WV-55 11.7 mi to Jordan Run Rd (CO-28/7). Turn L and go 0.9 mi to unpaved FR-19. Turn L and go 6 mi to the jct with FR-75. Keep L on FR-19 and go 3.7 mi (at 0.6 mi pass the Dolly Sods Picnic Area, L; at 1 mi is the *South Prong Trail*, L) to the *Red Creek Trail* access.

topography: Located S of the Dolly Sods Wilderness, the plains occupy the same broad plateau, but have a more diverse topography. Elevations are between 2,200 ft on Red Creek (the area's major drainage) and 4,790 ft on Mt Porte Crayon. Slopes and coves are heavily forested with northern hardwoods and conifers. Heath barrens and bogs cover the plains. **maps:** USGS Laneville, Hopeville.

starting out: Facilities are even more limited in this remote backcountry region than in the adjacent wilderness are to the N. There's no potable water source, and the only development is a small picnic area with tables, grills, and pit toilets beside FR-19.

activities: Hiking, Camping.

hiking: 4 trails wind through the lush forests and along the small creeks for a total distance of 17 mi. Along with gated FR-70, and FR-19/CO-45, the trails form a large outer loop with several trails that cut across its midsection, permitting shorter loops. Highlights

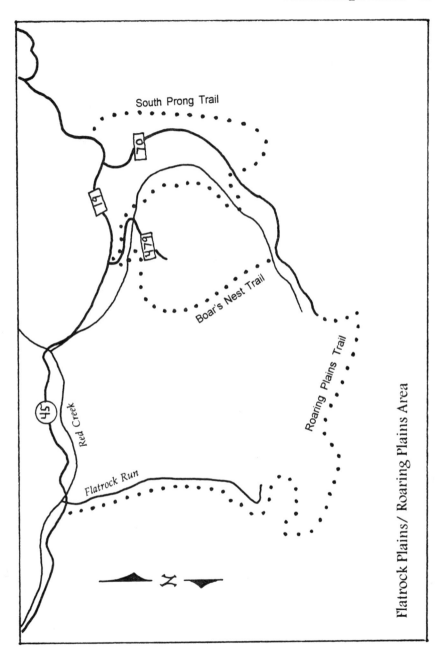

South Prong Trail

70

19

479

Boar's Nest Trail

Roaring Plains Trail

45

Red Creek

Flatrock Run

N

Flatrock Plains/ Roaring Plains Area

along the trails are the remote setting, fewer visitors than in the popular Dolly Sods Wilderness, superb views, and the native flora and fauna. Unlike in the wilderness, the trails here are blazed, through minimal use keeps them in a fairly primitive condition. Hiking is moderate to strenuous. Trailheads are located along FR-19.

camping: Primitive backcountry camping is permitted throughout the area. Although there's no car campground in the area, you can camp roadside along FR-75 and FR-19, where there are several sites.

Spruce Knob Area

At 4,861 feet, Spruce Knob is West Virginia's highest point. The rounded mountain summit overlooks a vast backcountry referred to as the Seneca Creek Area. The lofty elevation dictates the flora and fauna that can survive in the often harsh conditions of wind and weather that prevail here. Forests of wind-whipped red spruce cling to the highest elevations, surrounded by large treeless barrens of grassy sods and heaths of blueberry and huckleberry. On the lower slopes and in the coves a dense forest of northern hardwoods flourishes. An observation tower atop Spruce Knob permits one to survey this alpine landscape in all directions. The 20,000-acre backcountry to the north of Spruce Knob is a roadless area that resembles a designated wilderness in all but name. Only non-motorized travel is permitted, and hikers, backpackers, mountain bikers, and equestrians all take advantage of the vast trail network. Outside the backcountry is a car campground that makes an ideal basecamp for those not wanting to backpack or bikepack. A small lake stocked with trout rounds out the recreation facilities. The harsh weather requires preparation on the part of backcountry travelers. Come prepared for high winds, cold temperatures, and sudden storms. Roads are not cleared of snow in winter.

Franklin (E) is the closest town.

getting there: From the jct of US-33 and WV-55 next to the Seneca Rocks Visitor Center, turn S onto WV-33 and go 9.5 mi to Briery Gap Simoda Rd (CO-33/4). Turn R and go 1.8 mi to a jct. Keep L and go 0.6 mi to unpaved FR-112. Bear R and go 7.3 mi to a jct with FR-104. R it's 2 mi to the parking lot on top of Spruce Knob. L it's 6.5 mi to the Spruce Knob Campground and Spruce Knob Lake.

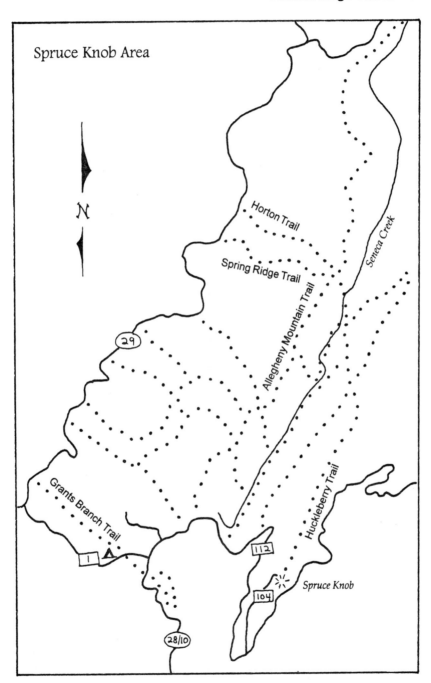

Spruce Knob Area

topography: A red spruce forest occupies the highest elevations in the region. In the valleys and on the lower slopes, the forest is a mix of northern hardwoods and conifers, predominantly hemlock. Elevations are between 3,840 on Spruce Knob Lake and 4,861 on Spruce Knob. Despite the lofty elevation, the terrain is not especially steep. **maps:** USGS Spruce Knob.

starting out: Facilities are at Spruce Knob Lake and at the summit parking lot, where there are pit toilets. The only potable water source in the area is in the campground.

activities: Hiking, Mountain Biking, Camping, Fishing, Cross-country Skiing.

hiking: With 18 trails that cover a total distance of just under 70 mi, the Spruce Knob backcountry has the largest trail network on the district. The trails are laid out in a compact grid to the N and W of Spruce Knob. The trails criss-cross and intersect at so many different points that hikes and loops of almost any length can be put together. Ambitious backpackers could spend days in the backcountry and never hike the same section of trail twice. Trail highlights are scenic views, wildlife, access to trout creeks, and the lush northern forest. The trails are extremely popular, and are used by mountain bikers and equestrians too. While this keeps the paths clearly defined and easy to follow, it can make parts of the backcountry feel uncomfortably crowded on peak weekends. The trails are blazed with blue diamonds and rectangles. Some creek crossings are improved with footbridges, others must be rock hopped or waded. Signed trailheads are at numerous locations, including the campground, and along CO-29 and FR-112. Parking is available at all of the trailheads. Hiking is easy to moderate on most trails in the area.

mountain biking: All trails in the area are multi-use, open to hikers, mountain bikers, and equestrians. Riders will encounter a variety of trail types, including unimproved road beds, 4WD roads, and single-track. Riding conditions vary from easy to strenuous, with most trails falling in the moderate range. Riding is also possible on the forest roads that provide vehicle access to the area, through these can get fairly busy on peak weekends. The rugged route from the Laurel Fork Wilderness to Spruce Knob Lake on FR-1 and FR-421 is an exception. It is a wonderfully scenic ride that passes through mountain meadows and hardscrabble farms. For more detailed trail info, see above under *hiking*.

camping: Low-impact backcountry camping is permitted throughout the area, except where posted. The vast trail network makes this one of the most desirable areas on the district for backpacking or bikepacking trips.

A primitive car campground is located near Spruce Knob Lake. 42 large sites are spread out across a heavily wooded hillside. The sites afford a high level of privacy. Each site has a picnic table, grill, and a lantern post. Pit toilets and a hand water pump are the only facilities. Most of the sites cost $7/night. Sites 31–42 cost $5/night. The campground is open Apr 15–Dec 1.

fishing: The best destination for backcountry anglers is Seneca Creek, a small drainage that flows down a mild to average gradient. It is a native brook and rainbow trout fishery. Cover is exceptional and the creek's rocky bed creates some nice pools. Access is from the *Seneca Creek Trail*, which follows it for 5 mi.

The other option is fishing for stocked trout on Spruce Knob Lake, a 25-acre impoundment that's the highest lake in WV. You can fish from the open shoreline or put a canoe on the water. Gas motors and swimming aren't permitted on the lake.

cross-country skiing: The lofty elevation of the entire region ensures heavy snowfall each year. Although most of the snowfall occurs between Nov and Mar, snowstorms in Oct and Apr are not uncommon. None of the roads in the area are cleared of snow. While this means that the roads are often excellent choices for nordic skiing, it also affects access. Several of the backcountry trails are also suitable for skiing. In general, those that follow a generally level route are best.

Blackwater Falls State Park

This 1,688-acre park straddles the magnificent canyon of the Blackwater River. The canyon walls, formed from Conoquenessing sandstone, rise precipitously hundreds of feet from the river. Although resort facilities—a lodge, cabins, picnic areas, tennis courts, and swimming area are all present—dot the park, most of the acreage remains blanketed by a cool, moist forest where rhododendron crowds the understory and mosses cling to slippery rocks. Wildlife flourishes in this sylvan setting: black bear, snowshoe hare, fisher, mink, muskrat, beaver, wild turkey, and of course white-tailed deer all inhabit the park. Just about every type of outdoor recreation is available, from hiking or cross-country skiing on a large network of trails to fly fishing for trout in the pools of the Blackwater River. And with the Monongahela NF adjacent, the possibilities for longer expeditions increase considerably. The park can also be used as a base for mountain biking, cross-country skiing, or backpacking trips on the *Blackwater River Trail* or on Canaan Mountain.

Davis (E) is the closest town.

contact: Superintendent, Blackwater Falls State Park, PO Box 490, Davis, WV 26260; 304/259-5216. wvweb.com/www/blackwater.html.

getting there: From WV-32 in downtown Davis, Turn W onto CO-29 and go 0.9 mi to the park entrance.

topography: The park occupies part of the broad plateau of Canaan Mtn. The Blackwater River bisects the park as it flows through a steep gorge. Elevations on the river are around 2,500 ft. The rolling uplands reach 3,225 ft. Forest cover is lush, with northern hardwoods, hemlock, and rhododendron all abundant. **maps:** USGS Blackwater Falls, Mozark Mtn.

starting out: The large lodge can serve as a useful base. Inside you can get a trail map, brochures, and other park info. Water, rest rooms, and a pay phone are also there. The rental center is another facility worth checking out. They rent cross-country skis, mountain bikes, and other outdoor gear.

activities: Hiking, Fishing, Cross-country Skiing, Camping, Mountain Biking, Canoeing/Kayaking.

hiking: A 12.5-mi trail network covers all corners of the park. In addition a 3-mi segment of the *Allegheny Trail* passes through the park, offering the possibility of longer backpacking trips and connections with the trails of the Monongahela NF. Park trails pass by scenic overlooks of the Blackwater River Gorge, through lush forests of hemlocks, rhododendron, and hardwoods, and past all the major rec facilities. The trails are well maintained, blazed, and easy to follow. Trailheads are signed and located at numerous locations around the park, including all the major rec areas. Hiking in the park is easy to moderate.

fishing: The 3.5-mi stretch of the Blackwater River between the bridge in the park and the jct with the N Fork is an exceptionally scenic cold water fishery. The river is large and tumbles around massive boulders on an average to steep gradient beneath the heavily forested, steep walls of the Blackwater River Canyon. Pooling is exceptional. This section of the river is stocked trout waters, catch-and-release only. Access is either from the bridge on CO-29/1 in the park (above the falls), or from one of the trails that lead to the river below the falls. Cover is dense, but the river is wide enough to permit easy casting.

cross-country skiing: Come winter, most of the hiking trails in the park are converted to cross-country ski tracks. Only a few trails are not suitable to skiing, which means that the same spectacular views and beautiful forest setting are available year round. Longer trips are possible by heading into the Canaan Mtn backcountry. From there, it's possible to continue S to Canaan Valley Resort SP and hook up with its own network of trails. For more specific info about the trails, see above under *hiking*.

camping: Although backcountry camping isn't allowed in the park, a short hike will put you in the middle of the adjacent Canaan Mtn Area of the Monongahela NF (see separate entry).

The park's developed car campground has 65 sites arranged in 2 large loops. One of the loops is in a large clearing with sites that offer little privacy. The other loop is in a forested area; privacy is better at these sites. In any case, the campground is most popular with RVers. Each site has a picnic table and a grill. Rest rooms with showers are centrally located. Sites cost $11/night, $14 with hookup. The campground is open May 1 to Oct 31.

mountain biking: Although the whole Davis area is a mountain biking mecca, riding in the park is restricted to 2 trails—the *Davis Trail* and *Dobbins Hill Trail*. The trails combine to cover a mile of terrain and are hardly worth describing since everyone who comes to the park to ride ends up in the vast backcountry of the adjacent Canaan Mountain Area of the Monongahela NF (See separate entry).

canoeing/kayaking: If there were a paddling sign posted at the put-in on the Blackwater River, it would read: for experts only. The 10-mi stretch of water between the SP and the take-out in Hendricks is almost continuous rapids, most in the class IV-V range, a few reaching class VI. Scouting individual rapids is necessary, particularly at the upper section, which is most difficult. Getting to the put-in requires almost as much effort as paddling the river. Access is via a steep trail near the start of the *Gentle Trail*, a short trail river L that leads to an overlook of the falls. To get to the water, start out on the *Gentle Trail*, but depart on a side trail L near the start and hike the half mile down to the overlook. The take-out is easy; it's at the WV-72 bridge in Hendricks. This is also the best place to check the water level. If this part of the river is runnable, then so is the rest of it. If the water is high here, forget it.

lodging: The park is home to both a lodge and cabins. The 55-room lodge is perched on the S rim of the Blackwater River Canyon, affording exceptional views. Each of the rooms has all the amenities you'd expect from a hotel. A restaurant is also in the building. Rates vary with the season; doubles range from $48 to $63/night. The lodge is open Mar 1–Dec 15.

For more privacy and seclusion, try one of the park's 25 deluxe cabins. The cabins are heated and open year round. Each one has a fireplace, kitchen, and bathroom with shower. The cabins are located in a forested corner of the park. Rates begin at $88/night for 2 people during peak season. Rates are lower for longer stays or during the off season. 4- and 8-person cabins are also available.

Timberline Resort

Located on the Allegheny Plateau just up the road from Canaan Valley State Park, Timberline Resort is right in the middle of West Virginia's skiing and mountain biking country. Although it's known primarily as a downhill ski resort, mountain biking and cross-country skiing trails are adding to Timberline's reputation. Since the resort opened its trails to mountain bikes during the off-season, it has quickly become one of the major stops in a region that's packed with great fat tire tracks. And each June, the resort hosts the 24 Hours of Canaan, arguably the most famous mountain bike race in the East. From May to October riders can use the trail network for free, as long as they sign a waiver and wear a helmet. In winter, nordic skiers head to the backcountry where there's a network of almost 20 mi of groomed cross-country ski trails. Bikers and skiers can take the chairlift to the summit, and a fully stocked activities center offers rentals and sales.

Davis (N) is the closest town.

contact: Timberline Four Seasons Resort, Canaan Valley, WV 26260; 304/866-4801; wvweb.com/www/timberline.

getting there: From Davis, drive S on WV-32 7.7 mi to Timberline Rd (CO-32-16). Turn L and go 2.5 mi. Turn R and go 0.2 mi to the lodge. • From the jct of WV-32 and WV-55 in Harmon, drive N on WV-32 10.5 mi to Timberline Rd.

topography: Timberline Resort is wedged between the Dolly Sods Wilderness and Canaan Valley SP. The terrain varies from gentle to steep, with elevations that range from 3,200 to 4,268 ft. Forest cover is intermittent, due to the resort nature of the area and the ski slopes. Most parts of the broad valley are open, while a deciduous forest covers the mountains. **maps:** USGS Blackwater Falls, Blackbird Knob.

starting out: Begin your visit in the activities center at the bottom of the mountain. That's where you'll pick up your trail pass. Nordic skis and mountain bikes are available for rent, and accessories are for sale. Water and rest rooms are here too.

activities: Mountain Biking, Cross-country Skiing.

mountain biking: Once the snow is gone and the ground has dried out, the mountain's network of trails and roads is converted to mountain bike tracks. 20 mi of trails include dirt roads, wide paths, and single-track. Highlights along the trails are the awesome mountain views and the woodland setting. A wide range of riding conditions are encountered on the varied terrain. Trails are clearly marked and easy to follow. A trail map is available in the mountain bike center. You can ride the chairlift to the top of the mountain for $5, or $15 for as many rides as you want. The biking season is from May to Oct. Hours are 8 AM to 8 PM daily. All riders must wear helmets.

cross-country skiing: A 17-mi nordic ski track network is separate from the downhill runs. Cross-country skiers can purchase a one-time lift ticket and access the backcountry trails from the summit. The varied terrain offers skiers trails that range from easy to challenging. All trails are clearly marked. Ski season is from mid-Dec to mid-Apr.

Canaan Valley Resort State Park

This large resort-style park encompasses more than 6,000 acres of alpine valley and mountain slopes in Tucker County. The park is surrounded by the Monongahela National Forest and it sits on the same plateau as the Dolly Sods Wilderness and the Canaan Mountain backcountry. Flora and fauna are more characteristic of northern latitudes than of the central Appalachians, with ecosystems that include northern bogs and heath barrens. A grove of maples and aspens is particularly attractive. White-tailed deer are abundant in the park and are frequently seen grazing on the golf course or at the edges of woodlands. Black bear are also present, though they're less numerous and more secretive. In addition to an extensive backcountry, the park offers numerous resort facilities, including a 250-room lodge, 18-hole golf course, and downhill ski area. With the park's cool temperatures in summer and heavy snowfall in winter, outdoor recreation is year round. The large network of hiking trails converts to cross-country ski tracks with the first serious accumulation of snow. Backpackers can connect park trails with the trails of the national forest via the *Allegheny Trail*, which passes through the park. And car campers can overnight in the developed campground.

Davis (N) is the closest town.

contact: Superintendent, Canaan Valley Resort & Conference Center, HC70, Box 330, Davis, WV 26260; 304/866-4121; wvweb.com /www/canaan_valley.html.

getting there: From Davis, turn S onto WV-32 and go 9.7 mi to the park entrance, R. • From the S: take WV-32 N 2.3 mi from its jct with WV-72 to the main park entrance, L.

topography: As its name suggests, most of the state park lies within a broad valley. The valley sits atop a plateau, however, with elevations averaging 3,200 ft. Large areas have been landscaped and mowed to accommodate the resort amenities. To the W and N steep, forested mountain ridges rise to elevations as high as 4,360 on Weiss Knob. **maps:** Blackwater Falls, Laneville.

starting out: With all the resort amenities, there's no lack of facilities in the park. Water, rest rooms, and pay phones are available at several locations. A good place to start is the nature center. You can pick up a trail map there, and they rent mountain bikes, cross-country skis, and snow shoes.

activities: Hiking, Cross-country Skiing, Camping, Mountain Biking.

hiking: The park's trail network covers 13 miles of mountain and valley terrain. The trails have been laid out so that numerous connections and different routes are possible. In addition to the park trails, a 3.3-mi segment of the *Allegheny Trail* passes through the park from N to S. For longer expeditions you can continue N on the trail to the Canaan Mtn Area or Blackwater Falls SP and join the vast backcountry trail network there. Highlights along the trails are exceptional mountain views, various forest types including the magnificent aspens and other N hardwoods in the Blackwater River area, and the broad alpine valley. Trailheads are signed and the trails are blazed and easy to follow. The trails are well maintained and kept clear by moderate to heavy use, except for the *Allegheny Trail*, which has slightly more primitive conditions. Hiking is easy to moderate on most trails; the *Bald Knob Trail* is strenuous. Trailheads are in various locations, including the nature center, lodge, and golf clubhouse.

cross-country skiing: 18 mi of trails are open to cross-country skiers and come winter this is one of the most popular activities in the park. Skiing on most of the trails is easy to moderate. Long tours are possible by following the route N out of the park in into the Monongahela NF and Blackwater Falls SP. See above under *hiking* for more detailed information. The season runs from Dec to Mar.

camping: Backcountry camping is not permitted in the park. If you want to backpack in Canaan Valley, however, you can camp in the Canaan Mtn Area of the Monongahela NF (see separate entry above) by hiking just 2 mi N of the park on the *Allegheny Trail.*
    Camping in the park is at a 34-site developed car campground that sits in the valley. The campground is popular with the RV set.

The area is mostly open with a scattering of tree providing some shade and at least a trace of backcountry atmosphere. The sites are small, and privacy is minimal. Each site has a picnic table and grill. Rest room/shower facilities are centrally located. Sites cost $16.50/night. The campground is open year round.

mountain biking: A single 3-mi off-road trail is open to mountain bikes. The white-blazed *Back Hollow Trail* starts out at the nature center and travels W toward the cabin area. Here it splits—one segment runs N to the lodge, the other ends at the cabins. Backtracking is necessary. The trail affords some nice views of the valley. Riding is easy to moderate. Riding on other trails in the park is not allowed.

lodging: A 250-room lodge provides luxury accommodations right in the park. The rooms don't have much of a rustic backwoods feel, but they do offer all the creature comforts. Amenities in the lodge include a health club, indoor pool, hot tub, and saunas. Rooms cost $86/night for a double in the summer, $58 in winter.

23 cabins offer somewhat more private lodging. The cabins are lined up along a street that seems a little like a suburban subdivision with a woodsy theme. The brown shingled cabins all have showers, fully equipped kitchens, and fireplaces. Rates start at $137 for a 2-bedroom cabin for 1 night. Rates are lower for longer stays.

Cathedral State Park

At only 133 acres Cathedral is one of the smallest state parks in West Virginia. But with most of that acreage covered by a magnificent old-growth hemlock forest, it boasts some of the state's largest trees. The forest's beauty and the scarcity of old growth in West Virginia earned for the park a designation as a National Natural Landmark. In fact, the park represents one of the last stands of mixed virgin timber in the state. Some of the trees reach heights of 90 feet and are up to 21 feet around. In all more than 30 tree species thrive in the park, in addition to 50 kinds of wildflower and 9 different fern species. White-tailed deer can often be seen. Recreational facilities in the park—in addition to the network of hiking trails—are a large picnic area with tables, grills, rest rooms, and water.

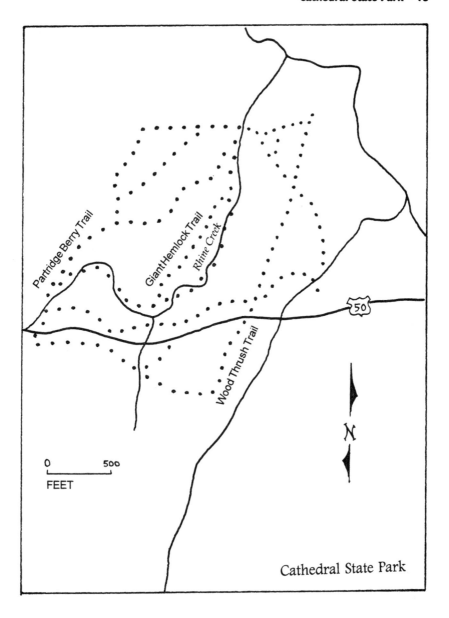

Cathedral State Park

Terra Alta (N) and Oakland, MD (NE) are the closest towns.

contact: Superintendent, Cathedral State Park, Route 1, Box 370, Aurora, WV 26705; 304/735-3771.

getting there: From the jct of WV-24 and US-50 just W of the MD state line, turn W onto US-50 and go 0.4 mi to the park entrance, R.

topography: The mostly level terrain is drained by several small creeks. Forest cover is hardwoods and hemlocks, with old growth covering large portions of the park. Elevations are between 2,460 and 2,620 ft. **maps:** USGS Aurora.

starting out: Water and rest rooms are both located in the park. Although there isn't a park office per se, you can pick up a trail map and park brochure at the entrance.

activities: Hiking, Cross-country Skiing.

hiking: The small network of hiking trails provides access to all corners of the park. The major highlight along the trails are the magnificent, towering trees they pass beneath. Trails are wide, level, and easy to follow. Footbridges and boardwalks provide dry crossings of creeks and wet areas. The trailhead is in the main parking lot. Trail jcts are signed. Hiking is easy and trail use is moderate to heavy.

cross-country skiing: Although there are hardly enough miles of trails to warrant an all-day outing, experiencing the forest in winter provides a whole different perspective. Skiing is easy and the wide, level trails are easy to follow.

Cheat Ranger District

Monongahela National Forest

The Cheat Ranger District covers 127,995 acres in Tucker, Randolph, and Preston Counties. The major landholdings are in the mountain uplands on either side of the Dry Fork River. A pair of large, continuous tracts of national forest land—the Otter Creek

Wilderness and Canaan Mountain Backcountry—are managed for wilderness protection and backcountry recreation. Wildlife that inhabits the forested mountain slopes, deep coves, and broad summits includes black bear, white-tailed deer, snowshoe hare, wild turkey, ruffed grouse, and many smaller mammals. Outdoor recreation is low-impact and trail oriented. Hiking, backpacking, mountain biking, and cross-country skiing are all popular on the district. Developed recreation areas are at Horseshoe Run and between US-33 and the Otter Creek Wilderness. Canaan Valley State Park and Blackwater Falls State Park are within the district's boundaries. The Potomac Ranger District and Greenbrier Ranger District are adjacent to the east and south, respectively.

Parsons is inside the district. Elkins (W) and Davis (E) are also nearby.

contact: Cheat Ranger District, USDA Forest Service, PO Box 368, Parsons, WV 26287; 304/478-3251.

getting there: WV-72 and US-33 are the primary highways that serve the district. To reach the district RS: From the bridge in downtown Parsons, drive N on US-219 0.7 mi to the entrance, R.

topography: The western portion of the Allegheny Plateau and a series of NE-SW mountain ridges SW of there are the district's major landforms. The Blackwater River, Dry Fork River, and the Cheat River are the primary drainages. Elevations are between 4,008 on Bickle Knob and 1,400 ft on the Cheat River at the Tucker/Preston County line. **maps:** See below under the separate areas.

starting out: The district RS is a good place to begin a visit to the region. Inside are trail maps and brochures for free, and USGS topo maps for sale.

activities: Hiking, Mountain Biking, Camping, Fishing, Cross-country Skiing.

hiking: The district inventory lists just under 161 mi of trails. Major trail concentrations are in 2 large backcountry areas—Otter Creek Wilderness and the Canaan Mountain Area. Trails in both areas offer outstanding opportunities for backpacking and wilderness solitude. Outside the wilderness, trails are multi-use, and mountain biking and cross-country skiing are both popular. Equestrian use is also permitted. The district's mountain topography is the chief factor in dictating trail profiles. Trails follow ridges, mountain slopes, and drainages. Hiking is often moderate to strenuous. Trails are generally well maintained, signed, and blazed, except in the wilderness, where primitive conditions prevail. Since more hikers use those trails than elsewhere on the district, however, paths are kept well defined and relatively clear.

mountain biking: Outside of the Otter Creek Wilderness, all trails on the district are open to mountain bikes. A vast network of forest roads—both open and gated—at least doubles the amount of mileage open to riders. The largest trail network is found W of Davis in the Canaan Mountain Backcountry. Trail connections to Blackwater Falls SP and Canaan Valley SP, as well as proximity to the Blackwater River Rail-Trail, greatly increase the number of ridable trails in the area. In fact, the whole Davis/Canaan Valley area is one of the major mountain biking hubs in West Virginia.

camping: Backcountry camping is permitted throughout the district on NF lands, except where posted. The Otter Creek Wilderness and the Canaan Mountain Area offer the best opportunities for extended backpacking, or, in the case of the latter, bikepacking expeditions.

There are also 3 developed campgrounds on the district, with varying numbers of facilities. The Stuart Rec Area offers the highest degree of development, with showers and electrical hookups for RVs. Horseshoe and Bear Heaven are semi-primitive and primitive camping areas, respectively. Camping is seasonal, except at Bear Heaven, which is open year round.

fishing: The best destination for backcountry fishing expeditions is the Otter Creek Wilderness. A native trout fishery, the eponymous creek flows through the wilderness from one end to the other. The Horseshoe Rec Area offers angling in a less remote location and on a stocked trout creek.

cross-country skiing: The Canaan Mountain Area's lofty elevation and location at the western end of the Allegheny Plateau translate into heavy annual snowfall. The mountain's broad summit and extensive network of trails and primitive roads make it the best destination in the Cheat RD for winter cross-country ski trips. The season runs from Nov to Mar.

lodging: The Deer Park Inn & Lodge (800/296-8430) is located W of the NF district near Buckhannon. Featured are a 19th-century farmhouse and a large log cabin-style lodge. The latter has a 6-foot fireplace inside and wrap-around porches outside. 100 acres of woodland surround the compound and isolate it from the outside world. Rooms are furnished with antiques and an atmosphere of rustic ease pervades both buildings. 2 suites and 4 bedrooms (each with private bath) are available in the 2 buildings. Rates are $90–$150/night on weekends, 20% less on weekdays.

In downtown Buckhannon is the Post Mansion Inn (800/301-9309). The renovated Civil War-era mansion was recently added to the National Register of Historic Places. The most surprising architectural feature is a turret, no doubt responsible for the building's nickname of "the castle." Inside, it's furnished with late-Victorian period pieces. Rates are $80/night for 2 people.

Horseshoe Recreation Area

Located in Tucker Country near the Cheat Ranger District's northern boundary, Horseshoe is an attractively landscaped recreation area beside a small creek. Featured are a picnic area with shelter, tables, and grills; large field for sports; swimming hole on Horseshoe Run; and attractive car campground. Backcountry travel is rather limited in the area, as only a handful of short trails extend outward from the recreation facilities. Fly fishing for trout is possible in the creek, and hiking or short backpacking trips are an enjoyable way to explore the wooded slopes of Stemple Ridge.

Parsons (SW) is the closest town.

getting there: From the W: From the jct of CO-7 and CO-1 NE of Parsons, turn E onto CO-7 and go 3.5 mi to the rec area entrance, L. • From the E: From US-219 turn W onto CO-9 and go 4.5 mi to CO-7. Turn L and go 1.5 mi to the rec area, R.

topography: Horseshoe run flows SW along the W slope on Backbone Mtn. Elevation in the campground is 1,733 ft. Mountains rise NW and SE from there. Peaks reach as high as 2,885 on Close Mtn. A forest of pines and hardwoods covers the mountain slopes. The rec area has been landscaped and a large grassy area is kept mowed.
maps: USGS Lead Mine.

starting out: There are water fountains and pit toilets in the picnic area. A pay phone is located in the picnic area.

activities: Hiking, Fishing, Camping.

hiking: 5 trails around the rec area cover a total distance of 6.7 mi. Individual trails range in length from 0.4 mi to 2.1 mi. Most of the trails are short out-and-back hikes. 3 of the trails connect to form a 3.6-mi one-way hike (backtracking is necessary). Highlights along the trails are scenic views and the woodland setting. Trails are blazed with blue diamonds. Hiking is moderate to strenuous. Trailheads are located in the rec area (at the self-pay station) and along CO-7 within walking distance of the rec area. If you're not camping, park in the picnic area.

fishing: Horseshoe Run is a small creek that flows down a mild gradient. It has a rocky bed with good pooling. The tree cover on both banks is excellent. The creek offers 2 mi of fishable water on NF land. It's stocked trout waters. Access is at the back of the picnic area where there's also a swimming hole.

camping: Although primitive backcountry camping is permitted on NF land in the area, without a large trail network the opportunities for backpacking are fairly limited. A shelter is located at the jct of the *Losh Trail* and *Dorman Ridge Trail.*

A very attractive primitive car campground is located next to Horseshoe Run. 13 large sites are spread out in a single loop. The area has been cleared and landscaped, but enough trees remain to provide shade and at least some measure of privacy. Each site has a picnic table, grill, and lantern post. There are rest rooms (no showers) and water spigots in the campground. Sites cost $7/night. Some of the sites can be reserved by calling 800/280-2267. An overflow camping area on the other side of the picnic grounds is just as popular as the main campground. This area is heavily forested, and offers a bit more privacy and a more rustic feel. The sites are smaller but have a picnic table and grill too. The campground is open May 9–Dec 1.

Canaan Mountain Area

Encompassing the broad mountain plateau west of Canaan Valley, the Canaan Mountain Area covers 13,500 acres of remote forested backcountry. It offers outstanding recreational opportunities for mountain biking, hiking, backpacking, and cross-country skiing in a primitive setting. The entire area is undeveloped except for an unpaved loop road that circles the mountain and provides access. The northern hardwoods, red spruce, laurel, rhododendron, and other ground cover that blanket the mountain's plateau and slopes provide sanctuary for a variety of wildlife. Black bear, white-tailed deer, and wild turkey are all present. Recreation centers around the extensive trail network, which is connected to the trails of Blackwater Falls State Park (N) and Canaan Valley State Park (S). The Otter Creek Wilderness is adjacent to the west.

Davis (E) is the closest town.

getting there: Main access to the area is via the 15.4-mi Canaan Loop Road, a primitive forest road that begins on WV-32 S of Davis and ends in Blackwater Falls SP. • Note: If you're starting in the SP, be aware that the first 5 miles are only passable in 4 WD vehicles with high ground clearance. • From the blue bridge in Davis: drive S on WV-32 3 mi to the unsigned road, R. At 0.8 mi come to a gate and the start of the backcountry.

topography: Unlike many of the summit ridges in the Alleghenies, Canaan Mtn has a broad plateau-like summit. Red Spruce and northern hardwood forests thrive in the cool, moist environment. The highest point—on Mozark Mtn—is 3,843 ft. Elevations on the Blackwater River drop to 1,800 ft near Hendricks. **maps:** USGS Mozark Mountain, Blackwater Falls.

starting out: There are no facilities in this large backcountry area. The proximity of Blackwater Falls SP and Davis makes getting supplies or setting up a base camp easy. Water, rest rooms, and pay phones are located in the SP.

activities: Mountain Biking, Hiking, Cross-country Skiing, Camping.

mountain biking: 15 mi of primitive forest road and almost 26 mi of single-track comprise the riding opportunities here. The trail layout is ideal for creating loop rides of various distances. The Canaan

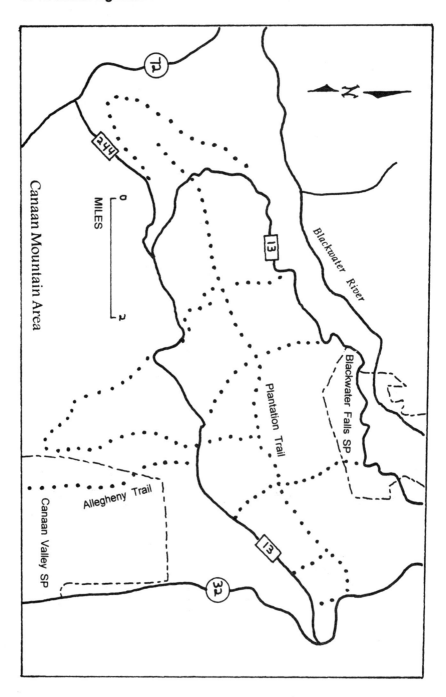

Loop Rd forms a 15-mi oval which is crossed longways and shortways by single-track. Highlights along the road and trails are the different forest communities, wildlife, and the remote mountain setting. Riding conditions vary, from easy gravel road to narrow footpaths that are have rocks, roots, and sometimes mud to keep things interesting. The popularity of this area keeps most of the trails clearly defined and easy to follow. Trailheads are signed and distances to trail jcts given. Riding is easy to strenuous, with most of the trails in the moderate range. Access is from WV-32 or Blackwater SP.

hiking: The network of 26 mi of trails is as good for hiking or backpacking as it is for biking. Trails range in length from several short connectors that are less than 1 mi to the 8.4-mi *Plantation Trail*, which follows the mountains summit from E to W. All other trails in the area cross this trail, so forming connections and creating loop hikes is not difficult. Hiking sections of FR-13 is necessary to create most of the loops. The *Allegheny Trail* passes through the area between Blackwater Falls SP and Canaan Valley SP, facilitating connections to the trail networks in those parks. Hiking on the trails is mostly easy to moderate, and heavy use keeps them easy to follow. For more info, see above under *mountain biking*. To reach the E end of the *Plantation Trail*, leave Davis and go S on WV-32 2 mi from the blue bridge to the trailhead, R.

cross-country skiing: Canaan Mountain's location atop the Allegheny Plateau guarantees heavy annual snows. And while Canaan Valley SP and Blackwater Falls SP get more press as nordic skiing destinations, for real backcountry remoteness, neither can match Canaan Mtn. The 15-mi open-ended loop formed by the Canaan Loop Rd (FR-13) offers perfect cross-country skiing conditions when there's 6 inches or more of snow on the ground. The road is virtually level for most of its route, and it forms numerous connections with the area's many trails. Included among these is the *Allegheny Trail*, which runs S to Canaan Valley SP and N to Blackwater Falls SP. The season runs from Nov to Mar.

camping: Primitive backcountry camping is permitted throughout the area on NF land. The size of this region makes it ideal for backpacking or bikepacking trips, though the dense forest understory can make finding a suitable site difficult in places. Trail shelters are located on the *Pointy Knob Trail*, *Railroad Grade Trail*, and near the jct of the *Allegheny Trail* and *Plantation Trail*. FR-13 offers some good roadside camping sites.

The closest developed campgrounds are in Canaan Valley SP and Blackwater Falls SP.

Otter Creek Wilderness

The second largest designated wilderness in the Monongahela National Forest, Otter Creek comprises 20,000 acres of mountainous terrain in Tucker and Randolph Counties. The area that is now wilderness was intensively logged around the turn of the century. The RR grades that form the base of the hiking trails are the main remnants from those days. The forest that covers the coves, slopes, and summits is predominantly northern hardwood and red spruce. Norwegian spruce has been planted as well, and rhododendron grows in impenetrable slicks in the understory. The wilderness is a natural oasis for wildlife and backcountry travelers. Among the former are black bear, snowshoe hare, and white-tailed deer. Recreation in the wilderness is no-impact, with the emphasis on hiking, backpacking, and fishing. Otter Creek is a native brook trout fishery whose acidity levels are kept in check by a limestone drum near its headwaters.

Elkins (SW) and Parsons (N) are the closest towns.

getting there: From the bridge in downtown Parsons, drive N on US-219 0.1 mi to a NF sign and jct. Turn R and then immediately L. Go 2.4 mi to a jct with FR-701. Keep R and go 2.7 mi through Fernow Experimental Forest to another jct. Bear L and go 0.6 mi to the Big Springs Gap trailhead. • From downtown Elkins: Turn E onto US-33 and go 10.8 mi to FR-91. Turn L and go 1.9 mi to a parking area. • From Hendricks, drive S on WV-72 to a parking area and access to the wilderness across an elaborate footbridge, R.

topography: Otter Creek flows N through the wilderness beneath rugged, steep mountain slopes. The terrain is most precipitous at the wilderness' N end near Big Springs Gap. Elevations are between 1,800 ft at the creek's mouth and 3,728 ft on McGowan Mtn. A northern hardwood forest blankets the wilderness. **maps:** USGS Mozark Mtn, Parsons, Bowden, Harman.

starting out: There are no facilities in the wilderness. A hand water pump is located at the Alpena Gap Trailhead on FR-91 at the jct with US-33 E of Elkins.

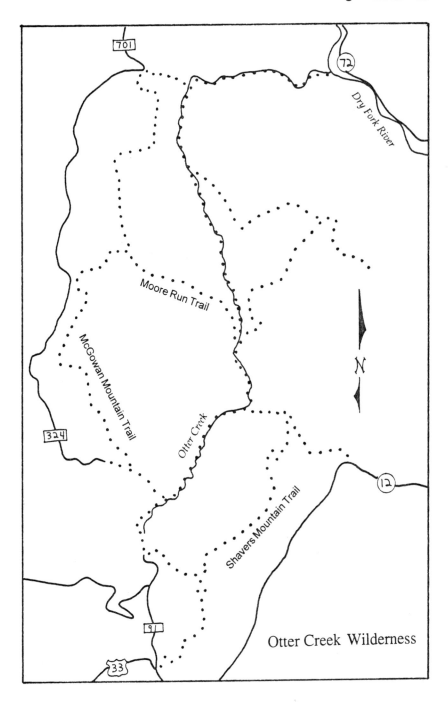

Otter Creek Wilderness

activities: Hiking, Fishing, Camping.

hiking: 11 trails that cover a total distance of 45 mi extend into all corners of the wilderness. As befits a wilderness area the trails are unblazed and unimproved. Creek crossings are by rock hopping or wading; during periods of high water fording Otter Creek may be impossible. The trails range in length from less than a mile to more than 11. Connections are numerous and forming circuits of many different lengths is possible. Highlights are the remote location, lush forest, wildlife, and mountain scenery. Hiking ranges from easy along Otter Creek to strenuous on the steeper mountain slopes. Trailheads are signed and are described above under *getting there.*

fishing: The headwaters of Otter Creek are on McGowan Mtn. From there it winds N and descends down an average gradient. It's a small to medium creek that flows through a forested canyon of startling beauty. Its course is rock filled and boulder strewn, and its many drops and plumes create outstanding pooling. Forest cover is thick. It offers 10 mi of fishable water for native brook trout. Access is from the *Otter Creek Trail*, which follows it through the entire wilderness.

camping: Primitive backcountry camping is permitted throughout the wilderness. Its large size and extensive trail network make it ideal for extended backpacking trips.

Bickle Knob Area

Wedged into a narrow strip of land between the Otter Creek Wilderness and US-33, the Bickle Knob area features a pair of campgrounds that make ideal base camps for exploration of Otter Creek. The larger of the two is Stuart Recreation Area. It has a large developed campground an a vast picnic area with shelters and dozens of picnic tables and grills. There are also large mowed fields for sports or other outdoor recreation. Just up the road is the Bear Heaven Campground, a small primitive camping area with minimal facilities. The area's scenic focal point is the eponymous knob. There's an observation tower on top that affords good views of the surrounding area.

Elkins (W) is the closest town.

getting there: From the jct of US-33 and US-250/US-219 in downtown Elkins, turn E onto US-33 and go 3.4 mi to Old Route 33 (CO-33/8). Turn L and go 2 mi (at 1.9 mi is the Stuart Rec Area entrance, L) to FR-91. Turn R and go 7.4 mi (at 3.8 mi reach FR-91A. L it's 0.2 mi to the Bickle Knob parking area) to the Bear Heaven Campground. Continuing E on FR-91 you reach a jct after 1.3 mi. L is FR-303 and 0.5 mi to a large parking area for the Otter Creek Wilderness. R it's 1.4 mi to US-33. On US-33 it's 10.8 mi W back to downtown Elkins.

topography: The area's mountainous terrain is defined by an E-W summit ridge that reaches an elevation of 4,008 ft on Bickle Knob. Shavers Fork flows N, defining the W edge of the area, the district, and the NF. Elevations on the river are as low as 1,800 ft. Forest type is northern hardwood with hemlocks and rhododendron also prominent. **maps:** USGS Bowden, Elkins.

starting out: Water is available at the Alpena Gap trailhead and in the Stuart Rec Area. Rest rooms and a pay phone are also in the latter. The Stuart Rec Area is open from 8 AM to 9 PM.

activities: Camping.

camping: Without hiking trails in the immediate vicinity, there really isn't an opportunity for backcountry camping. The adjacent Otter Creek Wilderness, on the other hand, is one of the best backpacking destinations in the state.

A couple of campgrounds are in the area, one developed, one primitive. The more primitive of the 2 is Bear Heaven. 8 sites are set back from the road in a heavily wooded area. Each of the large sites has a picnic table, grill, and lantern post. Privacy at the secluded sites is good. There are pit toilets, but no water. Sites cost $5/night. The campground is open all year.

The developed car campground at Stuart Rec Area has 26 large sites that are spread out across a wooded area. The campground is most popular with RVers, but tent campers will find that the sites afford a decent amount of privacy. Each site has a picnic table, grill, and lantern post. There's a shower/rest room facility near the entrance. The campground is popular, so expect crowds on most weekends. Sites cost $12/night. The campground is open May 9–Oct 6.

Greenbrier Ranger District

Monongahela National Forest

The largest district on the Monongahela National Forest, the Greenbrier encompasses 243,055 acres in two counties—Randolph and Pocahontas. The district's boundaries are formed by US-33 (N), the Potomac RD (E), the Marlinton RD (S), and US-219 (W). There are 4 developed recreation areas on the district; all are primitive and offer only very limited facilities. A single designated wilderness—the Laurel Fork Wilderness—occupies more than 12,000 acres on Middle Mountain and along Laurel Fork near the district's E boundary. The large backcountry areas between US-250 and US-330 are heavily forested mountain ridges cut by large, churning rivers. Among the former are Cheat Mtn, Shavers Mtn, Middle Mtn and Rich Mtn. Shavers Fork, West Fork Greenbrier River, East Fork Greenbrier River, and Laurel Fork are the major drainages.

With no large developed recreation areas on the district, outdoor recreation is centered around the vast network of trails, railroad grades, and forest roads. These remote paths and vehicle routes are a bounty for all backcountry travelers. Outside of the designated wilderness, all trails are multi-use. Hikers, backpackers, mountain bikers, and cross-country skiers will find literally hundreds of miles of one type of corridor or another to explore. And for those not wanting to camp in the backcountry, the two primitive campgrounds can be used as base camps.

contact: Greenbrier Ranger District, USDA Forest Service, Box 67, Bartow, WV 24920; 304/456-3335.

getting there: US-250 runs E–W through the center of the district, providing the main vehicle access. On the N boundary US-33 is another major access route. The district RS is located on US-250 in downtown Bartow.

topography: More than any other district on the Monongahela NF, the Greenbrier's topography is dominated by a series of long, NE–SW ridges and the rivers that flow in their shadow and drain them. Forest cover is primarily northern hardwoods and conifers, including the largest stands of red spruce in WV. Elevations in the district are between 4,800 and 1,800 ft. **maps:** See below under the individual areas.

starting out: The district RS is useful for free maps and brochures, and to check on current conditions. They sell NF maps and USGS topos too.

activities: Hiking, Mountain Biking, Fishing, Kayaking/Canoeing, Camping, Cross-country Skiing.

hiking: There are more than 30 trails on the district, including a 33.5-mi segment of the *Allegheny Trail.* Major trail concentrations are in 3 different areas: Cheat Mountain, Shavers Mountain, and Middle Mountain, including the Laurel Fork Wilderness. The *West Fork Rail Trail* is also on the district, where it parallels the W Fork Greenbrier River for 20 mi. The district's topography—long NE–SW ridges and rivers—to a large extent dictates the routes of the trails, many of which follow these rivers and ridges or descend from the latter to the former. One such trail is the *Allegheny Trail,* which between US-33 and US-250 follows first Glady Fork and then Shavers Mountain for a total distance of 24 mi. Trail maintenance in the district is spotty. Many trails are blazed and follow clearly defined paths, but a significant number have missing blazes, overgrown paths, or both. Trails within the wilderness are not blazed to help insure a primitive backcountry experience. With mountain slopes comprising so much of the district's terrain, hiking on most trails is moderate to strenuous. Trails that follow the major rivers tend to rate easy. The easiest long hike on the district is the *West Fork Rail Trail.*

mountain biking: Unlike Monongahela NF ranger districts such as the Gauley or Cheat, the Greenbrier doesn't have a well-known trail network that's favored by mountain bikers over hikers. Yet more than 100 mi of forest roads—many of them remote and closed to vehicles—provide ample riding opportunities. A certain amount of independent route planning and adventurousness is required, however, to put together backcountry rides. The rewards are isolation and often beautiful forest settings. The best spots for long rides are the roads and trails around the Laurel Fork Wilderness and the Cheat Mountain Area. Riding on most of the roads and trails is moderate to strenuous, since there are few level stretches of either on the Greenbrier RD. The *West Fork Rail Trail* is a popular trail that provides easy riding conditions.

fishing: Trout anglers will find some of the most remote and scenic backcountry rivers and creeks in the entire state on the Greenbrier

RD. These include major rivers such as Shavers Fork and the West Fork Greenbrier River, as well as smaller creeks such as Laurel Fork. There are waters that can be reached by car or mountain bike, and waters that can only be reached on foot. Each of the areas described below offers fly fishermen and other trout anglers some kind of fishing action.

kayaking/canoeing: Whitewater paddling on the district is on the West Fork Greenbrier River and Shavers Fork. Each of these is an outstanding whitewater river that passes through some stunning mountain scenery. The rivers are long enough that day and overnight trips are possible.

camping: Primitive backcountry camping is permitted throughout the district on NF land, except where posted. The Laurel Fork Wilderness offers the largest expanse of pristine backcountry on the district, and is ideal for backpacking trips. The area around the wilderness and the Cheat Mountain area are the best destinations for bikepacking.

The largest district offers the fewest choices to car campers, There are only 2 small, primitive campgrounds. One is between the 2 halves of the Laurel Fork Wilderness, the other is just a short distance from the district RS. Both are open all year.

cross-country skiing: Heavy winter snows transform many of the district's trails and roads into ideal nordic skiing tracks. The snows are heaviest from Dec–Mar, with storms occasionally occurring earlier or later. A wide array of conditions can be found, depending on location and trail surface. Generally, the backcountry forest roads and the *West Fork Rail Trail* offer the mildest grades and widest paths. Many of the longer trails offer more of a challenge and provide the added benefit of wilderness solitude. The *Allegheny Trail* between Glady and US-250 is one such route. The Middle Mountain Area around the Laurel Fork Wilderness offers a wide array of skiing options amidst beautiful mountain and forest scenery.

lodging: The 100-year-old Cheat Mountain Club (304/456-4627) is just about the perfect incarnation of a rustic lodge. Spartan but comfortable, the wood and stone lodge sits on almost 200 acres in the remote Cheat Mountain backcountry. Downstairs is a large communal area for dining, relaxing, and sitting by the fire. Upstairs are 10 simple bedrooms and rest rooms. But it's outside that the real attractions are. The lodge employs a full-time outfitter for activities such as hiking, mountain biking, cross-country skiing, canoeing, kayaking, and fly fishing. 5 miles of trails are located on the property and Shavers Fork is in the backyard. Rates begin at $160/night for 2 people. Or you can rent the entire lodge for a weekend or week (quite a few parties do this). Reservations at least 3 months in advance are recommended.

Another excellent option is the Cheat River Lodge (304/636-2301; wvweb.com/www/cheat_river_lodge.html). The 2-story, cedar-shingle lodge sits on the banks of Shavers Fork in a remote setting. A long screen porch runs the length of the building and provides excellent views of the river. Each of the simple, comfortable rooms has a private bath. Rates for 2 people are $53/night. Also available are 6 unique cottages built of wood and stone, each with 2 to 4 bedrooms, kitchens, stone fireplaces, hot tubs, and other amenities. Cottages sleep from 4 to 8 people. Weekend rates are $151/night.

Laurel Fork Wilderness

12,200 acres of forested mountain slopes and the bottomland along Laurel Fork comprise this primitive backcountry area. Because wildernesses are by definition roadless, Laurel Fork is divided into two halves—north and south. In between is FR-423 and a primitive car campground that makes an ideal base camp for exploring the wilderness and surrounding region. Three long, narrow, parallel ridges—Shavers Mtn, Middle Mtn, and Rich Mtn—define the local topography. Laurel Fork drains the slopes of the latter two. Within this area are wildlife such as black bear, white-tailed deer, snowshoe hare, and wild turkey. Recreation is low-impact backcountry travel. Hiking and backpacking are both popular, and Laurel Fork is a stocked trout creek that's perfect for backcountry fly fishing trips. Outside the wilderness, the large network of trafficless roads are ideal for mountain biking, and, in winter, cross-country skiing.

Wymer (N) is the closest town.

getting there: From the district RS in Bartow, turn E onto US-250 and go 2.5 mi to WV-28. Turn L and go 1.9 mi to FR-14. Turn L and go 15.3 mi (at 0.2 mi the pavement ends; at 8.8 mi reach FR-17, L; at 10.5 mi reach the start of the wilderness and a trailhead on gated FR-97, R) to FR-423. Turn R and go 1.4 mi to the campground.

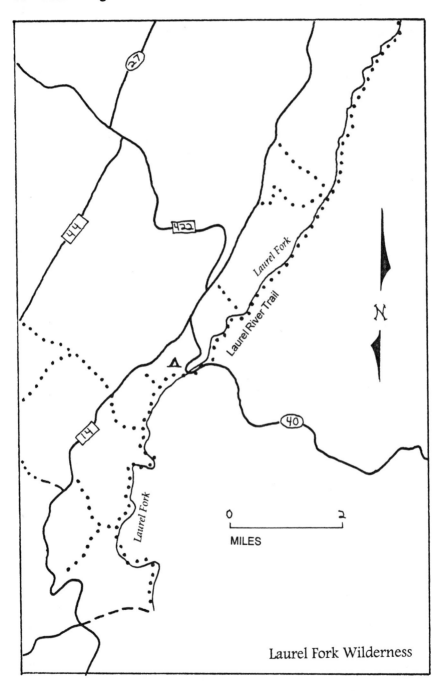

Laurel Fork Wilderness

topography: The Laurel Fork River flows NE through the wilderness between parallel mountain ridges. Forest cover of northern hardwoods and conifers is dense and lush. The terrain is generally rugged and steep, though milder slopes do occur. Elevations are between 2,850 on the creek and 4,400 ft. **maps:** USGS Glady, Sinks of Gandy.

starting out: The only facilities in the area are at the primitive campground, where there are vault toilets and hand water pumps.

activities: Hiking, Fishing, Camping, Mountain Biking, Cross-country Skiing.

hiking: 8 wilderness trails cover a total distance of 26 mi; The longest of these is the 18-mi *Laurel River Trail*, which follows the creek of the same name from the S end of the wilderness past its N boundary to FR-14. All other trails in the wilderness intersect with this main axis and connect it to FR-14. These spur trails are short, with lengths from 0.5–1.5 mi. Loop hikes are possible, but only by including segments of FR-14. The main attraction of the trails is the entrance they offer into the wilderness' deep forest. Laurel Fork is a beautiful trout stream and wildlife is abundant in the area. Trails are left in a primitive condition befitting the wilderness setting. There are no blazes and creek crossings are by rock hopping or wading. Hiking on the trails is easy to strenuous. Trailheads are along FR-14 and in the campground.

For additional hiking, it's possible to link the wilderness trails with trails that begin just outside its borders. 5 scattered trails provide another 20 mi of hiking or backpacking opportunity. One of the trails also connects with the section of the *Allegheny Trail* that runs between US-33 and the crossroads community of Glady. Access to these trails is at several locations along FR-14. The trailheads are signed, and, unlike the trails in the wilderness, they're blazed. Hiking is moderate to strenuous.

fishing: Backcountry fly fishing doesn't get much better than on Laurel Fork. The stream offers more than 15 mi of fishable water in a remote, (almost) roadless setting. The creek is small to medium in size, and flows down a mild gradient under excellent cover. It has a rocky bed and good pooling. Access is from the *Laurel River Trail*, which follows it from one end of the wilderness to the other. It's stocked trout waters. Fishing pressure is moderate to heavy near the campground, progressively lighter the further away you hike.

camping: The Laurel Fork Wilderness is one of the premiere backpacking destinations in the Monongahela NF. Primitive backcountry camping is permitted throughout the wilderness.

A primitive car campground is located on FR-423, the gravel road that divides the N and S portions of the wilderness. 14 sites are spread out around 2 large meadows, one on either side of the road. Scattered spruces provide a measure of shade, but for the most part the sites are in the open. The sites are very large and well spaced, and with so few of them, they offer plenty of privacy. Each site has a picnic table, grill, and lantern post. Pit toilets and a hand water pump are the only facilities. There's no fee to camp here. The campground is open all year, but water is off Dec 1–Apr 1.

mountain biking: Although bikes are not permitted within the boundaries of the wilderness, options do exist for riding on area roads and trails just outside the wilderness. FR-14, the main access road, is exceptionally scenic, with dense forest vegetation crowding it on both sides and blocking out the sun for most of the day. The route from the campground E to the Spruce Knob Area (see separate entry) on FR-423 and CO-40 passes through open mountain pastures that offer exceptional views. And W of FR-14 there's a vast and intricate network of forest roads—both open and gated—ripe for exploration. The mountainous terrain makes riding moderate to strenuous, even on maintained roads.

cross-country skiing: The same forest roads described above under *mountain biking* are suitable for ski touring from Dec to Mar when there's snow on the ground.

lodging: The Middle Mtn Cabins (304/456-3335) are owned and operated by the USFS. The 3 rustic cabins can sleep 11 people total. All 3 cabins must be rented at a time, regardless of how many people are in your party. The cabins are primitive, though the main cabin has kitchen appliances that run on gas. All cabins have stone fireplaces. A hand water pump and pit toilets are the only facilities. The cabins rent for $30/night or $168/week. The cabins are located at the S edge of the wilderness off of FR-14, 11.8 mi N of the jct with WV-28. The cabins are available from Apr 1 to Dec 15.

Island Recreation Area

The "recreation area" is a small primitive campground tucked into a forest of hardwoods and hemlocks on the N side of WV-28. The camping area sits on the bank of the East Fork Greenbrier River, which meanders south from Blister Swamp on the Randolph /Pocahontas county line. The *East Fork Trail* follows the river upstream into the backcountry. The trail is suitable for hiking or mountain biking, and the river is stocked with trout. With its easy access and location near the district RS and the town of Durbin, this is a good choice for a short stop if you don't have the time for a longer expedition into some of the district's remoter backcountry regions.

Durbin (W) is the closest town.

getting there: From the district RS in Bartow, turn E onto US-250 and go 2.5 mi to WV-28. Turn L and go 2.7 mi to the campground entrance, L.

topography: The E Fork Greenbrier River flows S through the heart of the area between Burner Mtn (elev 4,293) and Poca Ridge (elev 4,070). Forest cover is heavy, with deciduous species and hemlocks abundant. Elevation in the campground on the river is 3,000 ft.
maps: USGS Thornwood.

starting out: The only facilities in this primitive backcountry area are at the campground. There's a vault toilet there, but no potable water source.

activities: Hiking, Mountain Biking, Fishing, Camping.

hiking: The 8-mi *East Fork Trail* is the single trail that begins in the campground. It follows the E Fork Greenbrier River for its entire length, ending at a jct with FR-254. Highlights along the trail are access to the river for fishing, a sun-dappled forest setting, and wildlife. The trail is blazed, though it's route along an old RR grade is easy enough to follow anyway. Hiking is easy. The signed trailhead is in the campground.

mountain biking: The wide, level path of the *E Fork Trail* is as well suited for mountain biking as it is for hiking. The dirt path has few obstacles, and except for an unimproved river crossing, there's little to interrupt a pleasant ride through a scenic forest. At the end of the trail it's possible to turn onto FR-254 and connect with FR-112, one of the access roads to the Spruce Knob Area.

fishing: The E Fork of the Greenbrier River is a medium-sized river that flows down a mild to average gradient over a very rocky bed. Pooling is good, but water levels drop considerably in summer. Fly fishermen will find plenty of room to cast, despite good forest cover on both banks. Access is via the *East Fork Trail* described above. As you move upstream, the river becomes increasingly scenic and remote. It is stocked trout waters.

camping: Primitive camping is permitted anywhere in the backcountry, as long as it's on NF land.

A small primitive car campground is tucked back in the forest just off WV-28. The 6 sites are large and very well spaced from one another; privacy is excellent. Each of the sites has a picnic table, grill, and lantern post. There are pit toilets in the camping area but no water. No fee is charged to camp. The campground is open all year.

West Fork Rail Trail

One of the rails-to-trails conversions that have added immeasurably to outdoor recreation in West Virginia, the *West Fork Trail* travels 22 miles between trailheads in Glady (N) and Durbin (S). It follows the route of the former CSX Railroad through small farms and remote mountain forests. For most of its length it closely shadows the branch of the Greenbrier River for which it's named. During most of the year, a mountain bike is the perfect vehicle for exploring the trail. In winter, however, heavy snows turn the trail into a path through a white wonderland best suited to cross-country skis. Traveling on foot is another option, one that allows more time to observe the region's native flora and fauna. The trail also provides access to the West Fork, a beautiful mountain river prized by trout anglers.

Durbin (S) and Elkins (NW) are the closest towns.

getting there: To reach the N terminus: From the jct of Bemis Rd/Middle Mountain Rd (CO-22) and CO-27 in the crossroads community of Glady, turn S onto CO-27 and go 0.7 mi to a gate and the start of the trail. • For the S terminus: From the Greenbrier RD ranger station in Bartow, drive W on US-250 3.2 mi to CO-250/13, L (where a steel bridge crosses the river). There's room for a couple of cars to park.

topography: The river flows S between mountains to the E and W—Little Beech Mtn and Shavers Mtn, respectively. Terrain in the broad valley is undulating, with much of it cleared for farmland, especially at the N end. Beyond that, the mountain slopes are steeper and heavily forested, particularly on Shavers Mtn. Elevations on the river drop from 2,900 to 2,700 ft. On Shavers Mtn they reach 4,300 ft. **maps:** USGS Glady, Wildell, Durbin.

starting out: You can get trail info and a crude map at the Greenbrier RS on US-250 in Bartow. There are no developed facilities along the trail.

activities: Mountain Biking, Hiking, Fishing, Camping, Cross-country Skiing.

mountain biking: Mountain bikers outnumber other trail users on the *West Fork Trail*. The mild grade and wide corridor make riding easy, and on a bike it's possible to cover the entire trail in a single day—even roundtrip if no vehicle shuttle is available. Highlights along the trail are the remote mountain setting, wildlife, RR history, and access to the river. Cinders, crushed gravel, and small stones comprise the trail's bed. Trail use is light to moderate.

hiking: For hikers, the trail is a good destination for anything from a leisurely stroll to a backpacking expedition. Hiking the trail end to end in a single day would really be pushing it; in 2 days you can take your time and set up camp trailside. Other options are to join one of the FS trails that connect with the *West Fork Trail*. The most popular of these is the *High Falls Trail*—it leads 2 mi W to Shavers Fork and one of the most scenic falls in WV. Connections to the *Allegheny Trail* are also possible.

fishing: The West Fork is a medium to large river that flows down a gradient that varies from mild to average. The river bed is extremely rocky, and there are numerous pools, especially in the S half. Cover is excellent along most of the river. The river is stocked trout waters. Access is via the trail, though along the northern third it's out of sight of the river.

cross-country skiing: The same features that make the trail easy for bikers and hikers make it an ideal nordic track for skiers of all levels. The season runs from Dec to mid-Mar, though it varies depending on annual snowfall. When the snow is heavy, access is easier at the S terminus.

camping: Although there are no developed campgrounds and no designated sites along the trail, backcountry camping is permitted on NF lands. Sites aren't difficult to find, though you may have to travel a little bit away from the trail. Just be sure not to camp on private property (it's generally posted) before asking permission from the land owner.

Gaudineer Scenic Area

The Gaudineer Scenic Area is a small pocket of magnificent red spruce forest amidst a large backcountry area defined by Shavers Mountain. In one part of the area picnic tables and grills are isolated beneath stands of red spruce. To add to the natural beauty, several overlooks offer outstanding panoramic views to the west. Just up the road is a parcel of old-growth spruce forest where individual trees date to the middle of the eighteenth century. Outside of these special areas a forest of northern hardwoods and conifers blankets the mountain slopes, providing refuge for black bear and white-tailed deer. Although most visitors come for a short time to see the virgin spruce, the area is an excellent destination for longer backcountry trips. The *Allegheny Trail* follows the ridge line all the way north to the small community of Glady. (It continues N all the way to the PA state line). It offers opportunities for long day hikes or weekend backpacking excursions. In winter heavy snowfall makes it perfectly suited to cross-country skiing. Several trail connections to the *West Fork Rail Trail* add to the possibilities for lengthy trips.

Durbin (S) is the closest town.

getting there: From the E: from the district RS in Bartow, drive W on US-250 7.4 mi to unpaved FR-27. Turn R and go 1.8 mi to a jct. Turn L onto FR-27A and go 0.5 mi to the picnic and scenic area; or continue straight for another 0.75 mi to the trailhead to the *Gaudineer Trail* and access to the virgin spruce stands. • From the W: from the jct of US-219 and US-250, turn E onto US-250 and go 14.1 mi to FR-27. Turn L and follow the directions above.

topography: The topography of the area is defined by a pair of rivers, and a long mountain ridge. Shavers Mountain follows a NE-SW axis, with Shavers Fork and W Fork Greenbrier River on either side. The rivers flow in opposite directions, the former to the NE, the latter to the SW. Several distinct forest types are present. A red spruce forest blankets the higher elevations, while northern hardwoods and hemlocks occur at lower elevations. **maps:** USGS Wildell, Durbin.

starting out: This is a large primitive backcountry area with very limited facilities. You'll find a vault toilet in the picnic area, but there's no potable water source.

activities: Hiking, Camping, Cross-country Skiing.

hiking: Hiking in this area is on one of two trails: the *Allegheny Trail* and the *Gaudineer Scenic Interpretive Trail.* The first is the state's longest trail; it passes through this part of the district for 16.6 mi between the scenic area and Glady. It follows the ridge of the mountain on a path blazed with the familiar yellow rectangles. Highlights along the trail are the remote mountain setting, scenic vistas, and wildlife. The trail follows both old road beds and footpaths. Hiking is moderate to strenuous.

The other trail is a 0.5-mi interpretive loop that winds through stands of virgin spruce. The trail has been carefully constructed and is well maintained. Interpretive plaques along the route describe the ecology of an old-growth forest. The trail is blazed and easy to follow. It briefly joins the *Allegheny Trail.* Hiking is easy. Access to both trails is on FR-27 at the scenic area.

camping: Primitive backcountry camping is permitted throughout the area on NF lands, except where posted. There are 2 shelters located on the *Allegheny Trail.* Camping is not allowed in the Gaudineer Scenic Area itself.

cross-country skiing: The section of the *Allegheny Trail* described above is an ideal cross-country skiing track when there's snow on the ground. Due to it's high elevation, it receives a considerable amount of snowfall each year. The season usually runs from Dec to Mar. Skiing is moderate.

Cheat Mountain Area

This large remote backcountry area is defined by Shavers Fork, one of the most scenic rivers in all of West Virginia. It flows north along the eastern base of Cheat Mountain, a long narrow ridge drained by small feeder streams. Access is via an unpaved forest road that roughly traces the mountain's plateau. A network of other forest roads—in various states of repair—and hiking trails is concentrated in the southern half of the area. These permit exploration of the northern forest that blankets the mountain's slopes. Wildlife in the area is abundant and frequently seen. Recreation centers around the trails and Shavers Fork. The latter is one of the most prized trout rivers in the state. It's also a pretty popular whitewater run, punctuated by the High Falls, a riverwide drop that's a favorite of photographers. The area offers good opportunities for backpacking and bikepacking.

Durbin (SE) is the closest town.

getting there: From the district RS in Bartow, drive W on US-250 13.1 mi to unpaved FR-92, R. Access to the trails and river is from forest roads that branch off to the R and L. At 1.3 mi is gated FR-758, R; 2.2 mi is gated FR-789; at 2.3 mi is FR-759; at 3.2 mi is FR-405; at 4.1 mi is FR-47, R. Turn R onto FR-47 and go 2.2 mi to the end of the road at Shavers Fork. • From the jct of US-219 and US-250, take US-250 E 8.5 mi to unpaved Cheat Mountain Rd (FR-92), L.

topography: Cheat Mtn is a long, NE-SW ridge which falls off steeply on its NW slope. The SE slope is milder, and it's this that FR-92 runs along. Shavers Fork is the major drainage, with numerous feeder streams flowing SE off the mountain. Forest cover consists of hardwoods, hemlocks, and spruce, with rhododendron prominent in the understory. **maps:** USGS Mill Creek, Wildell, Glady.

starting out: There are no facilities in this primitive backcountry area.

activities: Hiking, Mountain Biking, Fishing, Kayaking/Canoeing, Camping.

hiking: A small network of 8 trails covers a total distance of 19 mi. All but one of the trails are located between FR-92 and Shavers Fork. The single exception is the *Chestnut Ridge Trail*, which leads W from FR-92. The trails are similar in configuration and in the hiking experiences they offer. All follow the heavily forested E slopes of Cheat Mountain. The main attractions on the trails are their isolation, the chance to encounter wildlife, and access to Shavers Fork, an exceptionally scenic river that's a favorite with fly fishermen. The trails follow both narrow footpaths and old road beds. The trails are blazed irregularly, and the signs at the trailheads may be missing. Hiking on the trails is moderate. Access to all trails is from FR-92.

mountain biking: Riding in the area is best suited to those with an adventurous streak who don't mind riding in less than perfect conditions. The easiest riding is on the relatively large network of unpaved roads that criss-crosses the backcountry. These are all open to vehicles, though traffic is usually light to nonexistent. Riding on the roads is easy to moderate; the drawback is that the scenery is rather plain compared to some of the lush stands of spruce and dense hardwood forests in the backcountry. More challenging and more rewarding riding is available on the gated roads and trails. Although these may be overgrown in places, with missing blazes and obscure routes, the payoff is in the surroundings. The terrain is not especially steep, but trail conditions are often primitive, so be prepared to do some work.

fishing: A medium to large river that flows through a remote forest setting, Shavers Fork is almost cinematic as a setting for fly fishing for trout. Area anglers know it, and it has become a popular destination. The river flows over a rocky bed down a mild to average gradient, with excellent cover provided on both banks by the deep forest. Catch-and-release regulations are in effect on the river below the access on FR-47. Only fishing with barbless hooks is permitted. There are additional access points on FR-49 and FR-210, both of which run E from FR-92.

kayaking/canoeing: Shavers Fork enters the area under the US-250 bridge and follows a twisting course N for 23 mi before leaving the NF at Bemis. For almost all of this distance it flows through near-pristine mountain backcountry; a CSX rail line that hugs its banks is just about the only trace of human presence. The run is seasonal, with water levels too low in summer to permit paddling. At normal water levels, rapids reach the class III-IV range in the latter half of the run, where most of the serious whitewater is, including the scenic High Falls, a runnable 15-foot drop. Paddlers not up to class III or IV water can still run the lesser whitewater on the first half of the run. There are take-outs river L at FR-47 and FR-210 (after FR-210 there's no turning back). These can also be used as put-ins for those wanting to quickly get to the serious stuff. The put-in is at the bridge on US-250. The last take-out for this section is at the CO-22 bridge in Bemis.

camping: Primitive backcountry camping is permitted throughout the area on NF land, except where posted. With access via the river or the extensive trail network, there are plenty of opportunities for backpacking or canoe camping. Car campers will find some suitable roadside areas along FR-92.

Kumbrabow State Forest

This 9,474-acre forest with the unusual name is West Virginia's most remote and most mountainous. Located in Randolph County just west of the Monongahela National Forest, its vast backcountry encompasses cool hemlock and hardwood forests and a native trout stream. The name was derived from parts of the names of three families—Kump, Brady, and Bowers—who led the way in the purchase of the land. The forest is kept in a primitive state, and its lush forests are a haven for wildlife. White-tailed deer, black bear, bobcat, wild turkey, and ruffed grouse are all plentiful. Recreation facilities are limited to a picnic area with stone shelters, tables, and grills; a small rustic campground; and 5 cabins. The best way to experience the forest is on the network of hiking trails, which winds through most regions of the forest.

Monterville (S) and Huttonsville (NE) are the closest towns.

contact: Superintendent, Kumbrabow State Forest, Box 65, Huttonsville, WV 26273;304/335-2219.

getting there: From the S or W: From WV-15 in Monterville, turn N onto Turkey Boone Rd (CO-45). Drive 4.8 mi (at 0.4 mi the pavement ends) to a jct inside the forest. Turn R and go 2.3 mi to the forest HQ. The campground is ahead another 2.1 mi • From the N or E: From the jct of US-250 and US-219, drive S on US-219 6.5 mi to CO-219/16. Turn R and go 3.5 mi to a jct. Turn L and go 2 mi to the campground, or 4.1 mi to the forest HQ.

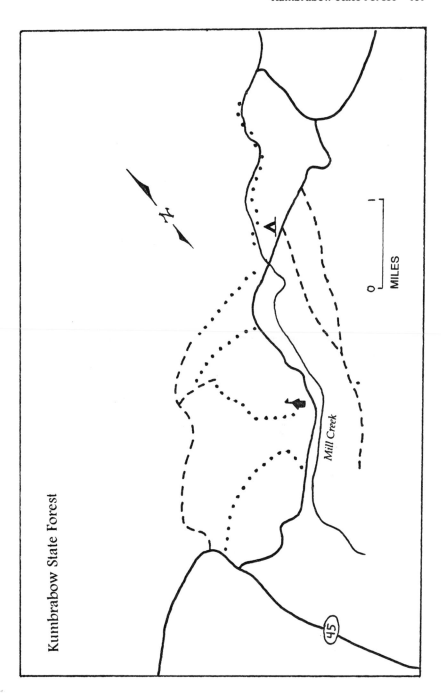

Kumbrabow State Forest

Mill Creek

MILES

45

topography: Located at the W edge of the mountains, the terrain is a combination of hills and mountain slopes. The drop-offs are steepest to the E and W. Forest cover is dense, and hardwoods are the primary species. Hemlocks are also present. Elevations are between 2,700 ft on Mill Creek—the area's major drainage—and 3,855 ft on Buck Knob. **maps:** USGS Adolph, Valley Head, Pickens.

starting out: A stop by the forest office is a good idea before heading into the backcountry. There you can pick up a trail map and get other park info. Facilities in the park are limited to hand water pumps and pit toilets; both are in the picnic area and campground.
Alcohol is not allowed in the forest.

activities: Hiking, Camping, Fishing.

hiking: A network of 8 trails winds through lush forests, along ridges, and across mountain slopes for a total of 12 miles. Most of the trails, none of which is more than 3.5 mi long, can be connected to form longer hikes. Highlights along the trails are wilderness solitude, a good chance to see wildlife, and ridgetop views. The trails follow a combination of single-track footpaths and grassy forest roads. Trails are blazed and trailheads are signed. Access is from the forest HQ, the picnic area, or near the campground. Hiking on the trails is moderate to strenuous. Trail use is light.

camping: The rustic 13-site campground is one of the most scenic car campgrounds in the state. Tucked away in a forest of hemlocks, hardwoods, and rhododendron beside Mill Creek, the large sites are spread out in 2 areas on either side of the creek. Privacy at the sites is excellent. Each site has a picnic table, grill, and stone fire place. The sites on the far side of the creek are arranged around a small meadow. Pit toilets and hand water pumps are the only facilities. Sites cost $7/night. The campground is located 2.1 mi past the forest HQ. It's open from mid-Apr to early Dec.

fishing: Mill Creek is a native brook trout fishery that flows through the park from end to end, a distance of about 4 mi. The small to medium creek flows NE down a mild to average gradient over a rocky bed. The forest cover is exceptional and fly-casters will find the conditions tight in many places. The creek is fishable year round, though the water gets pretty low in summer. Access is possible from the campground, the picnic area, or the forest HQ.

lodging: For a multi-day stay you can overnight at one of forest's 5 rustic cabins. The cabins are furnished, but have no running water. Each cabin has a stone fireplace, wood-burning kitchen stove, and a fully equipped kitchen. Lights and refrigerator are gas-powered. The cabins were constructed by the CCC in the 1930s. Pit toilets are in the area, and well water is available. The cabins sleep 4 and rates start at $55/night. Rates are lower for stays of more than 1 night. The cabins are open from around Apr 1 to Dec 1.

Snowshoe Resort

Snowshoe sprawls across 11,000 acres between Slatyfork and Cass in Pocahontas County. It's a full-scale resort with two massive lodges, several restaurants, a golf course, and enough mountaintop condominiums to make anyone but a land developer uneasy. In winter Snowshoe is one of the major downhill skiing destinations in the mid-Atlantic states. In summer the trails and roads that lace the mountain terrain—more than 100 miles of them—transform the mountain into one of the state's premiere mountain biking meccas. As befits a resort, you have to pay to ride, but where else will you have access to a trail network that includes dozens of miles of technical single-track that will test the mettle of even the best riders, screaming downhills runs, and winding roads that pass through mountain meadows overlooking spectacular vistas. When the clouds are sitting low in the valleys and you're riding 1,000 feet above them, the fee and resort atmosphere might just seem like acceptable compromises. The mountain biking season runs from the beginning of May to the end of October.

Slatyfork (W) and Cass (E) are the closest towns.

contact: Snowshoe Mountain Resort, PO Box 10, Snowshoe Rd, Snowshoe, WV 26209; 304/572-1000; wvweb.com/www/snowshoe.

getting there: From the jct of WV-39 and US-219 in Marlinton: Turn N onto US-219 and go 20.5 mi to WV-66. Turn R and go 0.7 mi to the resort entrance, L. • From Cass, turn W onto WV-66 and go 10.4 mi to the resort entrance, R.

topography: Snowshoe Resort is one of the highest elevation recreation areas in the state. It encompasses the headwaters of Shavers Fork and several mountain ridges, with elevations extending to 4,700 ft.

Even on Shavers Fork the elevation doesn't drop below 3,700 ft. The low point is in the valley where the golf course is located (3,350 ft) Despite development, most of the area remains forested with northern hardwoods and conifers, though large areas have been cleared to accommodate the resort facilities. **maps:** USGS Mingo, Cass.

starting out: Before heading out onto the trails, you need to purchase a trail pass ($8/day) at one of the biking centers. As part of the package you get a large, detailed trail map. Water, rest rooms, pay phones, and just about anything else you might want or need (including rental bikes and accessories) are widely available at different locations in the resort.

Helmets must be worn on the trails.

activities: Mountain Biking.

mountain biking: Ride the trails of Snowshoe long enough and you'll find just about every imaginable trail type and conditions: Gated roadbeds that wind leisurely through meadows or across ski slopes, rock-studded single-track paths that run through beautiful northern forests, unpaved roads leading to scenic views, and steep, steep downhills. All trails are well maintained and easy to follow. Trailheads and trail jcts are signed and the trails themselves are blazed. Difficulty ratings are assigned on a scale of easy, moderate, difficult, ratings that are reflected on the color-coded trail map. There are numerous access points along the main resort road, including at the entrance in the valley and on top of the mountain at the Silver Creek Lodge. Riding runs the gamut from easy to strenuous, with miles of trails in each category.

lodging: Just 2 mi down the road from the condo madness of Snowshoe Resort is Slatyfork Farm (304/572-3900), a 500-acre retreat tucked away in a scenic valley. The farm house is run as a B&B, with 5 separate rooms (only 1 has a private bath). Country furnishings and collectibles create a warm, comfortable atmosphere in the building. Weekend rates begin at $70/night for 2 people. Also available on the property are several rustic cabins. Rates for these start at $125/night on weekends.

Seneca State Forest

West Virginia's oldest state forest encompasses 11,684 acres of forested mountain slopes in Pocahontas County. The Greenbrier River flows past at the lower elevations, forming the forest's western boundary. The forest is managed for timber extraction, wildlife habitat protection, and outdoor recreation. A large network of hiking and biking trails; a small scenic campground; a picnic area with shelter, tables, and grills; and a small lake that is stocked with trout, bass, and bluegill are the main attractions. Away from the main rec areas you'll find a lush forest where hardwoods and hemlocks block out the sun and leave the forest floor in cool shade. Wildlife in the forest includes white-tailed deer and wild turkey.

Marlinton (SW) is the closest town.

contact: Superintendent, Seneca State Forest, Route 1, Box 65, Dunmore, WV 24934; 304/799-6213.

getting there: From the RR depot at Cass Scenic RR State Park, turn E onto WV-66 and go 4.6 mi to WV-28. Turn R and go 3.4 mi to a jct. Turn R, continuing on WV-28. Go 5.2 mi to the forest HQ.

topography: The Greenbrier River flows past the forest, forming much of its W boundary. Elevations on the river are around 2,250 ft. From there, the terrain rises to the E and S, reaching an elevation of 3,458 on Thorny Creek Mtn. The majority of the forest acreage is forested, with hemlocks, hardwoods, and rhododendron all present. **maps:** USGS Clover Lick.

starting out: Trail maps and other forest info are available at the main office. They also sell USGS topos for the area. Also there is a pay phone, and a spotless coin-operated shower/rest room in an adjacent building (for the use of campers and cabin guests only). The forest is open from 6 AM to 10 PM. The office is open weekdays from 8:30 AM to 4:30 PM; weekends and holidays from 10 AM to 2 PM.

activities: Hiking, Mountain Biking, Camping.

hiking: A network of 9 trails extends into every region of the forest, covering a total of 15 mi. In addition to these, both the 75-mi *Greenbrier River Trail* and the 330-mi *Allegheny Trail* pass through the forest, permitting hikes or backpacking trips of almost any length. Unmaintained dirt and gravel roads add another 13 mi of hiking potential. Highlights along the trails are mountain views, a remote forested setting, the scenic Greenbrier River Valley, and an abundance of wildlife. The trails follow a combination of single-track footpaths, old grassy roadbeds, and dirt roads, some gated and some open. Many of the trails intersect, permitting loops of various lengths. The trailheads are signed and the trails are blazed and generally easy to follow. Hiking on the trails is easy to moderate. Trail use is moderate, and some of the trails are open to mountain bikes.

mountain biking: Although the main riding attraction in the area is the *Greenbrier River Trail*, riders looking for single track or more technical conditions will want to check out the forest trails open to bikes. They include the forest's 7-mi stretch of the *Allegheny Trail*, another 3 mi of single track, and the 13 mi of unpaved forest roads. Many of the hiking trails are closed to bikes. Riding on the trails is moderate to strenuous.

camping: The SF is home to one of the more attractive primitive car campgrounds in WV. 10 sites are spread out in a heavily forested area where the dense understory of rhododendron provides excellent privacy at the large, well spaced sites. Each site has a picnic table, stone grill, and lantern post. Pit toilets and a hand water pump are in the campground, and campers can use the shower behind the forest office. The sites cost $7/night. The campground is open Apr 1–Dec 1.

lodging: The forest is home to 7 rustic log cabins constructed by the CCC in the 1930s. They're located in 2 areas: next to Seneca Lake and in a remote corner of the forest overlooking the Greenbrier River. The cabins are fully furnished, with stone fireplaces, wood-burning kitchen stoves, and gas stoves and lights. There's no running water, but pit toilets are available, and the shower behind the forest office is open to cabin guests. The cabins sleep from 3 to 8 people. Rates begin at $48/night, but drop for longer stays. The cabins are open from late Apr to early Dec.

Marlinton Ranger District
Monongahela National Forest

The Marlinton Ranger District covers 135,392 acres on either side of the Greenbrier River, which flows southwest through the district's center, dividing it in half. The mountainous terrain in the district's western half is remote, rugged, and steep. The region has been dubbed the "birthplace of rivers," since the Gauley, Elk, Shavers Fork, and Williams all begin here. District lands are adjacent to the Cranberry Wilderness and Cranberry Backcountry, and combine with them to create the largest continuous area of primitive outdoor recreation in West Virginia. The Highlands Scenic Highway provides the primary access to this area, and is an attraction in its own right. The area's high elevation and western location result in a climate that's characteristic of a rain forest, with up to 70 inches of rain annually. In winter, snows are equally heavy, and make the area a prime cross-country skiing destination. Wildlife abounds, and includes black bear, snowshoe hare, mink, white-tailed deer, and red fox. The eastern half of the district is characterized by long, narrow mountain ridges that are more modest than those to the west. The climate here is more moderate too, due to the mountains' "shadow effect."

Recreation on the district is exceptionally diverse. The multi-use trails—used by hikers, bikers, and skiers—are the main attraction, but the rivers, creeks, and campgrounds provide additional options for fly fishing, whitewater paddling, and camping.

Marlinton is the largest town on the district.

contact: Marlinton Ranger District, USDA Forest Service, PO Box 210, Marlinton, WV 24954; 304/799-4334

getting there: US-219 and WV-39 provide the major vehicle access to the district. The district RS is located on WV-39 E of downtown Marlinton.

topography: Steep mountain slopes forested with hardwoods and conifers comprise most of the district. The Greenbrier River is the major drainage. It flows SW through a valley that is broad in places. Elevations are between 2,000 ft on the Greenbrier River and 4,710 ft on Red Spruce Knob. **maps:** See below under the individual areas.

starting out: If you're visiting the district for the first time, a stop by the ranger station is worthwhile. They can supply you with maps and brochures of the district. You can also buy USGS topo maps inside. Another excellent source of information is the Marlinton visitors center, located in the restored RR depot beside the *Greenbrier River Trail*. It's on Main St in downtown Marlinton.

activities: Mountain Biking, Hiking, Cross-country Skiing, Camping, Fishing.

mountain biking: Both areas described below have networks of trails open to mountain bikes. The Tea Creek/Slatyfork area is the more popular. Indeed, it's one of the most popular fat tire destinations in the state. Most riding in these areas is on single-track trails that wind through mountainous terrain. Running through the center of the district, the *Greenbrier River Trail* is an exception. The 70-mi converted rail trail follows a wide path and gentle grade through the scenic river valley between Cass and Lewisburg. The trail is not a part of the NF and is described under its own heading.

hiking: Opportunities for both hiking and backpacking abound on the district. The largest network of trails is in the Tea Creek /Slatyfork Area, but the Middle Mountain Area is anchored by a single long trail that also provides access to the *Allegheny Trail*, at 330 mi the state's longest trail. Although easy hikes can be found, most paths wind through mountainous terrain that is rugged and steep in many places.

cross-country skiing: With substantial annual snowfall and a remote location, the Tea Creek/Slatyfork Area is one of the most popular destinations on the Monongahela NF for nordic skiers. Both trails and roads are used as ski tracks; the Highland Scenic Highway, which is not plowed, is a favorite starting point and can provide access to woodland trails such as the *Gauley Mountain Trail*. Another small network of groomed trails is located at the Elk River Touring Center. The season runs from Thanksgiving to around the middle of March.

camping: Primitive backcountry camping is permitted in both areas described below. With their extensive trail systems, there are plenty of opportunities for backpacking or bikepacking. A single trailside shelter is also at each location.

The district is home to 3 primitive car campgrounds, 2 in the Tea Creek/Slatyfork area, 1 in the Middle Mountain area. Facilities at each are limited to hand water pumps and pit toilets. They're all open from Mar 15 to Dec 15.

lodging: Located on US-219 in Slatyfork, the Elk River Touring Center (304/572-3771; wvweb.com/www/elk_river.html) features an inn with restaurant, farmhouse, and several cabins. As a base camp for mountain biking, cross-country skiing, and fly fishing trips, the compound can't be beat. In addition to housing the restaurant and outfitter's shop, the inn features 5 comfortable rooms, each with its own bath. Weekend rates are $80/night for 2 people. The farmhouse has 5 more rooms with 3 shared baths. Rates are $60/night. Next door are 3 cabins of various size. All have private baths. Rates are $125–$150/night. The touring center can provide rental equipment, guided trips, and lessons.

Tea Creek/Slatyfork Area

This is a vast backcountry area characterized by steep mountain slopes, cool mountain creeks, lush forests, and outdoor recreation possibilities to suit just about any taste. The area is bounded by US-219 (E), the Highland Scenic Highway (S), and the Gauley RD (W). It is adjacent to the Cranberry Wilderness, which is opposite FR-86, a rugged forest road. Mountain bikers, hikers, and cross-country skiers come from all over the East Coast to take to the vast trail network of single-track and forest road. Gil and Mary Willis of the Elk River Touring Center have been responsible for much of the region's popularity as an outdoor destination. They have mapped the area, run a farmhouse B&B and restaurant, and offer guided biking and skiing trips as well as rentals. In lieu of an on-site visitor center, their compound has become something of an unofficial outpost for visitors to the region. In addition to the trails, the Tea Creek campground serves as a car-accessible base camp to the area. There are a couple of top-notch trout creeks to be fished, and the Williams River, which flows through the area, is a popular whitewater run.

Marlinton (S) is the closest town.

getting there: From the jct of WV-39 and US-219 in Marlinton: Turn N onto US-219 and go 6.9 mi to the Highland Scenic Highway (WV-150). Straight on US-219 it's 8.8 mi to the Elk River Touring Center,

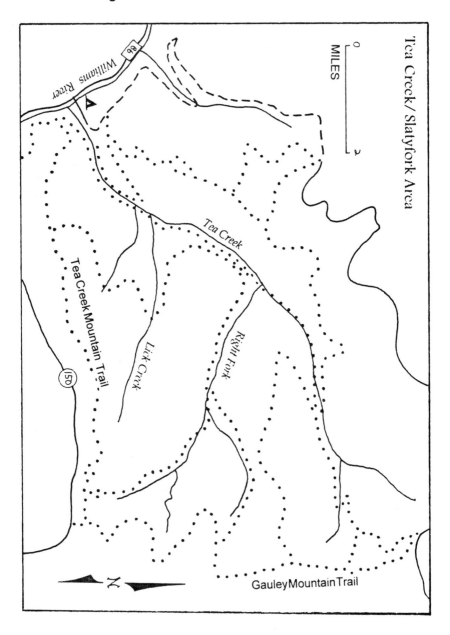

L. Or turn L onto WV-150 and go 8.9 mi (at 5 mi is the *Red Spruce Knob Trail*, L; 5.2 mi is the *Gauley Mtn Trail*, R) to access to the Tea Creek Campground. Turn L onto the gravel road and go 1 mi to the campground entrance, R. Note: WV-150 is often closed from mid-Dec to mid-March due to snowfall.

topography: The large backcountry is defined by Gauley Mtn, a long N-S ridge from which Tea Creek and the Gauley River flow W. A series of small, steep mountains line the area's S edge and provide the highest elevations—4,710 on Red Spruce Knob. Low point, on the Williams River at the campground, is 3,000 ft. The W slopes are generally the steepest in the area. The forest cover is a lush mixture of hardwoods and hemlocks. **maps:** USGS Webster Springs SE, Woodrow, Sharp Knob, (Webster Springs SW).

starting out: The Elk River Touring Center acts as something of an unofficial info center for this part of the district. You can buy trail maps there, or rent mountain bikes or cross-country skis. They also know the backcountry as well as anyone. A good trail map is available from the district RS. Water and vault toilets are located in the Tea Creek Campground.

activities: Mountain Biking, Hiking, Cross-Country Skiing, Fishing, Kayaking/Canoeing, Camping

mountain biking: The network of 17 trails located in the back-country between Slatyfork and the Tea Creek Campground covers a total of almost 50 mi. Of these, all are open to mountain bikes (a few, such as the lower *Tea Creek Trail*, are often unridable due to wet trail conditions). Most trails are single-track, though a few follow gated roads and old road beds. Rides of many different configurations are possible, making this the best fat tire destination on the district. Almost all riding conditions are encountered, from easy level grades without obstacles to steep descents and extremely technical single-track. The trails are blazed with blue diamonds; heavy use keeps them easy to follow in any event. Trailheads and trail jcts are clearly signed and large trailmaps on signboards provide useful overviews of the backcountry. Access to the trail network is from the Tea Creek Campground or at trailheads on FR-24. To reach the *Gauley Mtn Trail*: leave the Elk River Touring Center and go S on US-219 1.5 mi to unsigned FR-24. Turn R and go 3.5 mi to the trailhead, L. 0.2 mi further up the road is access to the *Tea Creek Trail* and a parking area, L.

hiking: Although the 50-mi backcountry trail network now gets most use from mountain bikers, it's still an excellent destination for hiking and backpacking. The large number of trails ensures that users are spread out over a wide area. The trails almost always seem empty, even when there are lots of hikers and bikers in the backcountry. Highlights along the trails are mountain views, the lush forest, and wildlife. Hiking is easy to moderate. See above for more detailed trail info.

cross-country skiing: From Thanksgiving to Mar the trails and roads that wind through this region of heavy snowfall are taken over by nordic skiers and snowshoers. The major skiing destinations are WV-150 (it's not plowed), the backcountry hiking/biking trails (*Gauley Mountain Trail* and *Red Spruce Trail* are favorites), and a 4-mi groomed trail network at the Elk River Touring Center. Skiers of all skill levels will find a suitable trail in this area.

fishing: Trout anglers can choose between a mountain creek that flows out of the backcountry mountains and a river that is paralleled by a road for almost 20 mi.

Tea Creek begins high up on Gauley Mtn and flows about 7 mi SW to a confluence with the Williams River at the Tea Creek Campground. It's small to medium in size and flows down a mild to average gradient. Cover is excellent and the stream bed is very rocky. Access is from the *Tea Creek Trail*, which follows it for its entire length. It's stocked trout waters. One of its tributaries, Lick Creek, is a native brook trout fishery. It offers fishing on a small backcountry creek where the only access is by wading.

The Williams River is the area's major drainage. Although access is at the Tea Creek Campground and along FR-86, most of the river flows through the Gauley RD. It is described below under the Cranberry Wilderness, which begins across the road from the campground and river.

camping: Backpacking is allowed anywhere in the Tea Creek backcountry. There's a shelter 0.7 mi from the upper end of the *Tea Creek Trail*. Sites along the trails are not difficult to find.

There are 2 primitive car campgrounds in the area—Tea Creek and Day Run. Tea Creek has 29 sites spread out in 2 heavily wooded areas between the Williams River and Tea Creek. The sites are large and well spaced, and the dense understory of rhododendron means that you won't have to see your neighbors. Each site has a picnic table, grill, and lantern post. Facilities are limited to pit toilets and a hand water pump. Sites cost $5/night. The campground is open Mar 15–Dec 15.

Less popular and slightly out of the way is the Day Run Campground. The 12 sites are large and isolated in a partially wooded area, offering a high level of privacy. Each site has a picnic table, grill, and lantern post. Facilities in the campground are pit toilets and a hand water pump. Sites cost $5/night. The campground is open Mar 15–Dec 15. To reach the campground: follow directions to the Tea Creek campground but turn R onto the gravel access road instead of L. Go 3 mi to FR-216. Turn R and go 1.2 mi to the campground entrance, L.

Another option for car campers is to overnight at one of 20 numbered roadside sites along FR-86 and the Williams River W of the Tea Creek Campground. These sites are spread out over 5 miles and offer just about the best that roadside car camping has to offer. The sites are isolated amid the heavy forest and dense understory of rhododendron that lines the river. Each site has a picnic table and fire ring. There's no fee to camp at the sites.

Middle Mountain Area

This primitive backcountry area occupies a long mountain ridge and a pair of smaller pockets of forested mountain terrain. A primitive car campground and a small roadside picnic area are the only developments on this part of the Marlinton Ranger District. The lack of amenities and the remoteness of the area keeps the numbers of visitors to a minimum and makes for ideal daylong or multi-day forays into the backcountry. A handful of multi-use trails are suitable for hiking, backpacking, and mountain biking. For those not wanting to overnight in the wilds, the Pocahontas Campground makes a convenient base camp.

Minnehaha Springs (NW) is the closest town.

getting there: The Pocahontas Campground is located on WV-92, 1.8 mi S of WV-39 and 13.6 mi N of CO-14 and access to the Lake Sherwood Rec Area. • Trail access at the Rimel picnic area is on WV-39 0.4 mi W of the jct with WV-92. • To reach the S end of the *Middle Mountain Trail*: From the jct of WV-92 and CO-16/1 N of White Sulphur Springs, go N on WV-92 6 mi to N Fork Rd (CO-14). Turn L onto the gravel road and go 0.5 mi to a low bridge across N Fork Anthony Creek. Roadside parking is available 0.2 mi further up the road.

topography: Middle Mountain is a long, narrow ridge that runs NE-SW and defines the area. Although there are a few steep slopes, in general the terrain is relatively mild. Elevations are between 2,450 at the campground and 3,559 on the mountain near the county line. A mixed hardwood/conifer forest covers most of the mountain. **maps:** USGS Lake Sherwood, Mountain Grove, Minnehaha Springs, Marlinton.

starting out: This area is primarily a large region of undeveloped backcountry. You'll find pit toilets and picnic tables at the Rimel picnic area. A hand water pump and pit toilets are located in the Pocahontas Campground.

activities: Hiking, Mountain Biking, Camping.

hiking: 3 trails in the area cover a total distance of 32.5 mi. The longest of these, 20-mi *Middle Mountain Trail*, follows the long ridgeline of the same name from the Rimel Picnic Area to Neola and the N Fork Anthony Creek. Mid-trail access is possible by hiking up the *Allegheny Trail* from the access on WV-92, 6.3 mi S of the Pocahontas Campground. Access to the *Two Lick Trail* is at the campground entrance. The trail is a 4.5-mi loop that winds through a scenic forest. The 8-mi *Laurel Creek Trail* is another loop—it begins in the Rimel Picnic Area. All trails are blazed and easy to follow. Hiking is moderate to strenuous. Highlights along the trails include scenic vistas, remote backcountry, and wildlife. There's an Adirondack-style shelter on the *Laurel Creek Trail.* All trailheads are signed.

mountain biking: The 3 main trails in the area—*Middle Mountain Trail, Two Lick Trail,* and *Laurel Creek Trail*—are all open to bikes. All 3 provide challenging riding on single-track trails that traverse mountainous terrain. Accesses are described above. Another loop, covering 12.5 mi, can be formed by connecting FR-55 and FR-345, open and gated forest roads, respectively. Access to the loop is 0.5 mi E of the Rimel Picnic Area on WV-39. Riding along all routes is moderate to strenuous.

camping: Primitive backcountry camping is permitted throughout the area on NF land. The *Middle Mountain Trail* offers the best opportunities for backpacking trips. There's also a shelter on the *Laurel Creek Trail.*

The Pocahontas Campground is a 9-site primitive car campground located on WV-92. The sites are set back in the woods and out of sight of the road, but the sounds of trucks rumbling through can still be heard. Fortunately, traffic on the road is relatively light. The large, well spaced sites offer a high degree of privacy. Campground use is light too, so you just might have it to yourself. Each site has a picnic table, grill, and lantern post. There are pit toilets and a hand water pump in the campground. A canopy of pines, hemlocks, and hardwoods offers shade and a rustic feel. The sites cost $5/night. The campground is open Mar 15–Oct 15.

Gauley Ranger District
Monongahela National Forest

The Gauley Ranger District encompasses 158,147 acres in Pocahontas, Webster, Nicholas, and Greenbrier counties. It is a region of amazing ecological diversity, vast natural habitats in a wild or semi-wild state, and outstanding opportunities for outdoor recreation. Wildlife abounds in the dense forest that covers most of the district's acreage, and sightings of black bear and white-tailed deer are common. Other mammals include bobcat, red fox, mink, and snowshoe hare. Of interest to the naturalist are the stands of pure red spruce found at the higher elevations and the Cranberry Glades botanical area, a series of bogs more typical of Canada than of central or southern Appalachia. Four major rivers—the Gauley, Williams, Cranberry, and North Fork Cherry—flow west through the district, draining the steep mountain slopes of the district's eastern half. The district is home to the 35,000-acre Cranberry Wilderness and the 26,000-acre Cranberry Backcountry, a semi-wild area from which machines and motor vehicles have been banished. These areas are a natural magnet for outdoor enthusiasts, who come to hike, bike, ski, fish, camp, canoe, and kayak—often combining several activities in a single trip. Access to this remote natural wonderland is via the 45-mile Highland Scenic Highway, a lightly traveled road that incorporates numerous scenic overlooks with access to all the backcountry areas.

Richwood is the largest town on the district.

contact: Gauley Ranger Station, USDA Forest Service, P.O. Box 110, Richwood, WV 26261; 304/846-2695.

getting there: 2 state highways that combine to form the Highland Scenic Parkway provide the major vehicle access to the district. WV-150 runs N–S along the E edge of the Cranberry Wilderness and WV-55/WV-39 runs E–W along the district's S boundary. • The Cranberry Visitor Center is at the jct of WV-55/WV-39 and WV-150. The district RS is on WV-55/WV-39 20.2 mi W of there.

topography: Terrain is mountainous throughout the district, with the highest elevations and steepest slopes occurring in the E half. The mountains are drained by the 4 rivers described above, all of which empty into the Gauley. **maps:** See below under each listing.

starting out: The Cranberry Visitor Center is the starting place for most visitors to the district. Inside you can pick up maps or brochures or check on current conditions. There are rest rooms, water, and a pay phone. A side room features exhibits on the area. You can also buy USGS topo maps. Hours are 9 AM to 5 PM daily during summer and on weekends the rest of the year. The Gauley RS is another source of information, though it isn't geared as much to visitors. It's open weekdays from 8 AM to 4:45 PM. Inside you can pick up maps and brochures that cover the district. USGS topos are also for sale.

activities: Hiking, Mountain Biking, Fishing, Cross-country Skiing, Camping, Kayaking/Canoeing.

hiking: Approximately 150 miles of hiking trails wind through the district. Most of these are concentrated in one vast network that connects the Cranberry Wilderness and the Cranberry Backcountry. Hikes of almost any length and configuration are possible here, from a short stroll on a boardwalk through the Cranberry Glades to a weeklong backpacking trips that may connect as many as a dozen trails. Scenic highlights along the trails are both dazzling and seemingly endless. The hiker who covers enough of the backcountry will encounter boreal and Appalachian forests, mountaintop vistas, alpine bogs, small headwater trout creeks, rushing whitewater rivers, and an abundance of wildlife. Conditions on the trails vary, but outside the wilderness the trails are almost uniformly blazed and the trailheads signed (except where bears have made a meal of the signs). Because of the mountainous terrain, hikers should be prepared for moderate to strenuous hiking, although easy stretches are encountered, and many of the roads make good footpaths too.

mountain biking: Although all trails in the district—with the exception of those in the Cranberry Wilderness—are open to bikes, the most popular destination by far is the Cranberry Backcountry. There the combination of technical single-track and unpaved roads (closed to vehicles) in a remote mountain location is unsurpassed. There are rides for riders of all skill levels, and the conditions for bikepacking are almost perfect. All of the highlights described above under *hiking* are accessible to mountain bikers as well.

fishing: The creeks and rivers that flow through the district provide trout anglers with a variety of conditions and challenges. In the Cranberry Wilderness are the headwaters of the Williams and Cranberry Rivers. These cold, pure creeks support small populations of wild trout. The creeks aren't stocked, and fishing them requires patience and a certain amount of effort, since they can only be reached by hiking trail.

As the creeks flow down the mountain they gain size and enter the Cranberry Backcountry, probably the most popular angling destination on the district. Here the Cranberry River and Dogway Fork provide miles of fishing on accessible, mid-sized trout waters. They're both regularly stocked, and regulations vary from one section of river to another. Fly-fishing and catch-and-release are both encouraged.

cross-country skiing: The uplands of the Cranberry Wilderness and Cranberry Backcountry receive just about as much annual snowfall as anywhere else in the state. Storms that dump a foot on the ground at a time are not uncommon. And since the region is so remote and even highway traffic so light, when it snows, the roads are simply left unplowed. For nordic skiers, this means that the Highland Scenic Highway is often one of the best cross-country ski tracks in the Allegheny Mountains. Added to that are approximately 100 miles of trails and roads suitable to skiing. Access is from the Cranberry Visitor Center, from which it's possible to access the entire network of ski trails. Maps of appropriate trails are available inside.

camping: The Gauley RD is one of the major backpacking and bikepacking destinations in all of WV. Although backcountry camping is permitted just about anywhere on NF lands, the trails and roads of the Cranberry Backcountry are the most popular destinations. A series of 7 shelters that line the Cranberry River and FR-76/FR-102 provide primitive accommodations for those who don't want to tent camp. The adjacent Cranberry Wilderness offers the best opportunity for backpacking solitude.

Car campers will find 4 different campgrounds to choose from. All are located in the W half of the district. Facilities are primitive, with just pit toilets and hand water pumps at each of the campgrounds. Some of the camping areas stay open all year.

For even more primitive car camping, there are designated roadside sites along the Cranberry River and Williams River. These have no facilities at all. Camping roadside outside of these sites is not permitted.

kayaking/canoeing: The main paddling action on the Gauley RD is on the Cranberry River and the Williams River. These are both seasonal rivers, with flows that drop too low in summer for river running. Both are hardcore whitewater rivers that require closed-deck canoes or kayaks, and plenty of experience. The payoff is a wild ride through some stunning mountain scenery.

lodging: In Marlinton is the Jerico B&B (304/799-6241). A farm house and 3 cabins—all tucked away in an attractive forest setting just outside of town—provide several different lodging options. The 5 rooms in the main house each have a private bath with a shared kitchen and living room area. Rates are $40–45/night. Each of the 3 log cabins is attractive and fully furnished, with kitchens and baths. One even has an outdoor hot tub. They sleep from 2 to 4 people. Rates range from $65 to 100/night.

Cranberry Wilderness

This 35,864-acre wilderness is one of the prize jewels of West Virginia's mountain backcountry. The wilderness was established in 1983, and since that time human impact has been virtually eliminated from the area and the forest is being allowed to return to a natural state. Already pure stands of red spruce tower over a carpet of moss so vivid and complete that it seems almost unreal. And the headwaters of the Cranberry and Williams rivers begin in these mountains, tumbling over mossy rocks through the cool, damp forest. The wilderness boundaries are formed by the Highland Scenic Highway (E), FR-86 and the Williams River (N), and FR-102 and the Cranberry Backcountry (W). The last area provides outdoor enthusiasts with an additional 26,000 acres of rugged mountain terrain where motorized vehicles are prohibited. Outdoor recreation

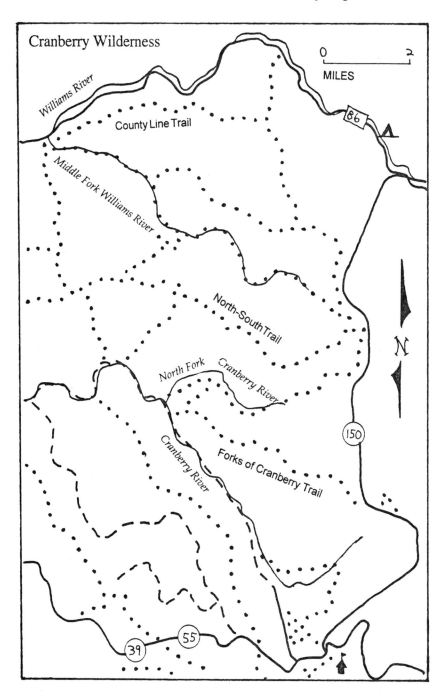

Cranberry Wilderness

Williams River

County Line Trail

Middle Fork Williams River

0   2
MILES

86

North-South Trail

North Fork   Cranberry River

Forks of Cranberry Trail

Cranberry River

150

N

39   55

in the wilderness centers around the vast network of trails, open to hiking and cross-country skiing. Backpacking trips are popular, and trout anglers can fish for native brookies in some of the purest, most remote waters in the state.

Marlinton (E) and Richwood (W) are the closest towns.

getting there: Main vehicle access to the wilderness is from trailheads located along the Highland Scenic Highway (WV-150). From the Cranberry visitor center, turn N onto WV-150 and go 3.3 mi to the *Forks of Cranberry Trail*; 3.7 mi to the *Cranberry Glades Overlook Trail*; 7.9 mi to the Big Spruce overlook; 8.4 mi to the *North-South Trail*, L; 9.9 mi to the *North Fork Trail*. • From the jct of US-219 and the Highland Scenic Highway (WV-150) S of Slatyfork, turn W onto WV-150 and go 12 mi to the *N Fork Trail*, R; 13.5 mi to the *North-South Trail*; 14 mi to the Big Spruce overlook; 22 mi to the end of the road and the Cranberry Visitor Center.

topography: Both the terrain and vegetation vary considerably in the wilderness. Flora includes red spruce forest, northern hardwood forest, and northern bog. While much of the region is mountainous, large portions of the upland terrain are fairly level. Highest elevation is on Sugar Creek Mtn (4,521 ft). The low point is 2,400 ft on the Williams River. Several smaller drainages flow W, including the Cranberry River. **maps:** USGS Webster Springs SE, Mingo, Lobelia, Webster Springs SW.

starting out: With no facilities of any kind in the wilderness, the Cranberry Visitor Center serves as a natural starting point if you need info, maps, water, or anything else before heading into the backcountry. It's located at the SE corner of the wilderness, and is open daily during summer and on weekends the rest of the year.

activities: Hiking, Camping, Cross-country Skiing, Fishing.

hiking: Certainly the best way to experience the diverse ecology of the wilderness is on foot. A trail network that covers almost 70 mi criss-crosses the wilderness and makes that possible. There are 10 trails in all, ranging in length from 1 mi to 9 mi. Since all of the trails connect with one another, it's possible to put together hikes of almost any length, from short leg-stretchers to multi-day backpacking trips. Numerous loop hikes are possible by combining 2 or more trails. And since many of the trails connect to the vast trail network in the Cranberry Backcountry, weeklong backpacking trips are quite feasible. The main attraction along the trails is the forest habitat—remote, isolated, remarkably diverse, and a haven to wildlife. Hiking conditions are primitive, with no blazes and most trail jcts unsigned, but following the popular trails is not difficult, since heavy use keeps the treadways clearly defined. Several of the trails follow RR grades and old road beds, others single-track paths. Signed trailheads are located along WV-150. Hiking is easy to strenuous.

camping: Primitive backcountry camping is permitted throughout the wilderness. Backpackers should be aware, however, that in places the spruce forest is so dense that locating suitable sites can be difficult.

cross-country skiing: Nordic skiers who want to make tracks through the wilderness backcountry face something of an embarrassment of riches. Since WV-150 isn't plowed during winter, it's often a cross-country skiing destination in its own right. As are the roads and trails that lead from the visitor center into the Cranberry Backcountry. Although there are dozens of miles of suitable skiing trails in the wilderness, getting to them often requires some effort, particularly if WV-150 is impassible in a vehicle. The best trails for skiing in the wilderness are those that follow old roads: the *North Fork Trail*, *North-South Trail*, and *Laurelly Branch Trail*. Skiing is moderate to strenuous. See above under hiking for further trail info.

fishing: With so much top-notch trout fishing in the creeks that surround the wilderness, the small creeks that drain the wilderness itself don't get much attention from trout anglers. It's understandable, since prime destinations such as the Cranberry River and Williams River are located just beyond the wilderness boundaries. But for the angler interested in fishing for native brook trout in a pure mountain setting that rivals any in WV for beauty, these small feeder streams are worth a try. The Middle Fork Williams River and North Fork Cranberry River both begin as headwater trickles in the wilderness. Both are exceptionally attractive, with plenty of cover and rocky, moss covered beds. Access is via the *Middle Fork Trail* and *North Fork Trail*, respectively.

Just N of the wilderness on the other side of FR-86 is the Williams River, one of the most popular destinations among trout anglers on the Gauley RD. The river is large, with massive boulders and rock formations creating some long, deep pools. Cover is exceptional, despite the presence of the forest road. Several different regulations are in effect on the river. Most of the river is regular stocked trout waters. 3 mi past the Tea Creek campground is the start of a 2-mi segment that's catch-and-release only. For directions and access, see the Tea Creek/Slatyfork Area above.

kayaking/canoeing: In addition to its popularity among fly fishermen, the Williams River enjoys a good reputation among whitewater enthusiasts. The run begins at the Tea Creek Campground across FR-86 from the wilderness' NE corner. Although the scenery isn't quite on par with that in the wilderness itself, it still rates pretty high. This is a seasonal run that's both easy to scout and easy to tailor to whatever length you feel like paddling, since FR-86 (it eventually becomes CO-46) shadows the river all the way to its confluence with the Gauley in Donaldson, a distance of 20 mi. The river is characterized by whitewater that gets up to the class III-IV range, which puts it firmly out of the reach of novices. The rapids are more or less continuous, particularly above the Three Forks of Williams where the heaviest whitewater is encountered. Below that the river calms down a bit, as it widens and flattens out.

Cranberry Backcountry

Adjacent to the Cranberry Wilderness, the Cranberry Backcountry is a 26,000-acre designated area of low-impact outdoor recreation. Although roads follow the major drainages, motor vehicles are prohibited. Instead the gated roadways are used by the mountain bikers, hikers, cross-country skiers, anglers, and equestrians who flock to this natural oasis. Throughout most of the backcountry a forest of hardwoods and conifers prevails, providing refuge for an abundance of wildlife. White-tailed deer are common, and more black bear sightings occur here than probably anywhere else in West Virginia. The ecology of the southeast corner of the backcountry is notably district from the rest of the backcountry. The upland bogs that cover approximately 750 acres there are far more common to Canada and the northern U.S. than to central Appalachia. Since few tree species can grow in the bogs' moist, acidic soil, shrubs and dozens of species of wildflowers are predominant. A short list includes cranberry, marsh marigold, pitcher plant, mountain laurel, rhododendron, cinnamon fern, skunk cabbage, and false hellebore.

Richwood (W) and Marlinton (E) are the closest towns.

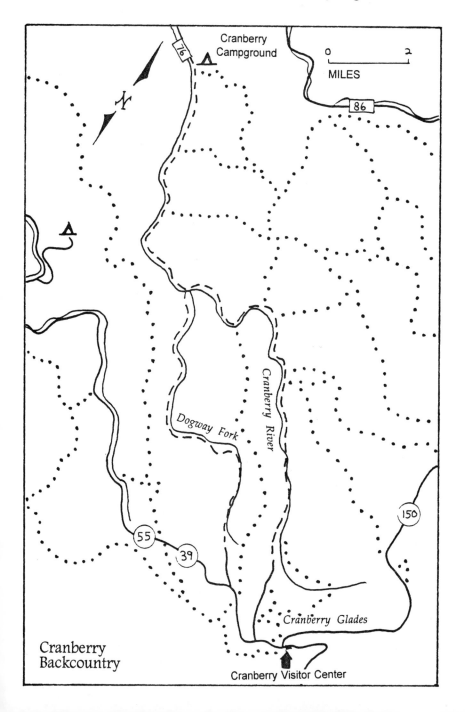

Cranberry
Campground

MILES

Dogway Fork

Cranberry River

Cranberry Glades

Cranberry Visitor Center

Cranberry
Backcountry

getting there: To reach the Cranberry Campground: From Richwood, turn E onto WV-55/WV-39 and go 0.5 mi to CO-76. Turn L and go 2.3 mi to unpaved FR-76. Turn L and go 10.2 mi to the campground and access to the backcountry. • To reach the Cranberry Glades access: Take WV-55/WV-39 W 0.6 mi from the visitor center to FR-102. Turn R and go 2.3 mi (at 1.5 mi come to a parking area for the Cranberry Glades) to the parking area. Another access is to Dogway Fork on FR-232.

topography: Terrain in the region varies from rugged and steep to moderate slopes and creek valleys. Elevations are between 4,260 at the S end of the area and 2,500 ft at the campground and lower end of the backcountry. A mixed deciduous/conifer forest covers most of the backcountry, with some clearings along the Cranberry River. **maps:** USGS Webster Springs SE, Lobelia, Camden on Gauley, Webster Springs SW, Hillsboro.

starting out: Trail maps, brochures, and other info are available in the Cranberry Visitor Center at the jct of WV-55/39 and WV-150. It's open daily in summer and weekends the rest of the year. Water and rest rooms are there too. Water is also available in the Cranberry Campground, though technically it's only for campers.

activities: Mountain Biking, Hiking, Fishing, Camping, Cross-country Skiing, Canoeing/Kayaking

mountain biking: This is one of the major fat tire destinations in the state. It's not hard to see why. All trails and backcountry roads are open to bikes, a total of 60 mi. (The *North-South Trail* is the only one that really isn't suitable to bikes). Rides of all difficulty levels are represented, from the easy grade of FR-76 and FR-102 along the Cranberry River, to 35 mi of technical single-track. Rides of almost any length are possible, and there are enough different loop rides to keep you busy for at least a week. Trail highlights are the forest setting, abundant wildlife, highland bogs, stocked trout creeks, and numerous bikepacking possibilities. Most rides start at the visitor center, Cranberry Campground, or at the gate on FR-232 just off WV-39/55 (3.9 mi W of the visitor center).

hiking: Hikers have virtually the same options as mountain bikers. For solitude and remoteness, the blazed footpaths will be most appealing. Several connections with the large trail network of the

Cranberry Wilderness (closed to bikes), makes them even more appealing. Trails are concentrated in 2 areas: SE of the Cranberry Campground, and in the Cranberry Glades area NW of the visitor center. At the Cranberry Glades a series of boardwalks loops through the rare bog environment. Trailheads are signed and the trails are blazed with blue diamonds. Hiking is moderate to strenuous, except on the gated roads, where it's easy. Trail use is heavy.

fishing: Trout anglers can choose from two exceptionally scenic creeks in the area that offer roughly 25 mi of fishable water. the Cranberry River is a medium sized creek that flows down a mild to avg gradient over a very rocky bed. It has exceptional pooling and good cover for most of its length. Access is from the gated roads that run beside it. Some special regulations apply on the river: for 4.3 mi from Dogway Fork to the N Fork Cranberry River it's artificial lures, catch-and-release only. The river is stocked. Fishing pressure is heavy.

Dogway Fork is a medium sized creek that flows down an avg gradient. Cover is exceptional, and pooling is generally quite good. Access is not as easy as on the Cranberry River, as the *Dogway Fork Trail* is out of sight of the creek for most of its length. The benefit is that fishing pressure is much lighter. From the dam to the creek's mouth (1.8 mi), artificial flies, catch-and-release only regulations are in effect. Dogway Fork is wild trout waters.

camping: The Cranberry Backcountry is the most popular camping destination on the district. Campers can choose between primitive backcountry camping, camping at one of 7 shelters spaced along the Cranberry River in the backcountry, or in the primitive car campground located at the lower access point.

Backpacking and bikepacking are both popular in the Cranberry Backcountry, with plenty of suitable areas along the trails and roads. The 7 shelters along the river provide one option, but tent campers can set up nearby if the shelters are full.

The Cranberry Campground is a primitive car campground located just beyond the boundaries of the designated backcountry at its lower (N) end. The 30 sites are large and well spaced, but privacy is minimized by the sparseness of the tree cover and the landscaping that has been done. The sites are arranged in 2 loops, one large and one small. Each of the sites has a picnic table, grill, and lantern post. Facilities are pit toilets and a hand water pump. Most sites cost $5/night; some cost $8/night during peak season. This is a popular campground that often fills on summer weekends.

(Sites are almost always available at Bishop Knob Campground, just up the road). The campground is open Mar 15–Dec 8.

Lower Cranberry River Area

Adjacent to the immensely popular Cranberry Backcountry, this area occupies the western portion of the Gauley Ranger District. It is an area characterized by 4 rivers considered by outdoor enthusiasts to be some of the best in the state. The Cranberry River flows through the heart of the area. A small primitive campground and a picnic area are built on the banks of the river. A second campground sits on a knoll overlooking the river. The other rivers are the Williams, the Gauley, and the Cherry. The first two form the area's northern boundary, while the Cherry forms the district's southern boundary. Recreation here is focused on the rivers, which are popular with both anglers and paddlers. A small network of trails open to hikers and mountain bikers add to the possibilities for outdoor recreation.

Richwood (S) is the closest town.

getting there: From downtown Richwood, turn E onto WV-55/WV-39 and go E 0.5 mi to CO-76. Turn L and go 2.3 mi to FR-76. Turn L onto the gravel road and go 3.1 mi to the Woodbine Picnic Area, L. 0.3 mi past the picnic area is the Big Rock Campground, L. Turn L at the campground onto FR-81 and go 5.4 mi to Bishop Knob Campground, R.

topography: The Williams River and the Cranberry River flow W through the area, and the N Fork Cherry River forms the S boundary. Elevations are between 2,158 ft at Big Rock Campground and 3,800 ft at the E edge of the area. A lush forest with hardwoods and scattered hemlocks covers most elevations. **maps:** USGS Camden on Gauley, Richwood, Webster Springs SW.

starting out: Information and maps are available at the district RS on WV-39/55 E of downtown Richwood or at the Cranberry Visitor Center. Water and rest rooms are at the Woodbine Picnic Area, as well as at the 2 campgrounds.

activities: Hiking, Mountain Biking, Fishing, Camping, Kayaking/Canoeing.

hiking: 4 trails cover a total of 14 mi around the 2 campgrounds. The trails can be connected, but only by hiking on forest roads. With lengths that range from 1.5 mi to 6 mi, they're best suited for day hikes. The adjacent Cranberry Backcountry or the long trails covered below under the Summit Lake Area are better suited for backpacking trips. Highlights along the trails are the remote forest setting and wildlife. Trails follow single-tracks and old road beds. The trails are blazed. Trailheads are dispersed. You can access the trails in the Bishop Knob Campground, the Woodbine Picnic Area, and on CO-7/6 W of the Big Rock Campground. Hiking is moderate.

mountain biking: All of the trails described are open to bikes. They can be ridden alone or in combination with the numerous forest roads—both open and gated—that lace the area. This is a much less popular area for riding than the Cranberry Backcountry, primarily because most of the main roadways are open to vehicles and the network of single-track is rather small. Still, it's worth a look, especially if the trails in the Cranberry Backcountry are congested. Riding is mostly moderate.

fishing: The Cranberry River flows through the center of this part of the Gauley RD, providing the main angling opportunity. Also in the area are the Williams River and the Gauley River, both of which flow W along the area's N boundary.

The Cranberry is a mid-sized stream that flows down a mild to avg gradient on a very rocky bed. Although FR-76 runs beside it for most of its length here, the forest cover is fairly heavy. Below the picnic area, the river leaves civilization until it empties into the Gauley just above that river's confluence with the Cherry. The entire distance from the Cranberry Campground to the Gauley River is 13 mi. Above the picnic area access is from FR-76; below the picnic area there's no access other than by wading or from FR-83 or the *Hinkle Branch Trail*, both of which end at the river. Fishing in the Woodbine Picnic Area is restricted to children and the handicapped from Mar 1 to May 31.

camping: Campers have 3 options for overnight trips in the area.

Primitive backcountry camping is permitted throughout the area on NF lands. Most backpackers on the district opt to camp in the Cranberry Backcountry or Cranberry Wilderness, since these areas have considerably larger trail networks.

The Big Rock campground is a small roadside camping area next to the Cranberry River. 5 large sites are shaded by hardwoods, but to the Cranberry River. 5 large sites are shaded by hardwoods, but their proximity to the road and the lack of any real forest cover minimizes privacy. Each of the sites has a picnic table, grill, and a lantern post. Pit toilets and a hand water pump are the only facilities. The fee is $5/night. The campground is open Mar 15–Dec 8.

The Bishop Knob Campground has 61 sites arranged in 2 large loops. Sites are well spaced, and the dense forest cover maximizes privacy in the campground. The campground gets little use compared to the more popular Cranberry Campground just down the road; it's a good choice when the other is full. Each of the sites has a picnic table, grill, and lantern post. Facilities are a hand water pump and vault toilets. The sites cost $2/night. The campground is open Apr 15–Dec 8.

There are several primitive roadside sites along FR-76 between the Cranberry backcountry and the Big Rock Campground. The sites are numbered and roadside camping at areas other than the sites is prohibited.

canoeing/kayaking: The Cranberry River is a seasonal run, since come summer the water drops too low to permit paddling. The run here is between the Cranberry Campground and a take-out on WV-55 at the confluence of the Gauley and Cherry rivers. This is a 13-mi run, but it can be broken up into 2 shorter runs of similar length by using the bridge beside the Woodbine Picnic Area as either a starting or ending point. Above the bridge the river is paralleled by FR-76; below it the river passes through undeveloped backcountry.

Each half of the run has its appeal and drawbacks. The whitewater is more intense on the first half of the run down to the picnic area. There are almost continuous class III-V rapids created by ledges and massive boulders. Some scouting is necessary, and the skill required to run this section disqualifies all but the most experienced paddlers. The main drawback is the road which follows the river the whole route, though the scenery is still quite attractive. The road does make scouting the river easy, and this is where to check to see if the water is high enough to make the run.

The lower half of the run is characterized by milder whitewater and gorgeous mountain scenery totally unspoiled by development. Rapids are class II-III and are interrupted by long sections of flat water. The most difficult rapids come about half way into the run. 2 mi above the take-out the Cranberry empties into the Gauley, a much larger river, but with rapids here of a similar difficulty. Take-out is river R under the bridge.

Summit Lake Area

This is a day-use area with a small scenic lake, picnic area, and adjacent campground. The lake is stocked with trout and is a nice place to spend a lazy day in a canoe. The campground provides yet another potential base camp from which to explore the area's trails or those in the adjacent Cranberry Backcountry. Apart from the lake, outdoor recreation here centers on 2 long trails that connect the rec area with the Cranberry Visitor Center and the upper access to the Cranberry Backcountry, Cranberry Glades, and Cranberry Wilderness. The trails run on either side of the North Fork Cherry River and WV-55/WV-39, which divides the backcountry in half. Also included here is the Falls of Hills Creek Scenic Area, where a series of boardwalks and wooden stairs leads 0.75 mile to three different falls. Access on WV-55/WV-39 apart from the rec area.

Richwood (W) is the closest town.

getting there: From Richwood, take WV-55/WV-39 E 7.1 mi to Summit Lake Rd (CO-39/5). Turn L and go 2.1 mi to FR-77, R and access to the lake and campground, L.

topography: The lake is cradled by low mountains that are covered by an Appalachian hardwood forest. Beyond that the terrain is more rugged and steep, with elevations that exceed 4,000 ft. **maps:** USGS Webster Springs SW, Fork Mountain, Lobelia.

starting out: You can pick up the district trail map and recreation brochures at either the Gauley RS or the Cranberry Visitor Center. Both are located on WV-55/WV-39. Water and rest rooms are at both locations, as well as in the campground.

activities: Hiking, Fishing, Canoeing, Mountain Biking, Camping.

hiking: A pair of long trails—19-mi *Fork Mountain Trail* and 17.5-mi *Pocahontas Trail*—provide the main hiking opportunity in the area. The trails follow similar E–W routes on opposite sides of the Cherry River. The former runs from WV-55/WV-39 1 mi E of the district RS to a jct with the *Pocahontas Trail* about 3.5 mi W of the Cranberry Visitor Center. The latter runs from the visitor center to a dead end on FR-99 NW of the lake and campground. Both trails cross roads several times, providing numerous other access points. Highlights along the trails are mountain views, the Falls of Hills Creek, a remote forest setting, and wildlife. Both trails are blazed and easy to follow. Their routes include both single-track and old road beds. Hiking is moderate to strenuous. Trail use is light. To reach the *Pocahontas Trail* access nearest the campground: turn R onto FR-77 at the rec area entrance and go 1 mi to the trailhead.

mountain biking: The best ride in the area is on the *Pocahontas Trail*, a long trail that can be ridden out and back or combined with the trails of the Cranberry Backcountry. The trail offers riding on both single-track and old road beds. The terrain is rugged in places, but most of the trail is manageable for riding. Riding is moderate to strenuous. See above for location of trailheads and a fuller description.

camping: Primitive backcountry camping is permitted throughout the area on NF land, except where posted. It is not allowed in the rec area outside of the campground.

The 33-site Summit Lake campground is set in a lush forest not far from the lake. The campground is most popular with the RV set, but the spacing of the sites and the forest cover adds a measure of privacy. Each site has a picnic table, grill, and lantern post. Pit toilets and hand water pumps are the only facilities. Sites cost $5/night. The campground is open Mar 15–Dec 8.

fishing: Summit Lake supports populations of largemouth bass and bluegill. In spring and fall the lake is stocked with trout. Fishing is either from the shore, which is mostly open, or from a boat. Boats with gas motors are not allowed.

canoeing: Although the lake is too small for any kind of lengthy paddling trip, the combination of mountain scenery and trout stocking make it an appealing destination for a short angling/paddling outing.

Cranberry Tri-Rivers Trail

West Virginia's most recent rails-to-trails conversion, the *Cranberry Tri-Rivers Trail* was dedicated on National Trails Day in 1997. The trail follows a 14.5-mile corridor between Richwood and Sarah's Tunnel, reputed to be haunted by the ghost of a woman who was murdered on the RR trestle that crosses the Cranberry River a short distance downstream. The eponymous three rivers are the Cherry, the Cranberry, and the Gauley. The rivers limn the western boundary of the Gauley Ranger District, amidst forested mountain slopes and almost complete isolation. The trail follows the Cherry and Gauley, and crosses the Cranberry on the RR trestle. It's a popular destination for mountain bikers, hikers, and cross-country skiing. It also serves as an access route for fishing trips on any of the 3 rivers.

Richwood (E) is the closest town.

contact: Richwood Area Chamber of Commerce, 50 Oakford Ave, Richwood, WV 26261; 304/846-6790.

getting there: The trailhead is in downtown Richwood at the corner of Oakford Ave and Railroad Ave. There's a small parking area next to the old RR depot. The Holcomb access is 5 mi from downtown Richwood on WV-55. There's a small parking area just before the bridge on the L.

topography: The trail environment ranges from a downtown district to town outskirts to forested mountain slopes. Elevations on the rivers range from 2,195 at the trailhead in Richwood to 1,901 ft at the confluence of the Gauley and Cherry. **maps:** USGS Richwood, Camden on Gauley.

starting out: You can get trail info at the Richwood Chamber of Commerce on Oakford Ave downtown. Hours are 10 AM to 2 PM weekdays. Although the trail begins in Richwood, many people prefer to start in Holcomb, beyond the rather plain first 6-mi stretch that passes through the semi-urban environs of Richwood. A small parking area is located just before the bridge that crosses the Cherry River. There are no facilities along the trail.

activities: Mountain Biking, Hiking, Fishing, Cross-country-Skiing, Camping.

mountain biking/hiking: Since the trail follows a former RR line, it's grade is mild from end to end, making either riding or hiking easy. Highlights along the trail are the RR history and the scenic views of the rivers. The surface is mostly crushed gravel, comfortable under either fat tires or hiking boots (sneakers are OK too). Currently trail use is light, but as it becomes better known it will probably rise.

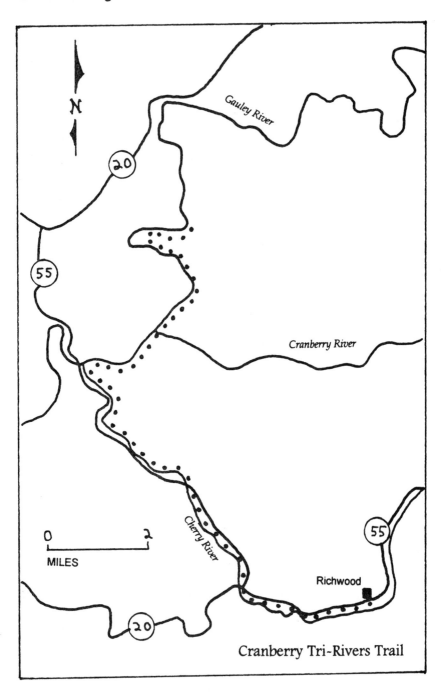

Cranberry Tri-Rivers Trail

fishing: The trail provides access to the 3 rivers for which it's named, though access is intermittent at best, since the RR grade is on a bluff that overlooks the rivers for much of its route. The 3 rivers are similar in their physical features, though their fisheries vary. Each of the rivers is large, and flows down a mild to average gradient. Pooling is excellent, with many pools (especially on the Gauley) too deep to be waded. Cover varies: it's best on the Cranberry, which flows W through remote backcountry before joining the Gauley. As for fish species, the Cherry and Cranberry are stocked trout waters. The Cherry also supports populations of smallmouth bass. The Gauley, on the other hand, provides habitat to fish that can tolerate warmer temperatures than trout. Popular catches are smallmouth bass, muskellunge, walleye, and catfish.

cross-country skiing: Although the trail doesn't receive the same amount of snow as in the Cranberry Backcountry or Cranberry Wilderness, when the snows do come, it becomes an almost perfect nordic track. The wide trail corridor and mild grade makes it suitable for skiers of all ski levels. And since the trail begins right downtown, getting to the trailhead isn't a problem.

camping: Although the trail is an ideal length for single-day out-and-back bike rides, hikes of the entire length require at least one overnight, and possibly two. Camping options are limited along the trail, though there are a handful of clearings where it would be possible to make camp. Be sure to avoid private property (it's generally posted), or ask first before pitching your tent.

Watoga State Park

The largest state park in West Virginia, Watoga sprawls across 10,100 acres of mountainous terrain on the eastern side of the Greenbrier River Valley. The 9,482-acre, completely undeveloped Calvin Price State Forest is adjacent to the south, nearly doubling the size of the remote backcountry. This vast tract of hardwood and hemlock forest is a boon to wildlife: white-tailed deer, red fox, black bear, wild turkey, and ruffed grouse all inhabit the lush woodlands. Recreation facilities and most of the hiking trails are concentrated in the northern half of the park, leaving much of the rest in a primitive state. Among these facilities are a picnic area with shelters, tables, and grills; a riding stables; swimming pool; 11-acre lake; cabins; two campgrounds; and a restaurant. Also in the area, but striking in contrast, is the Brooks Memorial Arboretum. Along the trails that wind through the area the naturalist can observe up close the botanical diversity of several different types of forest communities. A large trail network permits exploration of other parts of the park as well. And the adjacent Greenbrier River and *Greenbrier River Trail* add the potential for longer hike, bike, ski, or paddle trips.

The park's name is a modification of the Cherokee word watauga, "the river of islands." It refers of course to the Greenbrier, which forms the park's western boundary.

Marlinton (N) is the closest town.

contact: Superintendent, Watoga State Park, HC-82, Box 252, Marlinton, WV 24954; 304/799-4087. wvweb.com/www/watoga.html

getting there: E access: From Marlinton, drive E on WV-39 5.7 mi to Beaver Creek Rd (CO-21). Turn R and go 7.2 mi to the park's N entrance. • W access: From Marlinton, turn S onto US-219 and go 1.2 mi to CO-27. Turn L and go 2.2 mi to the Greenbrier River and a parking area for the *Greenbrier River Trail*. The state park is just across the bridge.

topography: The park occupies the valley and W slope of mountains that rise E of the Greenbrier River. The river forms the park's W boundary. Other drainages flow N and W to the Greenbrier. Hardwoods, hemlocks, and rhododendron account for must of the dense forest cover. Elevations are between 2,000 ft on the river and 3,211 ft. **maps:** USGS Denmar, Lake Sherwood.

starting out: Park HQ is reached via the N entrance. Maps and other park info are available at the park office. A pay phone is there; water and rest rooms are at several locations. A campstore next to the main office has a small selection of supplies.

activities: Hiking, Camping, Mountain Biking, Cross-country Skiing, Canoeing/Kayaking, Fishing.

hiking: The park's outstanding trail network covers 32 mi on 13 trails, including a 5.5-mi segment of the 330-mi *Allegheny Trail*. The 75-mi *Greenbrier River Trail*, a rail-trail that runs alongside the park on its W border, adds another hiking possibility. Trail highlights include exceptional views of the mountains and river valley, the botanical diversity of the Brooks Arboretum, and an abundance of wildlife. Trails follow a combination of narrow dirt footpaths and old road beds. Some loop hikes are possible by connecting several trails, though backtracking is also necessary along some of the trails. Trailheads are signed and the trails are blazed and easy to follow for the most part. Hiking varies from easy to strenuous, depending on topography. Rock hopping across small streams is necessary along some trails.

camping: Although primitive backcountry camping is not permitted in the park, the Laurel Run camping area offers similar conditions. This is a large clearing with sites indicated by a picnic table, grill, and fire place. To get there: Go 0.2 mi S of the S entrance on CO-21 and turn R onto a gravel road. Drive 1.3 mi to the end at the camping area. Sites cost $5/night.

The park itself has 2 separate developed campgrounds. The Riverside Campground has 50 sites in a semi-wooded area in a bend of the Greenbrier River. The sites are large, but squeezed together pretty tightly. Privacy is only adequate. Sites 20–50 offer the most privacy. Each site has a picnic table and grill. Shower/rest room facilities are centrally located. Sites cost $11/night, $14 with hook-up. The campground is open Apr 1 to mid-Dec.

Beaver Creek campground has 38 large, well-spaced sites in an area shaded by hardwoods and pines. Privacy at the sites is adequate to good. Each site has a picnic table and grill. Shower /rest rooms facilities are available. Sites cost $11/night, $14 with hook-up. The campground is open Apr 1–Oct 31.

mountain biking: Although bikes are prohibited on all of the single-track hiking trails in the park, they are allowed on several of the gated roads. The roads are not maintained and are very rough and rugged in places. They combine for about 7 mi of riding. One of the roads leads to the Ann Bailey Lookout Tower, with expansive views over the Greenbrier River. Riding on the roads is moderate to strenuous. For longer trips or more suitable riding conditions, try the 75-mi *Greenbrier River Trail*, which passes along the W edge of the park.

canoeing/kayaking: Paddling trips are popular on the Greenbrier River, which flows past the park along its W boundary. The park can be used as either a put-in or take-out for shorter trips, or as an overnight stop on longer trips. Conditions on the river are similar for the 75-mi stretch between Cass and Lewisburg: long flat pools interrupted every now and then by class I-II whitewater. The 10-mi distance from Marlinton to CO-27 is perfect for a day-trip. Put-in river L on the upstream side of the bridge in Marlinton.

fishing: The Greenbrier River is a warm water fishery with populations of walleye, sauger, and rock and smallmouth bass. The river can be fished by wading or floating. Access is from the bridge on CO-27 and then from the *Greenbrier River Trail*.

lodging: There are 33 cabins in the park; 24 are rustic log cabins, 9 are more modern wood-frame cabins. All are furnished and have stone fireplaces, kitchens, and bathrooms with showers. The cabins are spread out in 3 different areas of the park and offer a reasonable amount of isolation. The cabins can accommodate from 2–8 people. Rates begin at $65/night for 2 people during the spring/fall season. Summer rates are slightly higher and rates for stays of more than 1 night are lower. The modern cabins are open all year; rustic cabins are open from Apr 1 to Oct 31.

Greenbrier River
& New River Valleys

Greenbrier River & New River Valleys Key Map

1. Greenbrier River Trail
2. Lake Sherwood Rec Area
3. Blue Bend Rec Area
4. Greenbrier SF
5. Moncove Lake SP
6. Gauley River NRA
7. Carnifax Ferry SP
8. Hawks Nest SP
9. Babcock SP
10. Canyon Rim Area

11. Thurmond Area
12. Grandview Area
13. Glade Creek Area
14. Sandstone Falls Area
15. Little Beaver SP
16. Bluestone Lake WMA
17. Bluestone SP
18. Pipestem Resort SP
19. Camp Creek SP & SF
20. Twin Falls Resort SP

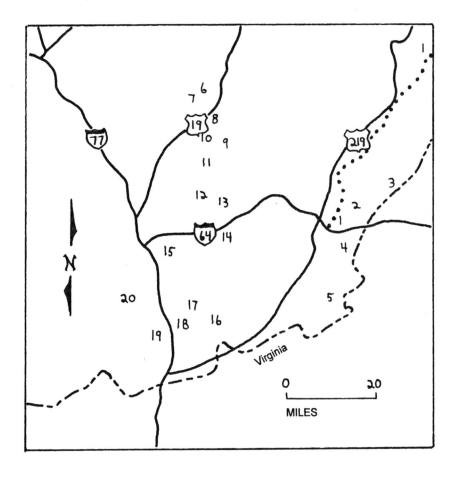

Weather & Climate Readings at Fayetteville

Month	Avg High F°	Avg Low F°	Precipitation (Inches)	Snowfall (Inches)
Jan	39	19	3.2	14.8
Feb	43	22	3.1	11.5
Mar	54	31	3.7	5.8
Apr	64	39	3.9	1.3
May	73	47	4.3	0
Jun	79	55	3.7	0
Jul	82	59	5.3	0
Aug	82	58	4.2	0
Sep	76	52	3.6	0
Oct	65	41	3.3	0.3
Nov	55	33	3.4	2.2
Dec	44	24	3.5	8.1

Introduction

Encompassing the southeastern corner of West Virginia, this region is defined by its two namesake rivers, the New and the Greenbrier. The landforms here are every bit as dramatic as those found to the north in the Potomac Highlands, if not more so. The terrain is mountainous throughout the area, but in places such as the New River Gorge, and the gorges through which the Gauley and Bluestone Rivers flow, the local topography takes on a drama and grandeur not often encountered on the East Coast. Deep fissures have been carved in the earth's surface, and the rivers flow through canyons whose walls rise as much as 1,000 feet.

Gentler terrain is encountered in this part of the state as well. As the Greenbrier River flows down out of the Potomac Highlands, it enters a broad valley of undulating hills that have been home to prosperous farms for the past tho hundred years. There are other contrasts between the rugged grandeur of the New River and the pastoral beauty of the Greenbrier River as well. First of all, the rivers flow in opposite directions. The Greenbrier flows south, beginning in the narrow valleys that separate the lofty ridges of the Allegheny Mountains. Its profile is not unlike that of the many large rivers that drain these uplands. The New, on the other hand, is unique. It doesn't flow down from the highest slopes of the Alleghenies; it cuts right through them, the only river in West Virginia to do so. This is because the river was flowing through this part of the continent before the Appalachian Mountains even existed. In fact, geologists surmise that the New is the second oldest river in the world—only the Nile predates it.

Public land in the region is a mix of national forest, national rivers, and a handful of state parks and state forests. Much of the private land that surrounds these public landholdings is agricultural, with dairy farms and crop farms both present. The region is not heavily developed, and travelers will find hundreds of miles of backcountry roads that wind through pastoral scenery and pass through small towns. Because more of the land is suitable to farming than in the more rugged mountains to the north, less of it is forested. Forests have been allowed to reclaim most of the public lands, however, and the oak-hickory and northern deciduous forests that are native cover large areas of backcountry. These woodlands provide haven for an abundance of wildlife in the area. White-tailed deer are the most common large mammal, and will almost certainly be seen on a trip into the backcountry. Other native mammals are black bear, red fox, ground hog, beaver, opossum, raccoon, grey squirrel, and cottontail rabbits.

More backcountry and adventure travelers visit this part of West Virginia than any other for two reasons: the New and Gauley rivers. Two of the wildest whitewater runs on the East Coast (or on the continent for that matter), they attract kayakers, canoeists, and rafters by the thousands. Whitewater rafting has become so popular that it's now a major component of the local economy. And for most visitors, paddling in a guided raft is the best way to experience the thrilling ride the rivers offer and the majestic scenery of gorges that surround them. Inexperienced or even intermediate paddlers will find the level of whitewater on these large, imposing rivers beyond their abilities, except on the upper New.

Of course there's more to the region than just whitewater. The New River Gorge in particular, which protects 53 miles of the river and the lands that surround it, offers a wide variety of backcountry recreation. Large trail networks cling to the river corridor and roam through the forested mountain slopes that rise to the top of the canyon. And the sheer rock faces of the Canyon Rim Area are a mecca for climbers, who can choose from more than 1,000 different routes. Anglers know the river as one of the best in the state for smallmouth bass, and float fish trips are popular on the sections between Hinton and Thurmond. Along the Greenbrier River is the *Greenbrier River Trail*, at 75 miles the state's longest rail-trail. Mountain bikers, hikers, and cross-country skiers all use this popular riverside trail that runs from Lewisburg into the mountains at Cass. And anglers and paddlers can use the trail to get on the river itself. The several state parks and state forests in the area round out the possibilities for outdoor recreation. All feature trail networks for hiking, and most have campgrounds that make useful base camps.

The area's climate fosters year round outdoor activities. Spring and fall, when the air is crisp and cool, are delightful. Summers can be hot and humid, but if you're on one of the big rivers or in a forest shaded by a canopy of hardwoods, temperatures will be cooler and generally comfortable. Winter brings cold weather and snow. From December to March, cross-country skiing and snowshoeing are the favored means of backcountry travel.

Greenbrier River Trail

This 75-mile multi-use trail is the jewel in the crown of West Virginia rail-trails. The state government and local conservation groups have done an admirable job of aggressively converting old, abandoned RR lines into greenways for hiking, mountain biking, cross-country skiing, and other outdoor recreation. And nowhere has the ideal of what a rail-trail can and should be been more fully realized than on the *Greenbrier River Trail*. Just as the C&O railroad that followed the grade once did, the *Greenbrier River Trail* links the Allegheny Mountains of Pocahontas County with the rolling farmland of the lower Greenbrier River Valley. The trail runs between the old railroad town of Cass and the pretty, historic town of Lewisburg. In between, it follows the river closely for most of its distance, crossing 35 trestles and going through 2 tunnels along the way. Most of the valley is exceptionally scenic, with small farms, a community or two, and forested mountain slopes along the route. In addition to activities on the trail, the river is a popular destination for paddling and fishing trips. Other recreation opportunities along the trail are available in Seneca State Forest, Watoga State Park, and the Blue Bend Recreation Area of the White Sulphur Springs Ranger District.

Cass, Marlinton, and Lewisburg are the only towns along the trail.

contact: Watoga State Park, Star Route 1, Box 252, Marlinton, WV 24954; 304/799-4087; wvweb.com/www/greenbrier_rt.html.

getting there: There are more than a dozen access points to the trail. The N terminus is at Cass Scenic RR State Park, even though the trail doesn't quite extend all the way into town. Park in the large parking lot across from the RR depot and follow WV-66 W 0.6 mi to a gravel road, L and a sign for the rail trail. • To reach the S terminus in Caldwell: From the W take I-64 to exit 169. Turn S onto US-219 and go 1.4 mi to downtown Lewisburg and the jct with US-60. Turn L onto E Washington St (US-60) and go 3.1 mi to Stonehouse Rd (SR-38). Turn L and go 1.3 mi to the trailhead and parking area. • From the E take I-64 to exit 175. Turn W onto US-60 and go 2.8 mi to Stonehouse Rd. Turn R and go to the parking area.

topography: The Greenbrier River flows S through a relatively narrow valley surrounded by modest mountain slopes. The land is a combination of pasturage, small towns, and patches of forest. Elevations on the river are between 2,450 ft in Cass and 1,850 ft near Lewisburg. **maps:** USGS Cass, Clover Lick, Edray, Marlinton, Hillsboro, Denmar, Droop, Anthony, White Sulphur Springs, Lewisburg.

starting out: Although there are no facilities on the trail per se, it passes through Watoga SP, Seneca SF, and several small towns. Water and rest rooms are available at each of these areas, as well as at the 2 endpoints.

activities: Mountain Biking, Hiking, Canoeing/Kayaking, Fishing, Camping, Cross-country skiing:.

mountain biking: A wide, level, 75-mi path that passes through some of the most scenic surroundings in the state is bound to be a magnet for mountain bikers. And so the *Greenbrier River Trail* is. The mild grade and well maintained treadway of crushed gravel allows you to pedal at your leisure and concentrate on the scenery rather than negotiating technical terrain and skirting obstacles. Trail conditions vary little from one end to the other. Riding is always easy (easier downhill, but not much of a struggle up), and with all the different access points you can ride almost any section of the trail you choose. And if you decide to bike the entire distance—whether one-way or return—camping trailside isn't a problem.

hiking: Hikers are far outnumbered by bikers on the trail, probably because on a bike you can cover more of the trail. But the trail offers hikers a scenic, easy-to-hike path through some beautiful mountain and valley terrain. In fact "hike" may be too strong a word: foot travel on the wide, level path is more akin to a leisurely stroll. Backpackers can bite off large chunks of the trail or hike the entire distance, camping at any of the designated sites along the way.

canoeing/kayaking: An ideal river for open canoes, the Greenbrier is characterized by long flat stretches punctuated by rapids in the class I-II range. This makes it perfect for novice paddlers wanting to get a first taste of whitewater or simply practice their technique.

Of course, since the Greenbrier flows through some of the most attractive scenery in this part of the state, paddlers of any skill level won't be disappointed. With numerous access points in the rec areas, towns, and bridges along the river, float trips of almost any length are possible. The character of the river doesn't change much along its course, except that what is already a large river in Cass is considerably larger by Lewisburg. The river can be paddled almost any time of year, except during summer dry spells. The best way to check water level is scout one of the access points.

fishing: Below Cass the Greenbrier River is a warm-water fishery that supports populations of smallmouth and rock bass, and walleye. The river is broad and shallow in most places, permitting easy wading. Float fish trips are also popular. Access to the river is from the trail.

camping: Backcountry camping is permitted along the trail on public lands. Designated sites are regularly spaced along the trail's entire length. They're marked with a tent icon and have a picnic table. Camping is permitted outside the sites, but since most of the land that surrounds the trail is private, finding a suitable site can be difficult. Developed campgrounds are located in Seneca SF and Watoga SP.

cross-country skiing: From Dec to Mar, when the snows come, the *Greenbrier Trail* is transformed into the longest nordic ski track in the state. At least 6 inches of snow should be on the ground before you head for the trail. Any less and the gravel surface becomes a problem. The N end of the trail gets considerably more snowfall than does the S end. See above under *mountain biking* for more details on the trail.

lodging: Since the trail travels through such a large area, many of the lodges listed elsewhere in this guide are suitable for outings on the trail. The General Lewis Inn and Jerico B&B are both just a couple of miles from the trail.

Another inn to consider is the Pence Springs Hotel (800/826-1829). It's located right on the banks of the Greenbrier River, albeit about 25 mi SW of the trail's S terminus. It's included here because it's a personal favorite. Established in 1897, the hotel has undergone many incarnations in the past 100 years, including a stint from 1947 to 1985 as a woman's prison. The large, colonnaded brick building sits on 400 attractive acres. Rooms are decorated in 1920's style and all have a private bath. 2 restaurants are also on the premises. Rates range from $69 to $95/night for 2 people. The hotel is open from Apr 1 to Dec 31.

White Sulphur Ranger District

Monongahela National Forest

The White Sulphur Ranger District encompasses 98, 254 acres in Greenbrier and Pocahontas counties. The district is the southernmost on the Monongahela National Forest. Its boundaries are formed by Virginia (E), the Greenbrier River (W), the Marlinton Ranger District (N), and the national forest boundary (S). The district is characterized by long, narrow ridges and the rolling uplands of the Greenbrier River Valley. Outdoor recreation on the district is focused at 2 areas: Sherwood Lake Recreation Area and Blue Bend Recreation Area. Both are located on water, with fishing, hiking, mountain biking, camping, and paddling the major activities. Outside of the rec areas, the large majority of district lands are forested, providing a haven for wildlife such as black bear, white-tailed deer, wild turkey, red fox, raccoon, opossum, and other small mammals. Interspersed with the NF holdings are private landholdings that are mostly agricultural. There are no large towns on the district.

White Sulphur Springs (S) and Lewisburg (S) are the closest towns.

contact: District Ranger, White Sulphur Springs Ranger District, 410 E Main St, White Sulphur Springs, WV 24986; 304/536-2144

getting there: Main highway access to the district is via I-64 and then WV-92, which follows the Greenbrier River and mountain ridges NE–SW. • To reach the district RS: from I-64 take exit 175. Turn E onto US-60 and go 4.1 mi to the RS in downtown White Sulphur Springs, L.

topography: The district's terrain includes mountain ridges and the broad valley of the Greenbrier River, which forms the W boundary. Ridges follow the NE–SW orientation typical of the Alleghenies. Middle Mountain is the most prominent. **maps:** See below under the separate headings.

starting out: The district ranger station on E Main St in downtown White Sulphur Springs can supply you with maps, brochures, and other info about the district. They sell USGS topos inside too. Office hours are weekdays from 8 AM to 4:30 PM. Next door is the White Sulphur Springs fish hatchery, with viewable holding pools.

activities: Hiking, Mountain Biking, Camping, Fishing, Canoeing /Kayaking.

hiking: Trail networks are major features at both of the rec areas described below. In addition to these, 2 of the state's longest trails pass through or by the district: the 330-mi *Allegheny Trail* and the 75-mi *Greenbrier River Trail.* Since the areas covered by the 2 trail networks are not especially large, the trails are best suited to day-hikes or short overnights.

mountain biking: All NF trails on the district are open to mountain bikes. Only the *Allegheny Trail* isn't suitable, since sections of it are simply too rugged for good riding. In addition to the single-track trails, several gated and open forest roads in the Blue Bend Rec Area are suitable for riding. Most popular, however, is the *Greenbrier River Trail,* which passes along the district's W boundary for its entire length. See the separate entry above for a full description.

camping: Backcountry camping is permitted throughout the district. There are suitable sites along the trails of each of the rec areas described below.

The district is home to a pair of car campgrounds, one at Blue Bend and one at Lake Sherwood. Both provide running water and modern toilets, but only Lake Sherwood offers showers. They're open year round.

fishing: Angling for both warm-water species and trout is possible on the White Sulphur RD. Lake Sherwood is the most popular destination. Backcountry enthusiasts, however, will probably prefer the more remote locales of the 2 trout creeks described below, one at each area.

canoeing/kayaking: Lake Sherwood provides the main paddling opportunity on the district. The 165-acre lake is best suited to day trips or combined boating/fishing trips. Paddling is also possible on the Greenbrier River, which passes through the district. It's described separately under the *Greenbrier River Trail.*

lodging: South of the district is Lewisburg, often referred to as West Virginia's prettiest town. On E Washington St downtown is the General Lewis Inn (800/628-4454). The 25-room inn is housed in a beautiful mansion that dates from 1834 and is on the National Register of Historic Places. The living room, dining room, and "memory hall" are overflowing with antiques, and the pleasant, comfortable rooms are furnished with period pieces. The on-site restaurant serves southern and country fare and is an attraction in its own right. Rates for doubles range from $64 to $92/night. Pets are allowed for $10 extra.

Lake Sherwood Recreation Area

A beautiful 165-acre alpine lake is the centerpiece of this recreation area and surrounding backcountry tucked up against the Virginia state line. The lake is the main attraction—there are several swimming and picnic areas as well as a bathhouse. Also on its shores is a large developed campground that makes this a favorite vacation destination. Away from the centers of activity, however, forested mountain slopes spread for hundreds of acres in all directions. A large network of trails winds through these wilds, providing possibilities for hiking and mountain biking trips, or just enjoying the wonderful mountain scenery. Among these is the *Allegheny Trail,* which crosses the state from north to south and connects many of the park and forest recreation areas in the mountainous eastern half of West Virginia. The rec area can be used as a base camp for long backpacking trips or as a stopping off point.

Neola (SW) is the closest town.

getting there: From the jct of WV-92 and N Fork Rd (CO-14) in Neola, take CO-14 E 9.5 mi (at 1.4 mi reach a trailhead and parking area for the *Little Allegheny Trail,* R; At 2.5 mi reach a parking area and access to the *Allegheny Trail,*R) to the rec area entrance.

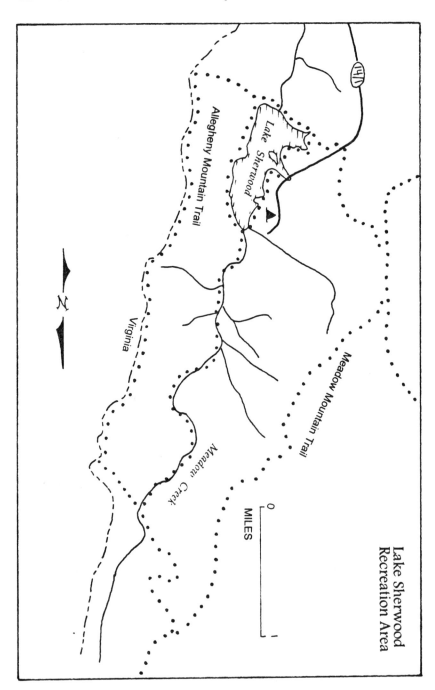

Lake Sherwood
Recreation Area

topography: Elevation on Lake Sherwood is 2,670 ft. The modest impoundment sits in a narrow bowl amidst forested mountain slopes. Elevations are highest along the VA state line, and top out at about 3,000 ft in the area. Slopes are generally modest. Forest cover includes northern hardwoods, hemlocks, white-pine, and rhododendron. large areas around the lake are landscaped and mowed. **maps:** USGS Lake Sherwood, Mountain Grove, Rucker Gap.

starting out: Facilities are clustered in several parts of the rec area. You'll find water and rest rooms at the trailhead parking area, campground, and beaches. There's no pay phone in the area. The rec area is closed from 9 PM to 7 AM.

Alcohol is not allowed around the beaches.

activities: Hiking, Mountain Biking, Camping, Canoeing/Kayaking, Fishing.

hiking: Hiking in the area is on an extensive network of trails that circle the lake and follow the ridges and drainages to its N. In all 7 trails cover 17 mi, not counting the *Allegheny Trail*, which skirts the rec area along its 330-mi route from Pennsylvania to Virginia. The rec area trails are laid out in a manner that facilitates loop hikes and backpacking trips: all of the trails can be connected to create hikes of various lengths without the necessity of backtracking or a vehicle shuttle. Highlights are scenic views of the lake and surrounding mountains, wildlife, and the remote forest setting, particularly along the border with VA. The trails follow a combination of single-tracks and old road beds. They're blazed and easy to follow. Trailheads are signed in the rec area, where there's a separate parking area for hikers and other trail users. Hiking is easy around the lake, moderate to strenuous on the ridgeline trails. Trail use is moderate, heavy around the lake.

The *Allegheny Trail* passes along the W edge of the area, sharing the *Meadow Mountain Trail* for 0.5 mi. The trail is blazed with yellow rectangles. It's accessible from the rec area via a 1-mi hike on the *Upper Meadow Trail*. From this jct it's an 8-mi hike S to the trailhead and parking area on CO-14. N from the jct it's a 14-mi hike to Watoga SP.

mountain biking: All rec area trails are open and suitable to mountain bikes. Several fairly long loops are possible by combining the *Meadow Creek Trail* with either the *Meadow*

Mountain Trail or the *Allegheny Mountain Trail*. Riding ranges from easy to strenuous on both loops. See above under *hiking* for more complete trail info.

camping: Primitive backcountry camping is permitted along the trails and throughout the NF, except where posted.

Car campers can overnight at the 97-site developed car campground, which is spread out along the lake in 3 separate areas. The campground is quite popular, and frequently fills on summer weekends. All 3 areas are similar, with a canopy of hardwoods and conifers providing shade over large sites. Privacy at the sites is adequate, but the sheer numbers of campers can leave you feeling a bit crowded. Each site has a picnic table, grill, and lantern post. Facilities include modern rest rooms with showers. There are pit toilets too. The sites cost $12/night. Some sites can be reserved—call 800/280-2267. At least part of the campground is open year round.

canoeing/kayaking: Lake Sherwood is one of the prettiest mountain lakes in WV. It isn't terribly large—long paddling trips aren't really a possibility—but the forested mountain slopes and seemingly endless sky create an atmosphere of bucolic serenity. This is compromised somewhat by the presence of the popular swimming beach, but that's the only part of the lakeshore that's developed. Boat launches are located near the entrance and in the campgrounds. Canoes are available for rent at the rec area.

fishing: Lake Sherwood is a warm-water fishery that supports populations of largemouth bass, tiger musky, bluegill, and bullhead and channel catfish. Anglers can fish from the long open areas along the shoreline, but fishing from a small boat is preferred. A canoe is ideal to cover the lake in a day.

Above Lake Sherwood, Meadow Creek is a small trout stream that flows down a mild to average gradient. Cover is excellent, and fly-fishermen will find casting conditions tight in many places. Access is from the *Meadow Creek Trail*, which follows it for about 2.5 mi to near its headwaters. Meadow Creek is stocked trout water.

Blue Bend Recreation Area

Encompassing the mountain slopes east of the Greenbrier River, the Blue Bend Rec Area includes a developed campground and picnic area with a large backcountry. The rec area itself is located on the banks of Anthony Creek, a stocked trout creek that also hasa popular swimming hole at a wide, slow bend. The area is very attractive, with the campground and picnic facilities (shelter, tables, and grill) nestled into a forest of hemlocks and northern hardwoods. The surrounding mountains are a refuge for wildlife such as white-tailed deer, black bear, and wild turkey. Hiking and biking trails provide access to the backcountry, and the nearby *Greenbrier River Trail* opens up options for longer trips.

White Sulphur Springs (S) is the closest town.

getting there: From the W: From I-64 take exit 169. Turn N onto US-219 and go 3.5 mi to Vago Rd (CO-21). Turn R and go 5.2 mi to Anthony Station Rd (CO-21/2). Turn R and go 6.3 mi (at 2.2 mi reach an access to the *Greenbrier River Trail* and trail access to Blue Bend area trails) to the rec area entrance, R. • From the E: from the jct of US-60 and WV-92 E of White Sulphur Springs, turn N onto WV-92 and go 9.1 mi to Little Creek Rd (CO-16). Turn L and go 2.7 mi to Big Draft Rd (CO-21/2). Bear L and go 1.1 mi to the rec area entrance, L.

topography: The Greenbrier River—the area's major geographical feature—flows S and forms Blue Bend's W boundary. Terrain to the E of the river is rugged and mountainous. Elevation rises from 1,900 ft on the river to 2,880 on Round Mtn. Greenbrier Mtn is at 3,121. Forest cover includes stands of hemlock amidst a northern deciduous forest. **maps:** USGS Anthony.

starting out: Water and pit toilets are in the rec area. A trail map and brochure are available at the district RS. The rec area is open from 7 AM to 10 PM.

activities: Hiking, Camping, Fishing, Mountain Biking.

hiking: A network of 3 trails traverses the mountain ridges and traces Anthony Creek to its confluence with the Greenbrier River. Total mileage is 14, and the 3 trails can be connected. To hike all 3 trails in series, backtracking is necessary on 2 of them. Even

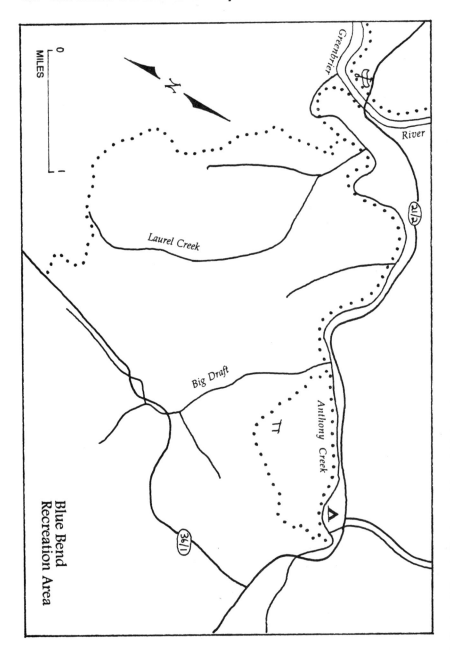

longer hikes are possible by connecting to the *Greenbrier River Trail*, which passes the area on the W bank of the river. Highlights along the trails include panoramic views, wildlife, and a stocked trout creek. An Adirondack shelter provides a backcountry camping option. The trails follow blazed single-tracks through hardwood forests. A scenic footbridge crosses Anthony Creek in the rec area; a crossing near the creek's mouth is unimproved, so wading is necessary. Hiking on the *Blue Bend Trail* is moderate to strenuous; hiking on other trails is easy to moderate. Trailheads are located at 2 different areas. The *Anthony Creek Trail* and access to the *South Boundary Trail* are at the E end of the bridge across the Greenbrier River. All area trails can also be reached from the main parking lot in the Blue Bend Rec Area itself. Most, but not all, trailheads are signed. To reach the S trailhead of the *South Boundary Trail*, go E from the rec area on CO-16/2 1.1 mi to Big Draft Rd (CO-36/1). Turn R and go 3.5 mi to a small parking area and trailhead, R.

camping: Campers in the area have several options. Primitive backcountry camping is permitted on NF lands except where posted otherwise. With the limited trail network, multi-day backpacking trips in the area aren't really feasible, unless you connect with the *Greenbrier River Trail*. An Adirondack shelter is located on the *Blue Bend Trail*.

The primitive car campground situated beside Anthony Creek amidst a shady grove of hemlocks and a dense understory of rhododendron is one of the most attractive in the Monongahela NF. The 21 sites are very large and well spaced, and afford a high degree of privacy. Each site has a picnic table, grill, and lantern post. Facilities include modern rest rooms (no showers), water fountains, and hand water pumps. Sites cost $7/night. The campground is open all year.

Blue Meadow is a camping area open to organized groups. Contact the district RS for information and reservations.

fishing: Anthony Creek is a medium to large creek that flows over a mild gradient through the rec area before emptying into the Greenbrier River, a distance of about 5 mi. Its bed is rocky, and pooling is very good. Forest cover is dense in most locations, with rhododendron, hemlocks and hardwoods all present. Access is from SR-16/2 (there are pullouts W of the rec area) or from the *Anthony Creek Trail*. It is stocked trout waters.

mountain biking: Although not nearly as well known as the nearby *Greenbrier River Trail*, the backcountry around the Blue Bend Rec Area offers some excellent riding trails. In addition to the hiking trails described above—all are open to bikes—riders can opt for the network of open and gated roads that wind into the mountains N of the campground. The main arteries here are FR-296, FR-297, and FR-139. The last begins across from the rec area entrance and climbs to 3,294 ft on Hopkins Mtn. From there it's possible to join the other 2 roads and ride back down to the Greenbrier River to where FR-296 rejoins the main road 2.9 mi W of the rec area entrance. Conditions vary from unpaved road to very rugged double track.

Greenbrier State Forest

5,100 acres of rugged woodlands in West Virginia's southeast corner comprise Greenbrier State Forest. Most of the forest occupies the ridge and slopes of Kate's Mountain; the Greenbrier River flows nearby to the west, but does not enter the forest. Although the towns of White Sulphur Springs and Lewisburg are just a few miles away, the area is best known for the sprawling, internationally famous Greenbrier Resort. The heavily forested mountain slopes of the state forest provide something of a contrast to the immaculately manicured golf courses and grounds of the Greenbrier. While falconry and tennis are among the outdoor pursuits offered at the resort, the main attraction in the forest is the network of trails—open to hikers and mountain bikers—that wind through the lush woodlands. The natural habitats in the backcountry support a diversity of wildlife, including white-tailed deer, wild turkey, and ruffed grouse. A small campground and a dozen cabins offer rustic accommodations for those looking to spend more than a day in the forest. Other facilities include an outdoor swimming pool (summer only), archery and muzzle rifle range, and picnic area with tables, grills, and shelters. The forest is open daily from 6 AM to 10 PM.

White Sulphur Springs (N) and Lewisburg (W) are the closest towns.

contact: Greenbrier State Forest, HC-30 Box 154, Caldwell, WV 24925-9709; 304/536-1944.

getting there: From I-64 take exit 175 (White Sulphur Springs). Turn S onto SR-60/14 and go 1.2 mi to the forest entrance.

topography: The forest occupies the slopes and drainage of a NE-SW mountain ridge. Elevations are between 1,850 ft on Harts Run and 3,115 ft on Roaring Mountain. The mountainsides are steep, particularly on the W slope. Most of the area is forested with hardwoods and conifers, except for the rec areas in the lower elevations. **maps:** USGS Glace, White Sulphur Springs.

starting out: If you're going to hike or bike the trails, you might want to pick up a trail map, available in the forest office. A pay phone is nearby. Water and rest rooms are at several locations.

Alcohol is not permitted.

activities: Hiking, Camping, Mountain Biking.

hiking: 8 trails wind through forested terrain on the ridge and western flank of Kate's Mountain. The trails are short, with most less than 2 miles, though longer treks are possible by combining two or more trails. Trails follow a combinations of seeded roadbeds and narrow dirt paths. For the most part they're well maintained. Hiking ranges from easy to strenuous. Trailheads are signed and trails are blazed and easy to follow. Access is from the main road that runs through the forest; the trails can be hiked uphill from the valley or downhill from the top of the mountain. A few overlooks on the top of Kate's Mountain offer panoramic views of the valley and surrounding mountains. It's almost 10 mi along the road from the forest office to the last trailhead on Kate's Mtn, with the last 6 mi of road unpaved.

camping: A small car campground is located not far from the forest's entrance. The area is quite attractive, with heavy forest cover of hardwoods and hemlocks providing shade and privacy for the 16 large sites. Each site has a picnic table and a stone grill. A bathhouse with showers is centrally located. Sites cost $11/night, $14 with electrical hookup. Half of the sites can be reserved in advance. The campground is open from Apr 15 to early Dec.

mountain biking: Although not a major biking destination, the forest can provide a nice alternative for bikers who come to the area to ride the immensely popular *Greenbrier River Trail*. Trails here are more technically demanding than the wide, level *GRT*. All of the forest's trails are open to both bikers and hikers, so the descriptions above under hiking apply equally to mountain bikers. One thing to keep in mind: most of the trails go up and down the relatively steep flank of Kate's Mountain, so riding uphill is considerably more difficult than riding down.

lodging: 12 log cabins that sleep 6 each provide lodging right in the SF. The cabins are rustic but modern, with electricity, a bath with shower, fully-equipped kitchen, and fireplace. They're available from Apr 15 to Oct 31. From mid-June to Labor Day rentals are on a week or 2-week basis only; at other times day rentals are accepted. Rates vary with the season and number of people. 2 people costs $65/night in spring and fall, $332/week in summer.

Moncove Lake State Park

Formerly a wildlife management area, this 896-acre recreation area and backcountry was designated a state park in 1991. The park centerpiece is the 144-acre lake, used for fishing, boating, and swimming. Surrounding it are wooded mountain slopes that provide habitat for white-tailed deer, red fox, wild turkey, and other small mammals. Recreation facilities in the park are a swimming beach, picnic area, car campground, and network of hiking/biking trails. Perhaps the park's main appeal is its isolation in a corner of West Virginia not often visited. An atmosphere of quiet serenity seems to pervade at all times.

Gap Mills (S) is the closest town.

contact: Superintendent, Moncove Lake State Park, Route 4, Box 73-A, Gap Mills, WV 24941; 304/772-3450; wvweb.com/www/moncove_lake.html

getting there: From WV-3 in Gap Mills, drive N 1 mi to CO-8. Turn R and go 5.5 mi to the park entrance.

topography: Elevation on the lake is 2,503 ft. The surrounding mountain slopes are blanketed with a forest of hemlocks and hardwoods. Mountain summits in the park do not exceed 3,000 ft.

maps: USGS Paint Bank, Glace.

starting out: You can pick up a trail map and other brochures in the park office. Water and rest rooms are also available in the park.

activities: Hiking, Mountain Biking, Fishing, Camping.

hiking: A small network of trails winds through the uplands that surround the small, scenic lake. Highlights along the trails are scenic ridgetop views, wildlife, and the remote, peaceful setting. Trails are blazed and trailheads are signed. Hiking is easy to moderate. Trailheads are in the campground.

mountain biking: All but one trail in the park are open to mountain bikes. The trails follow a combination of single-track and old road beds. In all, there are about 3 mi of ridable trails in the park. Riding is moderate. Access is from the campground.

fishing: Moncove Lake supports populations of largemouth bass, bluegill, and channel catfish. It can be fished from open places around the shore, or from a small boat. The latter option gives you the chance to cover more water and to explore the shoreline more completely.

camping: The developed car campground has 50 sites. Each site has a picnic table and grill. A bathhouse with modern toilets and showers is centrally located. Sites cost $11/night. The campground is open from Apr 15 to Oct 31.

Gauley River National Recreation Area

The headwaters of the Gauley River are located high in the mountains of Pocahontas County. Some 1,900 miles later, they empty into the Gulf of Mexico, after having joined the New, the Kanawha, the Ohio, and the Mississippi. Just a 25-mile stretch of the river between the dam on Summersville Lake and the small community of Swiss, however, has gained it an international reputation among whitewater enthusiasts. Here the river flows through a beautiful gorge while tumbling some 650 feet. And almost everyone who comes to visit the Gauley comes to raft, kayak, or canoe it. The river was paddled for the first time in the early 1960s; by the late 1980s it had become such a popular whitewater destination that the National Park Service designated it a national recreation area. The rec area remains largely undeveloped, with only a small camping area and large parking lot (to accommodate all the rafting company shuttles) at the put-in below the dam. There are plans to acquire land and add several more access areas downstream at the take-outs. For now, those lands remain in private hands, though property owners have allowed paddlers access in a few areas, particularly in Swiss.

Summersville (NE) is the closest town.

contact: Gauley River National Recreation Area, c/o New River Gorge National River, PO Box 246, Glen Jean, WV 25846; 304/465-0508; www.nps.gov.

getting there: From the jct of US-19 and WV-129 S of Summersville, turn W onto WV-129 and go 3 mi to the Gauley River NRA access road. Turn L and go 1.1 mi to the end of the road and a large parking area with river access and the campground.

topography: From Summersville Dam, the Gauley flows W through a narrow gorge with steep, 500-ft slopes. Most of the area is remote mountain forest, though there are a few homesteads along the route. Elevations on the river are between 1,380 ft at the put-in below the dam and 680 ft at the take-out in Swiss. **maps:** USGS Summersville Dam, Ansted.

starting out: Facilities at the NRA are limited. There are rest rooms and water at the dam tailwater parking area. Information about the river and NRA are available from the New River Gorge Canyon Rim Visitor Center on US-19 NE of Fayetteville. A pay phone is located just up the road from the put-in at the Summersville Lake Rec Area.

activities: Kayaking/Canoeing, Fishing, Camping.

kayaking/canoeing: The Gauley is indisputably one of the premiere advanced whitewater runs in the United States. Not only does it pass through beautiful mountain scenery, but its rapids are the stuff on which reputations and legends are built. In the 24-mi stretch from the Summersville Dam to the take-out in Swiss, there are 100 rapids that rate from class III to class V+. Most people who paddle the Gauley do so on rafts guided by professionals—for a very good reason: the skill needed to negotiate the many class IV-V+ rapids is beyond the abilities of all but the most advanced paddlers. If you belong to this group, you already know about this river. If, on the other hand, you belong to the majority who aren't ready to tackle this river alone in a kayak or canoe, you can still enjoy it by taking a guided trip with one of the rafting outfitters listed in the appendix. It probably goes without saying, but no one who has (or should have) doubts about his or her paddling abilities should be on this river without a guide.

While the river can be run at most times of year, there are distinct seasons on the river. Highest water is during the spring, and again in fall, when the Summersville Lake draw down takes place. This happens on 6 weekends (F-M) beginning on Labor Day.

The put-in is described above. To reach the take-out in Swiss: from the jct of WV-129 and the put-in access road: Take WV-129 W 7.1 mi to WV-39. Turn L and go 9.7 mi to South Swiss Rd (CO-19/25). Turn L and go 1 mi (at 0.7 mi the pavement ends) to where the 2 RR tracks meet. Turn R (across the tracks) and go 100 yds to a river access area.

fishing: Although fishing the Gauley requires a good deal of effort on the part of the angler, it can be done. Below Summersville Dam, the Gauley is a warm-water fishery with populations of smallmouth bass, muskellunge, and walleye. Probably the best way to fish the river is to hike down the *Fishermen's Trail* in Carnifax Ferry SP to the river. From there you can wade the deep pools or fish from the massive boulders that line the banks and fill the river.

The cold water that flows through the dam from the bottom of Summersville Lake creates ideal trout habitat in the dam's tailwaters. The river here is wide and powerful, especially during the fall draw down. Caution is necessary and anglers must stay downstream of the restricted area. Access is from the large parking area.

camping: A small primitive car camping area is located at the dam tailwater access area. There's nothing fancy or very appealing about the campground, but it does provide about the only place to overnight on the river. 18 closely spaced sites are lined along either side of a gravel spur. The sites are in the open and privacy is nonexistent. Each site has a picnic table and grill. Rest rooms and water are available. There's no fee to camp.

lodging: In downtown Summersville just a short drive from the Gauley River is the Historic Brock House (304/872-4887). The inn has been catering to guests for more than 100 years, and the Victorian building is listed on the National Register of Historic Places. Inside are 6 guest rooms, some with private baths. A wide wrap-around porch invites lazing at the end of the day. Rooms cost $70–$90/night for 2 people.

Carnifax Ferry Battlefield State Park

This 156-acre historical park sits on the northern rim of the gorge that overlooks the magnificent Gauley River. On September 10, 1861 the Union Army engaged the confederates on what was then a farm and forced their retreat to the river crossing known as Carnifax Ferry. The battle was a rebuff of the Confederate attempt to retake the Kanawha Valley and halt western Virginia's bid to become a state separate from Virginia. The park preserves the battlefield as a monument to that victory, and its appearance recalls the Civil War era, with wood fences and cannon still in place on the rolling uplands. Each fall the battle is reenacted in the park. Recreation in the park is rather limited, with a small network of hiking trails and a large, popular picnic area, but the adjacent Gauley River NRA adds the possibility of thrilling whitewater trips or fishing outings to the mix.

Summersville (NE) is the closest town.

contact: Superintendent, Carnifax Ferry Battlefield State Park, Route 2, Box 435, Summersville, WV 26651; 304/872-0825; wvweb.com/www/carnifax_ferry.html.

getting there: From US-19 S of Summersville, turn W onto WV-129 and go 4.5 mi to Carnifax Rd (CO-23). Turn L and go 0.7 mi to the park entrance.

topography: The park occupies an upland plateau and the precipitous slopes of the Gauley River gorge. Elevations are between 1,220 ft on the river and 1,700 at the highest point in the park. Large portions of the park have been kept clear of forest to help illustrate the array of lines and battlements during the Civil War.
maps: USGS Summersville Dam.

starting out: The park office doesn't keep regular hours; stop by the park museum before taking to the trails, however, and you can pick up a trail map, brochure, and check out the exhibits. Water and rest rooms are available in the picnic area.

activities: Hiking, Fishing, Kayaking.

hiking: 5 miles of trails wind across the battlefields, through the woods, and on one, down a steep, steep incline to the Gauley River 500 ft below. Highlights along the trails are the views of the river and gorge, and the area's historical significance. Trails follow both narrow paths and old roads, including one that was used for retreat by the Confederate soldiers. The trails are worn and easy to follow. Trailheads and jcts are signed. Hiking is easy to strenuous; the toughest trails lead to the river. Trail access is at the main parking lot.

fishing: The Gauley River is a warm-water fishery. Sport fish that inhabit the river include smallmouth and white bass, tiger muskies, and walleye. Access to the river is via any one of 3 trails that lead from the park uplands down paths of varying steepness. As it passes the park, the Gauley is a large, powerful river. Although its pools are generally too deep for wading, the massive boulders that line its banks and crowd its channels are suitable for casting from. The other option is to float-fish the river. Just keep in mind that it's not without reason that the Gauley is reputed to be one of the hairiest whitewater rivers in the East.

kayaking: The park is used as a put-in/take-out by ardent paddling enthusiasts. Ardent because you have to really love the sport to hump a kayak down (or worse, up) the steep quarter-mi *Fisherman's Trail* that leads from the parking lot to the river. (Hauling a canoe would require both love and madness.) Your reward once you reach the river is to be right above Pillow Rock rapids, a class V. From here it's about an 18-mi trip to the take-out in Swiss. See the separate entry for Gauley River NRA for complete details.

Hawks Nest State Park

The main appeal of Hawks Nest State Park is the magnificent views it affords of the lower New River Gorge. This appeal is so strong, in fact, that the park receives half a million visitors each year, making it the second busiest park in the state. The park encompasses 276 acres of the gorge's northern rim and the precipitous slopes that fall away to Hawks Nest Lake, a man-made impoundment on the New River. The park is geared toward taking in the scenery, whether with binoculars or a camera. Short paved trails lead to two overlooks and a tram takes visitors to the bottom of the gorge. Even the railroad trestle that crosses the lake somehow manages to be more scenic than obtrusive. Other facilities include a lodge perched on the edge of the canyon rim, a picnic area, small nature center, and tennis courts. A small network of trails permits access to the lush forest that blankets the gorge's steep slopes. The canyon is 585 ft from rim to water. What is now known as Hawks Nest was once called Marshall's Pillar, after the chief justice of the Supreme Court, who visited in 1812. Ansted (E) is the closest town.

contact: Superintendent, Hawk's Nest State Park, PO Box 857, Ansted, WV 25812; 304/658-5196; wvweb.com/www/hawks_nest.html.

getting there: From the jct of WV-16 and US-19 in Fayetteville, turn N onto US-19 and go 6.8 mi to US-60. Turn W and go 7.7 mi to the park entrance, L. A second access and overlook is another 0.6 mi further down the road.

topography: Spectacular. Steep mountain cliffs rise from the lake. Forest cover is heavy, a mix of northern hardwoods, pines, hemlocks, and cedars. Elevations are between 835 ft on the lake and 1,300 ft on the rim. **maps:** USGS Fayetteville.

starting out: Park trail maps and info are available in the lodge, which also acts as the park office. Water and rest rooms are available at both the lodge and the second overlook, as well as at the bottom of the gorge next to the tram stop.
Alcohol is not permitted in the park.

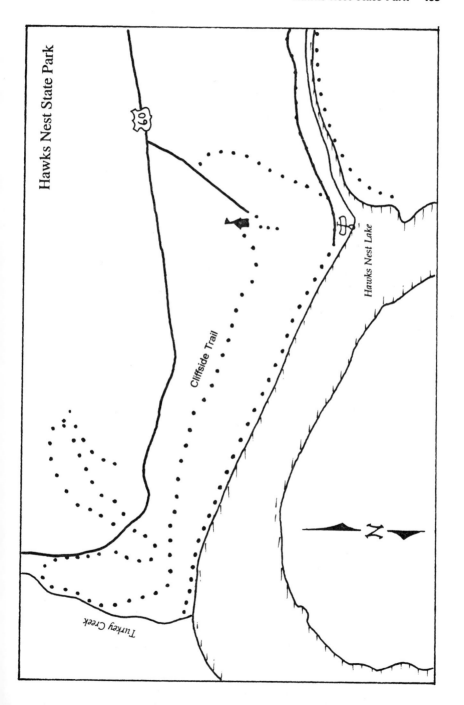

activities: Hiking, Canoeing/Kayaking, Fishing.

hiking: For such a small park, Hawk's nest has a pretty decent trail network. It centers on a pair of trails that parallel the shoreline of Hawks Nest Lake—one at lake level, the other at the rim of the gorge. A couple of other trails lead to the overlooks that offer spectacular views out over the lake and gorge, and another trail leads down the steep slope from the lodge to the lake. Combined, the trails cover about 3.5 mi. Hiking on the trails varies; generally it's easy, but steep sections do occur. Treadways include paved sections, steps, and some single track. Highlights along the trails are the views and the cool forest setting. Access is from either of the overlook parking areas or from the boat ramp parking area.

canoeing/kayaking: A park boat ramp makes it possible to put a canoe or kayak on Hawks Nest Lake and explore the park and gorge from its bottom. The lake is a long, narrow impoundment that covers 250 acres. While its size precludes long trips, the setting is so scenic that its worthwhile for shorter excursions. The banks of the lake are heavily forested, and rise steeply on all sides to the canyon rim. When the leaves change in autumn, the scenery is postcard perfect. To reach the boat ramp: from the main park entrance, turn R onto US-60 and go 1.5 mi to a Rite Aid. Turn L 180 and go about 100 yds a jct. Turn L (passing back under US-60) and go 2.1 mi (at 0.2 mi the pavement ends) to the boat ramp.

fishing: Hawks Nest Lake supports both warm-water and cold-water species of sport fish. Among the species you can fish for are trout, smallmouth bass, crappie, and tiger muskies. Angling can be done either from a boat or from the shoreline. If you choose the latter, you can hike along the *Fisherman's Access Trail*; it begins at the back of the boat ramp overflow parking area and follows the lakeshore W for almost a mile to Turkey Creek.

lodging: The main appeal of the 31-room Hawk's Nest Lodge is the awesome views it affords of the lake and gorge. The lodge itself is rather run of the mill, with rooms not unlike those found in the big hotel chains and architecture reminiscent of many junior high schools. A dining room and outdoor swimming pool are part of the package. Rates for a double range from $46 to $60/night depending on the season. The lodge is open year round.

Babcock State Park

Babcock State Park sprawls across 4,127 mountainous acres on the eastern rim of the New River Gorge. The park doesn't offer canoeists and kayakers access to the river, but it does offer a myriad of other outdoor recreation possibilities: a network of hiking trails, mountain biking loop, developed campground, picnic areas, stocked trout creek and lake, and, in winter, cross-country skiing. Facilities include cabins for overnight stays; a restaurant; a large picnic area with shelters, tables, and grills; and a grist mill. The oft-photographed grist mill, which is the park's centerpiece and identifying feature, is a recent recreation of the mill that once operated on Glade Creek, just a stone's throw from where the present one sits.

Rainelle (E) is the closest town.

contact: Superintendent, Babcock Lake State Park, HC 35, Box 150, Clifftop, WV 25831; 304/438-3003; wvweb.com/www/babcock. html.

getting there: From the jct of WV-16 and US-19 in Fayetteville, turn N onto US-19 and go 6.8 mi to US-60. Turn E and go 9.3 mi to WV-41. Turn R and go 3.1 mi (at 1 mi is Clifftop Loop (CO-11/4) and the entrance to the campground, R) to the park entrance, R.

topography: The park stretches E from the New River. Away from the steep slopes of the gorges, park topography is relatively mild. A lush forest of hemlocks, hardwoods, and rhododendron occupies most of the park's acreage. Mosses and ferns are prominent in the understory. Elevations are between 1,000 ft on the New River and 2,267 ft. **maps:** USGS Thurmond, Fayetteville.

starting out: The park office can supply you with a trail map and other info about the park. A restaurant and small gift shop are also at the site. Water and rest rooms are located in the park office and also at the picnic area.

activities: Hiking, Mountain Biking, Fishing, Camping, Cross-country Skiing.

hiking: The park has a network of trails that covers a total of 13 mi, all in the parks developed E half. The trails take in many of the park's highlights, including scenic vistas, lush forest, and a stocked trout creek. Not on any of the routes is the New River, which is beyond their reach on the park's W boundary. Trailheads are signed. The trails follow a variety of treadways, including rugged single-track, an abandoned RR grade, and narrow footpaths. The trails are blazed and generally easy to follow. Signed trailheads are located at several different locations. The campground, picnic area, and park office are all good starting points. Improvements along the trails include wooden ramps, footbridges, and shelters. Trail use is moderate to heavy.

mountain biking: Bikes are prohibited on most park trails. Only the 2.5-mi *Narrow Gauge Trail*—a former RR grade where remnants of the rail line still remain—is open to bikes. The real draw for riders is a 12-mi loop that can be made by connecting two of the park's primitive, unpaved roads. From the grist mill and parking area, the Old Sewell Rd runs W all the way to the New River. There it joins the Old State Rd (CO-19/33) which turns S and then E outside the park before looping back to the starting point. This route passes through the undeveloped part of the park; the scenery is excellent and the chance to observe wildlife is good. Riding on the roads and trail is moderate.

fishing: Anglers can choose between a beautiful mountain creek and a small lake, both stocked with trout. Glade Creek is a mid-sized creek that flows down an average gradient over a very rocky, boulder strewn bed. A dense forest crowds the banks and the creek passes through a very scenic gorge before joining the waters of Mann's Creek, which flows about 3 miles to the New River. Glade Creek provides about 2 mi of fishable water. Access is via the *Fisherman's Trail*, which follows its N to the confluence with Manns Creek.

Boley Lake is a 19-acre impoundment in a scenic setting. The lake can be fished from a path that its perimeter and provides access to open spots or from a small boat. Canoes or row boats are available for rent on the lake.

camping: The 51-site car campground is situated in a corner of the park away from most of the activity. Although the sites are large and well spaced, most of the forest cover has been removed from the campground, which has the effect of minimizing privacy.

Shade is provided by the scattered hardwoods, hemlocks, and pines that still remain. Each site has a picnic table and grill. Rest room/shower facilities with hot water are available. Sites cost $11/night, $14 with hook-up. The campground is open mid-Apr to Oct 31.

cross-country skiing: With 6 inches of snow on the ground, the gated park roads suddenly become ideal cross-country ski trails. The trails are not groomed and most park facilities shut down in winter, but this only makes the setting more perfect for a backcountry ski trip. The same loop used by mountain bikers during the warm months is a good route. Also, several of the hiking trails are suitable for skiing. These include the *Narrow Gauge Trail, Wilderness Trail,* and *Manns Creek Gorge Trail.* Skiing in the park is easy to moderate.

lodging: The 26 park cabins are isolated in 2 different areas. Cabin construction includes log and wood-frame structures. If you can, get a log cabin by Glade Creek. These offer the most privacy and are in an exceptionally scenic setting, with a very nice fly fishing creek just out back. Each of the cabins has a bath with shower, kitchen, and wood-burning stove. They sleep from 2 to 6 people. Rates for 2 people begin at $56/night in the spring/fall season. Multi-day and weekly rates are also available. The cabins are available from Apr 15 to Oct 31.

New River Gorge National River

Created in 1978 by an act of Congress, the New River Gorge National River protects 53 free-flowing miles of the river and the slopes that rise—precipitously in places—from its shores. The river has a long history, longer in fact than any other river on earth except for the Nile, a fact which frequently causes comment about the irony of its name. Geologists estimate that the river has been following its present course for about 65 million years. Until a little over a hundred years ago, however, long sections of it were uninhabited and inaccessible. The region's rich coal deposits eventually led to the construction of a railroad through the gorge in 1873, and boom towns such as Thurmond soon followed. When the coal ran out the miners and coal companies left, and today the RR tracks are used by the Amtrak train that passes through the

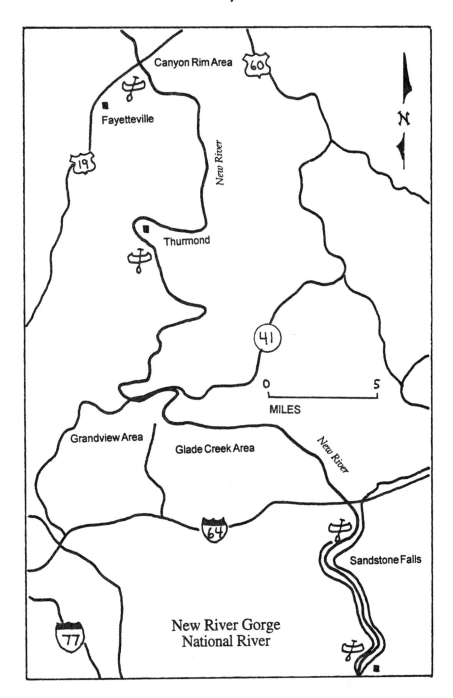

gorge daily. Remnants of that earlier era still abound, however, in ghost towns such as Thurmond and the mine sites at Kaymoor.

Although the region's history is compelling, most people who visit the New River Gorge today come for outdoor adventures. Few are disappointed. There's greater variety and opportunity for adventure sports and backcountry travel here than anywhere else in the state. First of all, the New is generally regarded as one of the premiere whitewater runs in the East, and the pilgrimage of paddlers from all points of the compass attests to the fact. The crags at the gorge's northern end are as highly regarded by climbers as any other walls east of the Rockies, and more than 1,000 routes have been put up. Hikers, backpackers, and mountain bikers come to travel into the backcountry on a vast network of trails. And anglers can cast for warm-water species such as smallmouth bass in the deep waters of the New or fish for trout in its many tributaries. And finally, backcountry enthusiasts of all types can spend a weekend, a week or longer in the gorge, camping at one of the primitive campgrounds beside a trail or on a remote stretch of the river.

Hinton (S), Beckley (W), Oak Hill (W), and Fayetteville (N) are the closest towns.

contact: Superintendent, New River Gorge National River, P.O. Box 246, Glen Jean, WV 25846; 304/465-0508; www.nps.gov.

getting there: US-19 roughly parallels the river to the W, providing the easiest access to all of the areas described below. I-64 crosses the river and gorge below the Grandview area.

topography: At the S end of the New River Gorge the river's flood plain is wide and the mountain slopes are moderate. As the river flows N it enters the gorge, with precipitous walls that rise more than 1,000 ft from the river in the Grandview area. Although some development exists along the river, most of the acreage is covered by a mixed deciduous forest. **maps:** See below under the different areas.

starting out: The Canyon Rim Visitor Center is the information center for the New River. Inside you can get free maps and brochures, buy guide books or maps, and check out the exhibits on the area's history, geology, and ecology. It's open daily from 9 AM to 5 PM. 3 other visitor centers—at Grandview, Thurmond, and Glen Jean—are open seasonally and usually only on weekends. Maps and brochures are available at each. Rest rooms and water are located at many of the recreation areas described below.

activities: Hiking, Kayaking/Canoeing, Camping, Rock Climbing, Fishing, Mountain Biking.

hiking: Although the New River Gorge is most famous for the challenges offered by its whitewater and rock climbing routes, most independent travelers experience its backcountry on the extensive network of hiking and biking trails. Throughout the gorge 23 trails cover a total distance of 43 mi. These include trails that follow the river on old RR grades, trails that wind along the canyon rim and afford spectacular views, and trails that lead away from the river and permit exploration of the gorge's fascinating geology, ecology, and history. Trail conditions and types vary considerably. Some are excellently maintained, with elaborate systems of steps and boardwalks. Others are primitive, with unsigned trailheads and difficult or obscure treadways. Picking up a copy of the large fold-out trailmap in one of the visitor centers will help you select and follow individual routes.

Major trail concentrations are in the Canyon Rim, Grandview, Thurmond, and Glade Creek areas. Connections are possible between the Canyon Rim and Thurmond areas on long rail trails, but otherwise the trail networks are discrete. Hiking along the trails ranges from easy to strenuous. Trail use is light to heavy, depending on location.

kayaking/canoeing: The New River is West Virginia's largest and most famous whitewater river. In its 53-mi course from Hinton to Fayetteville, the river drops 750 ft. Conditions vary considerably on different sections of the river, however, making different types of paddling trips possible.

On the upper sections between the Bluestone Dam and Thurmond, the wide river is characterized by long flat stretches interrupted every so often by rapids in the class II-III range. While some of these are long and will tax the skills of intermediate paddlers, they are not so severe that they can't be run in an open canoe. This makes possible multi-day paddling trips with a night or two spent in the backcountry. And you simply will not find a more dramatically scenic river in the East. In fall especially, when the leaves turn and cloak the towering walls in red, orange, and yellow, the sight is simply magnificent.

From Thurmond to Fayette Station, on the other hand, the

scenery is no less spectacular, but if you're running this section your thoughts will be elsewhere. That's because this run has the biggest whitewater in West Virginia. The river here is massive and the individual rapids pack so much power that mistakes can be deadly—fatalities have occurred here. While most people are best off running the lower New in a guided raft, for accomplished kayakers or canoeists there's just no better destination in the eastern United States.

camping: Backcountry camping is permitted throughout the national river, except where posted otherwise. Sites must be established at least 100 ft from the river or any road.

There are 6 primitive, car-accessible camping areas in the gorge. These are all small and barely a step up from backcountry camping. The only facilities at most are pit toilets. Most have no potable water source. There is no fee for camping at any of these areas and all are open year round.

rock climbing: The walls of the New River Gorge have had more routes put up on them than anywhere else in West Virginia. Well over 1,000 routes exist, ranging in difficulty from 5.0 to 5.13. Most of these are clustered on a handful of walls in the Canyon Rim Area. Since the gorge is one of the premiere climbing destinations in the East, efforts have been made to accommodate the thousands of climbers who come to the crags every year. Trails lead from large parking areas to the bases of the walls; pit toilets have been erected; and several guides to the area's many routes have been published. These latter are available from the visitor center or one of the local outfitters (see appendix for listings). Climbing is possible year round, but spring and fall are the best times of year.

fishing: The New River is a warm-water fishery known among anglers for its healthy populations of smallmouth and striped bass, walleye, and muskellunge. Several fishing strategies are possible on the river. For backcountry anglers, the most satisfying may be a float fishing trip. This is possible along any stretch of the New between Hinton and Thurmond. Considerable skill with a canoe is necessary, however, as the long pools are interrupted occasionally by class II-III rapids. Of course short sections of the river between individual rapids can also be fished in this manner. The other option is to fish from the shore or from the massive boulders that crowd parts of the river. Wading, on the other hand, is risky, as the New is very big water that is too deep in most places and too fast in others.

Trout anglers can fish the creeks that flow down off the slopes on either side of the New. These small to medium creeks can be reached by hiking trail, road, or in some cases, by wading only. Most of the creeks are stocked trout waters.

mountain biking: 4 trails that cover a distance of 19 mi are open to mountain bikes. These all follow former RR grades in the area between Thurmond and Kaymoor near Fayetteville. Most of the trails follow the river, affording excellent views and access. Other highlights are the mine remains around Kaymoor and the RR town of Thurmond. Since all the trails are straight, out-and-back riding is the norm. All of the trails connect, making rides of almost 40 mi possible. Bikepacking is also possible, as there are several primitive camping areas along the routes. Riding on the trails is easy to moderate. Trail use is moderate among bikers, but hikers are also a presence.

lodging: Just 2 miles from the Canyon Rim Visitor Center in downtown Fayetteville is the White Horse B & B (304/574-1400; wvweb.com /www/white_horse_bb/web.html). Listed on the National Register of Historic Places, the 22-room inn was built in 1906 by a Fayette County Sheriff. Although the building's exterior is attractive, it's the interior that draws the most notice. The rooms are smartly, but conservatively, furnished and the bright, spacious atmosphere contrasts with the sense of overdone clutter found in many B & Bs. The dining room, with a restored mantle and French ceiling-to-floor mural, is alone worth a visit. 7 guest rooms, some with private bath, are available. Call for rate information.

Another option is Dogwood Ridge Farms (304/658-4396), located just E of the Canyon Rim Area in Hico. The neo-colonial building sits on 60 acres of lawn, woods, and ponds. Inside are 3 guest rooms furnished with period pieces. Each room has a private bath and private deck. Rates are $65–$80/night for 2. A separate 3-bedroom cottage that sleeps 8 is also available. It has a fully equipped kitchen and private deck with hot tub. Rates begin at $100/night for 2 people.

Canyon Rim Area

Most people begin a visit to the New River Gorge National River in the Canyon Rim Area. The park visitor center is here, as is the steel arch bridge—longest in the world—that is one of the gorge's signatures. Of course there are other, natural hallmarks as well. Like the furious whitewater that draws kayakers, canoeists, and rafters from all over the East Coast. And the sheer cliff faces and precipitous slopes that rise 1,000 feet from river to canyon rim. And the railroad grades that were once conduits for the region's rich deposits of coal, but are now transformed into rail-trails used by mountain bikers, hikers, and other adventurers. Coal was once king here, and some of the remnants of its heyday are still present in the vicinity. Mine shafts and the ghosts of buildings can be seen along some of the trails. At Kaymoor a large sign reads: *Your Family Wants You to Work Safely, Section 53 Must Be Observed.* Another cautions about the danger of accidents and displays the running tally of such mishaps that was kept. The large trail network here is the most extensive of anywhere in the gorge. And the vast majority of the more than 1,000 climbing routes that have been put up are on the walls that rise from both banks of the river in the Canyon Rim Area. As the river narrows between Thurmond and Fayette Station, the whitewater more extreme than anywhere else on the New.

Fayetteville (W) is the closest town.

getting there: From I-77, take exit 48. Turn N onto US-19 and go 19.9 mi to the visitor center, R (just across the iron bridge and 2 mi NE of Fayetteville). Directions to other access points are given below under the appropriate activities.

topography: The gorge here is extremely rugged and steep, with exposed cliff faces common. Elevations in the area are between 850 ft on the river and 1,900 ft on the canyon rim. Forests of hardwoods and hemlocks cover most of the acreage. **maps:** USGS Fayetteville.

starting out: The NR's main visitor center is here, open daily from 9 AM to 5 PM. Inside are exhibits on local history, geology, and ecology. You can also pick up trail maps and brochures for free, or purchase USGS topo maps. Rest rooms and water are on the premises. The building sits perched on the gorge's eastern rim, affording awesome vistas.

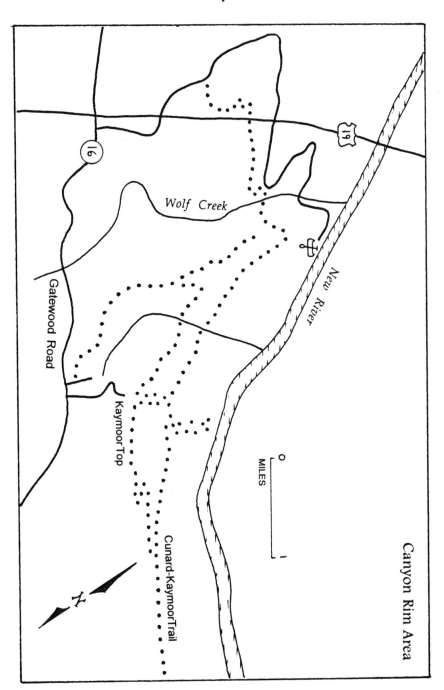

activities: Hiking, Rock Climbing, Fishing, Camping, Mountain Biking.

hiking: Area trails fan out on the gorge's W slopes. 6 interconnected trails cover a total distance of almost 14 mi. Several loop hikes are possible, as are long out-and-back hikes. Highlights are panoramic views of the gorge and bridge, as well as remnant mines and structures left over from the region's coal mining heyday. Trails follow a combination of roadbeds, narrow single-track footpaths, and even a long flight of wooden steps that leads from Kaymoor down to Kaymoor Bottom on the river. Hiking is moderate to strenuous. Creek crossings are improved with footbridges, and trailheads are clearly signed. To reach the trailheads, leave the visitor center and drive 1.6 mi S on US-19 to Fayette Station Rd. Turn R and go 2.8 mi to a parking area beside Wolf Creek and the trailhead to the *Kaymoor Trail.* 2 additional trail accesses are described below under *mountain biking.*

rock climbing: The E and W walls of the gorge contain more than 1,000 climbing routes. The walls range in height from about 60 ft to more than 125 ft. All are within a short drive of the visitor center. As climbing has become more popular in the gorge, trails have been blazed leading from the parking lots to the walls. Climbers of all skill levels will find suitable routes, ranging from 5.0 to 5.13. A description of individual routes is beyond the scope of this book. Although the visitor center can provide you with some information about the different areas and routes, the best bet is to stop in at one of the outfitters and ask or purchase one of the area climbing guides.

fishing: Anglers can choose between a stocked trout creek and the New River. Wolf Creek is a medium-sized creek that flows down the gorge's W side on a steep gradient. Massive boulders, moss-covered rocks, and frequent ledges create a tantalizing series of pools that harbor the trout that are stocked in the creek. Forest cover along the creek is exceptional, with hemlocks, rhododendron, and hardwoods all prominent. Access is from the trailhead parking area for the *Kaymoor Trail* or near the creek's mouth at Fayette Station. From there, you can wade upstream, climbing over the boulders as you go.

Fishing in the New River is for smallmouth and largemouth bass. The easiest access is from the trails and roads that parallel the river. Anglers can cast from the shore or from the house-sized boulders that line its banks and channel.

camping: Backcountry camping is permitted throughout the area on national river lands, except where posted otherwise.

A small primitive car camping area is located in an area called Brooklyn a mile past the Cunard river access. 3 sites sit on a bluff overlooking the river. Each of the large sites has a picnic table, grill, and lantern post. The sites are well spaced, and forest cover adds to the degree of privacy. A vault toilet is in the area, but there is no drinking water available. To get there, follow the directions below to the Cunard access. From there, take the dirt and gravel road at the right 1.1 mile to the camping area.

mountain biking: Just one trail in the area is open to mountain bikes, the 6.5-mi *Cunard–Kaymoor Trail*. As its name suggests, it follows a one-way route between Kaymoor and Cunard. The trail follows a combination of old roadbed and single-track through a lush forest setting. Panoramic views of the New River on one side and sheer cliff faces on the other elevate the scenery to the level of spectacular. The trail is mostly level, and ends at river level at the Cunard boat access. From there you can pedal the continuation of the trail all the way to Thurmond (see the next section for details).

To reach the Kaymoor trailhead, take WV-16 E out of Fayetteville 0.8 to Gatewood Rd (SR-9). Turn L and go 1.9 mi to Kaymoor #1 Rd (SR-9/2). Turn L and go 0.9 mi to the trailhead. • To reach Cunard: instead of turning L onto Kaymoor #1 Rd, continue on Gatewood Rd another 2.6 mi to a NPS sign for Cunard. Turn L and go 1.8 mi. Turn L and go less than 100 yds. Turn L again and go 1.7 mi down a narrow, winding gravel road to the access.

Thurmond Area

Although today it's a near-ghost town that only about 10 families call home, there was a time when Thurmond was one of the state's leading towns. It boomed in the early decades of the century, when revenues from coal made millionaires of its residents. In addition to quick wealth, the innumerable vices associated with boom towns flourished in Thurmond. Across the river was "southside," site of the famous Dun Glen Hotel (1901-1930) and infamous goings-on that included prostitution, drinking, gambling, and violence. One poker game is reputed to have run for 14 years. The

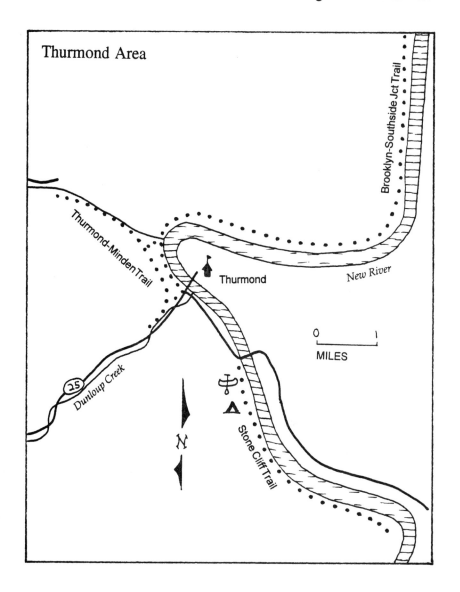

Thurmond Area

reason for the town's split across the river was that Captain W.D. Thurmond, the town's namesake and founder, would not abide vices in his town. More recently, the town again enjoyed a brief prominence, when John Sayles chose it as a stand-in for Matewan in the film of the same name. If you've seen the movie, you'll recognize the setting where Sid Hatfield and the miners shot it out with the coal company's hired guns. The original RR depot and the buildings that lined that RR tracks still remain and serve as a sort of living museum of the days when railroads and coal ruled West Virginia. Outdoor recreation in the area centers on the river and on a network of multi-use trails that wind along its western bank.

There are limited supplies in Thurmond. Hilltop (W) is the closest town.

getting there: From I-77, take exit 48. Turn N onto US-19 and go 7.2 mi to WV-61/WV-16. Turn R and then immediately L and go 0.5 mi to the Glen Jean Visitor Center. Turn L onto WV-25 and go 6.1 mi to the Thurmond Depot shuttle stop and parking area. The visitor center is across the bridge in the old RR depot.

topography: The terrain in this part of the gorge is rugged and steep, but the walls of the gorge are less precipitous than to the N. Elevations are between 1,120 on the river at Thurmond and 2,800 on area summits. Forest cover is heavy in the area, with a mix of hardwoods and hemlocks covering most of the mountain slopes. **maps:** USGS Thurmond.

starting out: There are a couple of visitor centers in the area, both housed in buildings that were central to the area during its coal-mining heyday. In Glen Jean the visitor center occupies the former Bank of Glen Jean building. The Thurmond visitor center in the former RR depot, where furnishings from the period are still on view. Both operate on restricted schedules and are usually only open on summer weekends.

activities: Hiking, Mountain Biking, Kayaking/Canoeing, Fishing, Camping.

hiking: A network of 5 trails covers 13 mi on the W bank of the New River. All but 2 short connectors are multi-use trails that are as popular with mountain bikers as they are with hikers. 2 of the 3 longest trails closely follow the New River for about 7 miles, providing easy access to the river. Area highlights are the town of

Thurmond, the New River, and the converted rail-trails. Most trail mileage is on old RR grades, though some single-track and roadbed is also encountered. Hiking is easy to moderate. Access is from the parking area just before the bridge. The *Brooklyn-Southside Jct Trail* begins across the road from the shuttle parking lot behind a RR sign that says Southside Jct. You have to cross the tracks to reach the trail.

mountain biking: Except for a pair of short connector trails, all trails in the Thurmond area are open to mountain bikes. These include a pair of riverside trails that parallel the New for almost 10 miles between Cunard and an old homestead S of Thurmond. For even longer rides, you can continue N past Cunard to Kaymoor (see previous section for details). A third trail runs perpendicular to the 2 riverside trails, following a scenic route up a creek and across several railroad trestles. Riding on the trails is easy to moderate, with surfaces that include dirt single-track, old roadbed, and a section of dirt and gravel road. Bikes can be rented from Thurmond Supply right next to the RR tracks for $25/day.

kayaking/canoeing: The Dun Glen Day Use Area just S of Thurmond acts as both a put-in and take-out. Which you use it for depends greatly on your skills as a paddler and on how much of a challenge you're up for. The New River changes character considerably at Thurmond. The 15-mi run from McCreery to Thurmond is not unlike the sections above it: long flat stretches punctuated every now and then by rapids in the class II-III range. This section is runnable in open canoes and is ideal for overnight paddling trips. Access to the put-in is described in the next section below.

Below Thurmond, the whitewater increases in intensity and you can leave the open-deck canoes at home. This is heavy water, with 18 rapids in the 14-mi stretch to Fayette Station, 4 of them class V. Although the New starts out as big water all the way up at the Bluestone Dam, by the time it squeezes into the gorge below Thurmond and churns through the major rapids, it's the biggest water in the state. This is no place for novices, or even intermediate paddlers, which is why most people who experience this part of the New do so in a guided raft. If you have any doubts about your abilities, don't test them here. To reach the take-out at Fayette Station, leave the Canyon Rim Visitor Center and go 1.6 mi S on US-19 to Fayette Station Rd. Turn R and go 3.8 mi to the end of the road at the river and parking area.

fishing: Anglers can choose between a stocked trout creek and the New River. Dunloup Creek flows down into the New on its W flank. The medium-sized creek follows a mild to average gradient through dense forest cover where rhododendron is prominent. The creek is shallow for most of the year, but intermittent rock ledges do create some nice pools. The creek is stocked trout waters. Railroad tracks that parallel the creek add a scenic touch and evoke the area's history. Access is from WV-25, which follows the creek from Glen Jean to Thurmond. Pullouts along the road once you enter NPS land provide parking.

Access to the New is on the W bank S of Thurmond. First a short access road and then a trail parallel the river, providing the best access in the area. The heavy water N of Thurmond makes float trips for extremely adventurous and skilled paddlers only. The best bet is to cast from shore or wade the shallower parts of the river.

camping: Primitive backcountry camping is permitted anywhere in the national river, except where posted otherwise.

Stone Cliff primitive car camping area is just upriver from Thurmond. 3 sites are spread out in a grassy clearing beside the river. Each site has a picnic table and grill. Rest rooms are in the area, but there's no potable water source. There's no fee to camp, and the area is accessible year round. To get there turn R at the Depot shuttle parking area and go 1.5 mi to a bridge across the New River, L. Don't turn, but drive straight onto a gravel road and enter the camping area.

Grandview Area

For 50 years, Grandview was a state park (a designation which still appears on many maps). In 1990 it was added to the New River Gorge National River. Perched high above the river on the gorge's western rim, the park offers spectacular panoramic views of the river and surrounding area. Although most of the upland plateau is forested with hardwoods and conifers, a large area near the visitor center has been landscaped and is used for picnics or casual outdoor recreation. Wildlife that might be seen in the wooded areas includes white-tailed deer, red fox, cottontail, red squirrel, and black bear. A small network of hiking trails winds along the edge of the rim, providing an up-close view of the geology that formed the deep cut in the earth's surface. The

Grandview area is open daily from 8 AM to 10 PM.
Beckley (W) is the closest town.

getting there: From I-64 take exit 129B. Turn N onto WV-9 and go 4.8 mi to the entrance to the Grandview area.

topography: The Grandview area is one of the steepest, most rugged section of the New River Gorge. The top of the gorge towers 1,200 ft above the river. Elevations are 1,200 on the New and 2,400 ft at the visitor center and overlook. Large sections of the park have been cleared and landscaped, though most of this area is blanketed with a lush forest that includes hardwoods, pines, hemlocks, spruce, and rhododendron. **maps:** USGS Prince.

starting out: The visitor center can provide you with trail maps and other info about the NR. Rest rooms and water are located here too. The large landscaped grounds are a perfect place for a picnic. A pay phone is at the amphitheater.

activities: Hiking.

hiking: 5 trails cover about 4.5 mi on the gorge's rim. The attraction here is not an extensive network of trails that lead into the backcountry, but the views the short trails and spurs provide of the gorge. Several overlooks perch on the gorge's rim, offering the best views of the magnificent geology that the river has created. The trails are clearly marked and easy to follow. Hiking is easy to moderate. Access is from the visitor center parking lot or the Turkey Spur Overlook.

Glade Creek Area

Between Sandstone Falls and the WV-41 bridge near the community of Prince, the New enters more rugged topography and receives the waters of two scenic mountain streams, Meadow Creek and Glade Creek. The latter was once the site of the town of Hamlet. The construction of the railroad bridge across the river brought the town to life in the '20s, when there was a saw-mill, post office, doctor's office, boarding house, club house and 25 to 30 residences. During the depression the mill closed, and today

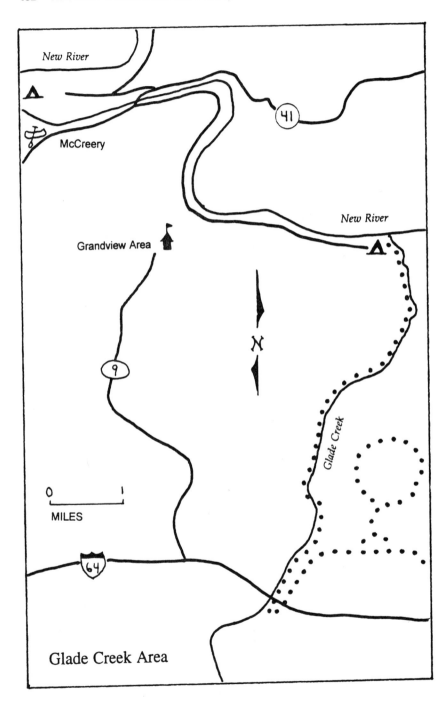

New River

McCreery

41

New River

Grandview Area

N

9

Glade Creek

0   1
MILES

64

Glade Creek Area

the area has been reclaimed by forest. A small picnic area and primitive campground are now located at the exceptionally scenic site at the mouth of Glade Creek. The creek is stocked with trout and a hiking trail follows the former RR grade along its banks. Paddlers will find several river accesses nearby, as well as numerous areas suitable for camping beside the river.

Beckley (SW) is the closest town.

getting there: From the jct of US-19 and WV-41 in Beckley, turn N onto WV-41. To get to the Glade Creek camping area and trailheads, go 8.6 mi (at 4.7 mi continue past a jct with WV-61; at 7.5 mi reach a boat ramp on the New at McCreery) to a bridge across the New and the access road to the Glade Creek area, R, just before the bridge. (To reach the Army primitive camping area, cross the bridge and turn immediately L. Go 2 mi to the end of the dirt and gravel road at the New River and the camping area). Bear R onto the dirt and gravel road. At 1 mi reach the Grandview Sandbar boat access and primitive camping area, L. 5.5 mi further down the road reach Glade Creek and a parking area for trailheads and a day-use picnic area. The primitive camping area is to the L.

topography: Both the New River and Glade Creek flow N through steep forested mountain slopes. Hardwoods, hemlocks, and rhododendron are most prominent. A wetland with beaver ponds is located near the S edge of the area. **maps:** USGS Prince.

starting out: Facilities in this remote backcountry area are quite limited. There's no potable water source, but pit toilets are located at the Glade Creek Rec Area.

activities: Hiking, Fishing, Kayaking/Canoeing, Camping.

hiking: 4 trails cover 14 miles in the area. The *Glade Creek Trail* is the anchor and provides access to the other 3, all of which intersect. It follows a narrow gauge RR route where timber was once carried from the mountain top to the mill in Hamlet. The trails can be hiked in series, but backtracking on the *Glade Creek Trail* is necessary. Highlights along the trails are Glade Creek, a stocked trout creek; Kates Falls; wildlife; and mountain scenery. Hiking is moderate to strenuous. Creek crossings are improved with footbridges. Trails aren't blazed, but are easy to follow. Access is from the picnic area/primitive camping area at the end of Glade Creek Rd.

fishing: Glade Creek offers 6 mi of fishable water on one of the most attractive streams in the New River Gorge. It flows N from Glade Creek Reservoir before passing under I-64 and entering the NR. From there it continues to tumble N over a mild to average gradient. Its course is extremely rocky, with lots of small and large pools. Forest cover is lush and dense, providing deep shade and a challenge to fly casters. Access is via the *Glade Creek Trail*, which follows the creek up the mountain. It's stocked trout waters.

The New River is also accessible from Glade Creek Road. There is a small area on the banks from which it's possible to cast, or the river can be waded in the shallower parts. Float fishing trips are also possible.

kayaking/canoeing: The Glade Creek Area is near the end of the 15-mi section of the New between Sandstone Falls and McCreery. Like the section above it, this part of the river features long stretches of flat water punctuated by a handful of class II-III rapids. Open-deck canoes are suitable, and the stunning scenery and abundant campsites make this one of the best stretches of the New for overnight paddling trips. The take-out is river L about a mi past the bridge below Prince. For directions to the put-in, see the next section below.

camping: Primitive backcountry camping is permitted throughout the area on NPS lands, except where posted otherwise. Good campsites can be found along the trails at the Glade Creek Area.

If you're car camping, you can choose from 3 different primitive car camping areas in the vicinity. The Grandview Sandbar area has 12 sites spread out along the river's edge. Access to the river is easy, making this a good choice for canoe/kayak camping. The sites are large and well spaced, offering a good degree of privacy. Shade is provided by dogwoods and bottomland hardwoods. The sites are largely unimproved. The camping area is open year round.

The Glade Creek area features 5 large sites that are very well spaced. The area is in a heavily forested area at the edge of the New River. Each site has a picnic table. Privacy is very good here. There are vault toilets in the area.

A third possibility for camping is the Army primitive camping area located on the other side of the New River. There are no designated sites here, just a large clearing behind a bend in the river with a wide sand beach. There's a vault toilet in the area.

Sandstone Falls Area

The falls that are the end of this section of the New lend the area its name and attract the most visitors. The river is wide here, more than a quarter-mile across, and the falls extend from one bank to the other. The drop varies from 10 to 25 feet at different points on the river, and there is no more spectacular sight or convincing proof of the power of moving water elsewhere on the New. The falls can be seen from an overlook high above the river on WV-20 north of Hinton, or experienced up-close on the series of boardwalks and footbridges that have been built across the islands that crowd the river below the falls. In addition to sightseeing, outdoor recreation here centers around the river. Unlike further north in the gorge, there's no extensive trail network here leading into the backcountry. The area below the falls is popular with anglers, and canoeists and kayakers can run the 10-mi section of river above the falls or put in just below them for trips of various length. The falls themselves cannot be run.

Hinton (N) is the closest town.

getting there: From I-64 take exit 139. Turn S onto WV 20 and go 10.7 mi through the town of Hinton and across the bridge to Madams Creek Rd (SR-21/3). Turn R and go 100 yds to Sandstone Falls River Rd (SR-26). Turn R again and go 8.2 mi (at 3.9 mi pass the Brooks Falls Day Use Area) to a parking area at Sandstone Falls.

topography: The river valley here is broad, and while the surrounding terrain is mountainous, the slopes rise more gradually to their peaks than further N. The most compelling geologic feature is the river-wide falls. Elevation at this point on the river is 1,290 ft. **maps:** USGS Meadow Creek.

starting out: Facilities on this stretch of the river can be found at Brooks Falls, Sandstone Falls, in the town park below the dam, and in the town of Hinton.

activities: Canoeing/Kayaking, Fishing, Camping.

canoeing/kayaking: The section of river from just below the dam to the unrunnable Sandstone Falls is 10 mi long. It's characterized by a few class II-III rapids with long stretches of flat and class I water. Open-deck canoes can handle all of the rapids, and the wide river and long flat stretches give paddlers a chance to admire the picturesque mountain scenery. The heaviest water is at Brooks Falls, a runnable river-wide falls that can be scouted from Hellem's Beach river L. The first put-in for this part of the New is just below the dam at a municipal park river R in Hinton. The last take-out above the falls is at a small day-use area on the L bank, 0.7 mi above the falls and the rec area parking lot. A large sign visible from the river marks the location. The put-in below the falls is 0.2 mi past the Sandstone Falls parking area.

fishing: The area just below the falls is a popular spot with local anglers. Access is easy from the small network of trails and boardwalks that wind through the islands located at the base of the falls. Anglers can also get a line in the river from one of the day-use areas located along Sandstone Falls River Rd.

camping: Since this is the most developed stretch of the New River Gorge, it also offers the fewest opportunities for backcountry camping. With only a couple of short trails, backpacking isn't really an option and canoe/kayak campers will find more isolation along the stretch of river below the falls.

Car campers will find 5 sites at the Sandstone Falls Rec Area. They're wedged onto a narrow strip of grass between the parking lot and road. The sites are small and offer no privacy at all. Each site has a picnic table, grill, and lantern post. Pit toilets are located in the parking area. The sites are accessible year round and there's no fee to camp there.

Little Beaver State Park

This 562-acre park is located in Raleigh County 5 miles east of Beckley. With the New River Gorge just a few miles up the road, the small park is generally overlooked by hardcore outdoor enthusiasts. In fact, its purpose is closer to that of a county park than to a state park with a large backcountry. Recreation in the park centers on the 18-acre lake; it's stocked with trout, and row boats and paddle boats can be rented at the park office. A small network of hiking trails laces the woodlands that surround it. There is also a picnic area with shelters, tables, and grills. Beckley (W) is the closest city.

contact: Superintendent, Little Beaver State Park, Route 9, Box 179, Beaver, WV 25813; 304/763-2494; wvweb.com/www/little_beaver.html.

getting there: From I-64 take exit 129 and turn S onto CO-9. Drive 1.8 mi (at 0.5 mi the road becomes WV-307) to the park entrance, L.

topography: The lake is the park's most prominent geographic feature. On its shore are modest mountain slopes covered in a thick canopy of hardwoods and northern conifers, with rhododendron abundant in the understory. Elevation on the lake is 2,414 ft. The surrounding hills don't exceed 2,600 ft in the park. **maps:** USGS Prince, Shady Spring.

starting out: You can pick up a trail map and other info at the park office on the lake. Boat rentals are available. Water and rest rooms are there too.

activities: Hiking, Fishing.

hiking: The park features 4 trails that cover 5.5 mi of lakeshore and forested uplands. Beginning from the office near the dam, the trails fan out beyond the lake's S shore. The trails follow dirt footpaths and old RR grades. Loop hikes are possible, as is connecting more than one trail. Trailheads and trail jcts are signed. Hiking is easy to moderate.

fishing: Little Beaver Lake is stocked with trout monthly. Anglers can fish the lake from the shoreline—there are scattered open areas—or from a small boat. The latter option is better, since it allows you to cover more water. The lake is small, however, and can feel pretty crowded on weekends.

Bluestone Lake Wildlife Management Area

The vast Bluestone Lake WMA sprawls across 17,632 acres that surround the lake and the New River just above the lake. The lake itself covers an area of 2,000 acres. It was created when a dam was constructed across the New River at Hinton. Away from the dam, the lake and lower stretch of the New River Valley are exceptionally scenic, with forest mountains rising from the water on all sides. Recreation at the WMA focuses on the water, where boating and fishing are both popular. Wildlife is abundant in the uplands and around the clearings in the river's flood plain. White-tailed deer, red fox, bobcat, wild turkey, and mink are all present. Since it's managed primarily as wildlife habitat, most of the WMA is left in a primitive state. The recreational facilities found in the state parks are absent here. About the only development is the series of primitive camping areas located on both shores of the lake and river. There are 300 sites in all, and each of the areas also offers boat access to the water.

Hinton (N) is the closest town.

contact: Resource Manager, Bluestone Lake, 701 Miller Ave, Hinton, WV 25951; 304/466-1234. • Superintendent, Bluestone Lake Wildlife Management Area, 2006 Robert C Byrd Dr, Beckley, WV 26241; 304/637-0245.

getting there: There are half a dozen different access points to the WMA on either side of the New River. To reach the WMA office and HQ: from Hinton take WV-3 S 5 mi to WV-12. Continue straight onto WV-12 and go 8 mi to CO-21/2. Turn R and go 3 mi to the HQ building, R. • Access to the areas on the E bank is from roads that connect to WV-12. To reach these areas, follow the directions below under *camping* to any of the different areas. All the routes are signed.

topography: Most of the WMA occupies the broad floodplain of the impounded New River. Most of the land immediately around the lake's perimeter is unforested, though the slopes that rise from the floodplain are blanketed with a hardwood forest. Elevation on the lake is 1,410 ft; higher elevations exceed 2,800 ft S of Bertha. **maps:** USGS Pipestem, Forest Hill, Peterstown, Lerona, Hinton.

starting out: You can pick up a map at the WMA HQ on weekdays. Fishing licenses are also sold there. Facilities at the WMA are limited. You'll find vault toilets at the primitive camping areas. Water is available at a few of the areas from hand water pumps, but at others, there's no potable water source. Alcohol is not permitted at the WMA.

activities: Canoeing/Kayaking, Fishing, Camping.

canoeing/kayaking: Paddling is on both the lake and the lower, flatwater section of the New River. 2,000-acre Bluestone Lake is one of the most scenic lakes in West Virginia. The lake's profile is long and narrow, and the slopes that rise from its edge are rugged, mountainous, and almost entirely undeveloped. In autumn, the setting is especially exquisite. Paddlers can put in or take out at any of the primitive camping areas described below. The last rapid on the New is near the mouth of Indian Creek; if you put in above there, remember that you'll have to paddle against a pretty strong current to take out at the same place. The lake is just about the right size for a full day's paddle, though with so many camping options along the shore, weekend trips are tempting too. The only big drawback to the lake is the fact that it's open to powerboats. Although you'll probably have to endure the whine of their motors for at least part of any trip, the most popular area is up by the dam, where water-skiing is permitted—far from most of the camping areas.

fishing: The lake provides a warm-water habitat for a variety of sport fish. Largemouth, smallmouth, and striped bass; crappie; bluegill; channel catfish; and muskellunge are all regularly caught. You can fish the lake from shore—the camping areas offer long stretches of treeless bank—but you'll be happier in a canoe. Not only can you cover more water, but you can explore the lake's isolated corners that are inaccessible from shore.

camping: Aside from a handful of gravel roads, really the only development on the WMA is a series of primitive camping areas that line the shores of the New and Bluestone Lake. Campers can choose from any of 4 different areas on the N shore of the New River. Sites at all areas cost $5/night. Areas are described here from N to S.

Bertha Camping Area. 55 sites are spread out across a very large clearing beside the river. Each site has a picnic table. There are pit toilets, but potable water is not available. There isn't much shade, but the sites are far away from each other and offer plenty of privacy. To get there: from the jct of WV-3 and WV-12, follow WV-12 S 6.2 mi to Seminole Rd (SR-21-2). Turn R and go 3.7 mi to a fork. Bear R and go 1.7 mi to a church and an unsigned jct. Turn L and go 1.9 mi down a winding dirt and gravel road to the camping area.

Shanklins Ferry Area. 76 sites are spread out across several large clearings. Each of the sites has a picnic table. Privacy at the sites is good. There are pit toilets, and a hand water pump is near the entrance. To get there: from the jct of WV-3 and WV-12, take WV-12 S 14.9 mi to WV-24. Turn R and go 2.7 mi to a crossroads. Continue straight onto Shanklins Ferry Rd (SR-24/3). Go 2 mi and turn L onto an unpaved road. Go 1 mi to the start of the camping area.

Cedar Branch has 24 sites spread out across a large area by the river. Each site has a picnic table. The site offer an adequate amount of privacy. There are pit toilets, but no water. To get there: Follow directions above to Shanklins Ferry, but instead of turning L at the unpaved access road continue another 2 mi to another unpaved access road. Turn L and go 1 mi to the entrance.

Indian Creek: 50 sites spread out across a large area beside the river near the mouth of Indian Creek. Each site has a picnic table. Water is available from a hand pump and there are pit toilets in the area. To get there: From the jct of WV-3 and WV-12, take WV-12 S 8 mi to CO-21/2. Turn R and go 5.5 mi to a jct with a dirt and gravel road. Turn R and go 1.5 mi to the camping area.

lodging: Located just minutes away in Pipestem, the Walnut Grove Inn (800/701-1237; wvweb.com/www/walnut_grove_inn) features a circa-1850 farmhouse set on 38 peaceful acres. The cozy stone and wood inn has 4 guest rooms furnished with Victorian and French period pieces. Rates are $65/night for 2 people during the peak season. A 7-course gourmet breakfast is included.

Bluestone State Park

Located at the northwest corner of 2,000-acre Bluestone Lake, the park's 2,000 acres of flood plain bottom land and rugged upland are part of almost 20,000 publicly owned acres that surround the lake and are managed for outdoor recreation and wildlife habitat. Park and lake are located south of the historic town of Hinton in

Summers County. Recreation naturally centers around the lake; boating and fishing are the most popular activities. The park has access to both, plus a small network of hiking trails, 3 separate camping areas, 25 cabins, a picnic area, and an outdoor swimming pool. Wildlife in the dense woodlands that surround the lake includes white-tailed deer, wild turkey, mink, red fox, and bobcat.

Hinton (N) is the closest town.

contact: Superintendent, Bluestone State Park, HC 78, Box 3, Hinton, WV 25951; 304/466-2805; wvweb.com/www/bluestone.html.

getting there: From I-77 take exit 14. Turn E and follow signs 2.6 mi to WV-20 (Athens Rd). Turn L and go 17.5 mi to the park entrance., L. From I-64, take exit 139. Turn S onto WV-20 and go 15 mi to the park entrance, R.

topography: Park terrain includes the river's narrow floodplain and the mountain slopes that rise on either side. Elevations in the park are between 1,409 ft on the lake and 2,400 ft near Sand Knob. The terrain is steep in places, particularly on the S shore. **maps:** USGS Pipestem.

starting out: You can pick up a trail map and brochure in the park office/store. Water, rest rooms, and a pay phone are there too. Facilities are also available at the swimming pool. The park is open daily from 6 AM to 10 PM.

activities: Camping, Canoeing/Kayaking, Fishing, Hiking.

camping: Campers have 2 options in the park—a pair of car campgrounds or a primitive camping area on the New River that can only be reached by boat. Canoe or kayak camping is possible an any of the camping areas.

Medor Campground is located beside the Bluestone River in the vicinity of the outdoor pool. 31 smallish sites are spread out across a semi-wooded area in the river's flood plain. The sites offer only a small degree of privacy. Each site has a picnic table and grill. Water and rest rooms with showers are located in the camping area. Sites cost $11/night, $14 with hook-up. The campground is open from the end of Apr to Oct 31.

The Old Mill Camping Area has 47 sites in a more rustic and

primitive setting. The small sites are numbered, but do not have picnic tables or grills. Hardwoods provide shade and a moderate level of privacy. The Bluestone River flows past the campground. Water and outdoor showers are available. There's also a boat launch in the camping area. Sites cost $7/night. The campground is open from Memorial Day to Oct 31.

canoeing/kayaking: Bluestone Lake is a 2,000-acre impoundment that backs up water on both the Bluestone and New River. Despite the fact that it owes its existence to a dam, the lake is one of the most scenic in West Virginia. Development along the mountainous shoreline is almost nonexistent, with forests of hardwoods and conifers blanketing almost all of the acreage, most of which is publicly owned. The profile of the lake is long and narrow, befitting rivers that flow bewteen rugged mountain slopes. The SP is located at the upper end of the portion of the lake on the Bluestone River. Both day and overnight paddling trips are possible. Although power boats are a presence on the lake, their numbers are usually relatively small. In addition to the boat ramp in the SP, there are numerous access points on the Bluestone Lake WMA. The WMA also has an abundance of primitive camping areas, all accessible from the water.

fishing: Bluestone Lake is a warm-water fishery that supports populations of largemouth, smallmouth, and striped bass; crappie; muskellunge; and channel catfish. Although fishing from the shore in the SP is possible, with limited room and no chance to cover more than a very small part of the lake, it isn't really desirable. The only satisfactory way to cover such a large body of water is from a boat. If you're determined to fish from the shore, you'll find much more room on the Bluestone Lake WMA.

hiking: The park isn't really a major hiking destination, though 6 mi of trails wind through the forested uplands that overlook the lake. The trails are concentrated in the area between the cabins and camping areas. A couple of different loop hikes are possible, though small sections of road make up part of the routes. The main appeal of the trails is the scenic views they afford and the cool forest setting. Hiking on the trails is easy to moderate. The trails are blazed with signed trailheads located on the main park road. Trail use is moderate to heavy in summer.

lodging: The park is home to 25 attractive cabins that can accommodate from 2 to 6 people each. The wood-frame cabins are fully furnished; each has a stone fireplace, kitchen, bath with shower, and central heat. Rates for 2 people start at $67/night during the peak season. Off-season and stays of more than one night are discounted. The cabins are available year round.

Pipestem Resort State Park

This 4,023-acre park straddles the Bluestone River and the magnificent gorge through which it flows. The setting is one of the most scenic in southern West Virginia, and the park manages to preserve it in an almost pristine state while providing the amenities of a large-scale resort. Among those amenities are an 18-hole golf course, 9-hole par three golf course, miniature golf course, riding stables, a pair of lodges, and 25 cabins. For the backcountry enthusiast, there's a network of hiking trails, the Bluestone National Scenic River, and an abundance of wildlife in a backcountry that remains relatively intact. Although the park encompasses a section of the gorge, most of its acreage sits on the plateau that extends southeast from the canyon rim. The park occupies a part of Summers and Mercer counties. The unusual name refers to the stem of a plant that was used by Native Americans to fashion pipes.

Princeton (SW) and Hinton (NE) are the closest towns.

contact: Pipestem Resort State Park, Box 150, Pipestem, WV 25979; 304/466-1800; wvweb.com/www/pipestem.html.

getting there: From I-77 take exit 14. Turn E and follow signs 2.6 mi to WV-20 (Athens Rd). Turn L and go 9.2 mi to the park entrance, L.

topography: The terrain in the park includes a little bit of everything: steep forested slopes, undulating hills, landscaped and mowed areas, and a golf course. The Bluestone River is the major drainage, and its spectacular gorge presents the park's steepest and most rugged terrain. Despite the resort atmosphere, large areas of the park remain forested. Elevations are between 2,960 ft on Pipestem Knob and 1,500 ft on the river. **maps:** USGS Pipestem, Flat Top.

starting out: Trail maps and other info are available at the park HQ. Rest rooms, water, and pay phones can be found at several locations in the park.

activities: Hiking, Mountain Biking, Cross-country skiing, Fishing, Camping.

hiking: The park's large and popular trail network consists of 16 trails that cover a total distance of 14 mi. Most of the trails are short—the longest is the 2.7-mi *River Trail*—but 2 or more can be joined together to form longer hikes. The trails take in all of the park highlights: panoramic views of Bluestone Canyon, the Pipestem Knob Tower, the Bluestone National Scenic River, and the forested backcountry. The trails follow both old roadbeds and narrow footpaths. Heavy use keeps them clearly visible and easy to follow. Trailheads are signed and are located at several places around the park. Hiking on almost all of the trails is easy to moderate. Note: part of the trail network is on the far side of the Bluestone River. The only way across is to wade.

mountain biking: 5 trails are open to mountain bikes, for a total distance of about 6.5 mi. It's actually further than that if you take into account that the 2.7-mi *River Trail* is a dead end that must be backtracked. The trails can be linked together to form an approximate loop ride of about 8 mi. Trails are single-track and dirt road beds (closed to vehicles). Riding is easy to moderate, except on the *River Trail*, which is steep and involves an unimproved river crossing. Rides can begin from the lodge or the nature center.

cross-country skiing: Although the annual snowfall is rather modest, when there's snow on the ground several trails are open for cross-country skiing. These are concentrated in the area of rolling terrain between the nature center and the lodge. The trails are blazed and easy to follow. Skiing is easy to moderate.

fishing: Although the banks of Long Branch Lake always seem to be teeming with anglers pulling stocked trout from its waters, backcountry enthusiasts will want to leave the madding crowd behind and head down to the Bluestone River. Flowing through the bottom of a 1,000-ft canyon, this is one of the most beautiful rivers in the state. The large river flows down a mild gradient over a very rocky bed. The forest of hemlocks and hardwoods that line the banks provides shade and adds to the scenery.

camping: The only option for campers in the park is a large developed car campground the is most popular with RVers. The 82 sites are rather small and crowded together. The area is only sparsely wooded, which keeps privacy to a minimum. Each site has a picnic table and grill. Rest rooms with hot showers are centrally located. Tent sites, which offer almost no privacy at all, cost $11/night. Half of the sites can be reserved by calling 800/CALL WVA. Some sites remain open throughout the year.

lodging: 2 lodges and 25 cottages are located within the park. The 113-room McKeever Lodge resembles a large hotel, but the views it affords from the canyon rim make up for what it lacks in character. Rates for a double are $68–94/night. The lodge is open year round.

The smaller and more rustic Mountain Creek Lodge sits on the banks of the Bluestone River at the bottom of the gorge. The lodge can't be reached by car; you either have to take an aerial tramway from the Canyon Rim Center or go on foot or mountain bike the River Trail. (If you choose the latter be prepared to wade across the river—there's no footbridge.) There are 30 rooms in several connected buildings. The lodge is open from Apr 1 to Oct 31. Rooms cost $58/night for 2 people.

The park's cottages are wood-frame construction with porches or balconies. Each of the heated, furnished cottages has a kitchen, bathroom with shower, and fireplace. The cottages come in 2-, 3-, and 4-bedroom configurations. Rates for a 2-bedroom range from $78/night in winter to $98/night in summer. The cottages are available year round.

Camp Creek State Park & State Forest

This pair of adjacent backcountry areas encompasses just under 6,000 acres near the southwestern edge of the Allegheny Mountains. Recreational facilities are confined to the 500-acre state park. These include a pair of campgrounds; a picnic area with shelters, tables, and grills; and a hiking trail. The 5,500-acre forest, on the other hand, is completely undeveloped except for the large network of unimproved roads that wind across the ridges and parallel the drainages. Outside of the park rec areas a hardwood forest covers most of the acreage, providing haven for wildlife that includes white-tailed deer, red fox, ruffed grouse, and wild turkey. Several cascading water falls add a scenic touch to the forest setting and provide opportunities for nature photography. The forest roads are particularly popular with mountain bikers.

Princeton (S) is the closest town.

contact: Camp Creek State Park, P.O. Box 119, Camp Creek, WV 25820; 304/425-9481; wvweb.com/www/camp_creek.html.

getting there: From I-77 take exit 20. Turn S onto US-19 and go 0.3 mi to Camp Creek Rd (SR 19/5). Turn R and go 1.8 mi to the park entrance.

topography: Narrow drainages flow S and E, cutting through uplands that semi-mountainous. The slopes are blanketed with a forest of hardwoods and hemlocks. Large areas in the valleys have been landscaped to accommodate park amenities. Elevations are between 2,000 ft and 2,900 ft. **maps:** USGS Odd, Flat Top, Matuaka.

starting out: If you want to pick up a trail map or get other info on the park and forest, the park office is a good place to start. Water and rest rooms are available at several locations. The park is open daily from 6 AM to 10 PM.

activities: Hiking, Fishing, Mountain Biking, Camping.

hiking: The only designated trail in the state park or forest is the 2.5-mi *Farley Branch Trail.* It combines with a section of rough road to form a loop that passes the campground, picnic area, and a scenic falls. The trailheads are signed and the trail is blazed. In addition to that, there are roughly 50 additional mi of trails and forest roads that lace the backcountry. Conditions on these vary from primitive to graded roadways, but the lack of blazes and signed trailheads is consistent. Be sure to bring a trail map and topo map if you decide to venture deep into the backcountry. The extra effort is worth it, as there are scenic falls along the route and an abundance of wildlife in the wooded uplands. Hiking is mostly moderate.

fishing: A pair of mountain creeks are stocked with brookies, rainbow, brown, and golden trout. Camp Creek is an attractive creek that flows through a mixture of meadow and forest from the N boundary to the S, a distance of about 5 mi. The creek is mid-sized, with a mild to average gradient. Rhododendron slicks crowd the banks in places, making fly-casting difficult. Access is via an unpaved road that begins in the primitive camping area.

Mash Fork flows W through the forest and park before joining Camp Creek near the entrance. It too is a small to medium creek that flows down a mild to average gradient. Cover is generally good, except where the creek passes by the campground. The creek can be fished for about 4 mi. Access is via a dirt road that runs beside it for all of its length in the park and forest.

mountain biking: None of the park/forest trails or roads are closed to mountain bikes, which means there's plenty of terrain to explore. The downside—for riders who like to have a definite route mapped out in advance, at least—is that navigating most of the trails is something of an adventure, since they're logging roads that don't show up on any maps. The park/forest trail map does show the main arteries, however. Most of the 50 miles of potential riding is on roads in various states of repair, with some single-track too. The best riding and the largest concentration of trails is in the NE quadrant. Ride up past the Blue Jay camping area to access the trails. Riding is moderate to strenuous.

camping: Campers can choose between two car campgrounds, one primitive and the other developed. Both are open from Apr 1 to Oct 31. Backcountry camping is not allowed.

The Blue Jay primitive camping area features 12 sites nestled among the trees that line Camp Creek. Located at the end of a dirt road, it's tucked away from the main areas of activity. The well-spaced sites and forest cover afford a high degree of privacy. Each site has a picnic table, grill, and lantern post. Pit toilets and water fountains are the only facilities. Sites cost $7/night.

The 25 sites in the developed campground are spread out across a large open area beside Mash Fork and shadowed by two steep ridge lines. Some shade is provided by tall hemlocks, pines, and hardwoods. The large sites are well spaced, and privacy is adequate. Each site has a picnic table, grill, and lantern post. A central bathhouse has hot water showers. Sites cost $14/night.

Twin Falls Resort State Park

This large park and resort complex sprawls across 3,776 acres of rolling countryside and mountain slopes in Wyoming County southwest of Beckley. Like nearby Pipestem Resort SP, Twin Falls incorporates resort recreation and facilities into a large and scenic backcountry. For nature lovers, the melding of the two may seem relatively successful here, as the resort complex is low key and an atmosphere of woodsy isolation prevails—even on the golf course, where deer are often seen grazing. Other amenities are a lodge, outdoor swimming pool, cottages, developed campground, picnic area, and tennis courts. Backcountry recreation focuses on the trail network, which provides access to the more primitive corners of the park. Park wildlife includes red fox, wild turkey, and rabbits. Also one the grounds is a pioneer farmstead that has been restored to a circa 1830 condition.

contact: Superintendent, Twin Falls Resort State Park, Route 97, Box 1023, Mullens, WV 25882; 304/294-4000; wvweb.com/www /twin_falls.html.

getting there: From I-77 take exit 42. Turn S onto WV-16/WV-97 and go 3.9 mi to WV-54. Turn R and go 13.4 to WV-97. Turn R and go 5.3 mi a fork. Bear L, continuing on WV-97 for 0.8 mi to the park entrance.

topography: Despite the presence of a golf course and other resort facilities, the park retains a backcountry feel. The main reason is the lush forest of hardwoods, hemlock, and rhododendron that blankets the rest of the acreage. Black Fork ambles SW through the park's center. Elevations on the foothills reach 2,500 ft and drop to 1,900 ft on the creek. **maps:** USGS McGraws, Mullens.

starting out: Stop by the park HQ to pick up a trail map or other info before you begin exploring the area. Rest rooms and water are inside. The park is open daily from 6 AM to 10 PM.
　　Alcohol is not permitted.

activities: Hiking, Camping.

hiking: Aside from the resort facilities, the main recreation draw in the park is the large trail network. 9 trails cover a distance of 20 mi, taking in many of the park highlights along the way. These include mountain views, scenic falls, and the restored pioneer farm. Although the trails can be linked by hiking sections of park road, they have not been laid out to facilitate long loops. Trailheads are scattered throughout the park, so some backtracking and moving around is necessary to hike all the trails. Most of the trails follow single-track treadways that are clearly defined, blazed, and easy to follow. Hiking is easy to moderate.

camping: A developed car campground has 50 sites nestled in a heavily wooded area. The sites are not particularly large or well spaced, but the tree cover provides an adequate degree of privacy. Each site has a picnic table and grill. Rest rooms with hot showers are located in the campground. Sites cost $11/night, $14 with hook-up. Some of the sites can be reserved. The campground is open from Apr 1 to Oct 31.

lodging: Lodging is available in the park in either a lodge or cottages. The 20-room lodge is a rectangular brick building that overlooks the golf course. The rooms are clean and function, and the lodge itself has something of a homey atmosphere. A restaurant and conference rooms part of the complex. Rates for a double begin at $55/night during peak season. The lodge is open year round.

Each of the 13 heated cottages is furnished, with a kitchen, bathroom with shower, deck, and stone fireplace. Cottages are available to sleep 4, 6, or 8. Rates for the smallest start at $94/night during the peak season. Off-season and stays of more than one night have lower rates. The cottages are available year round.

Ohio River Valley

Ohio River Valley Key Map

1. Tomlinson Run SP
2. Coopers Rock SF
3. Lewis Wetzel WMA
4. Valley Falls SP
5. Tygart Lake SP
6. Watters Smith Memorial SP
7. North Bend Rail Trail
8. North Bend SP
9. Audra SP
10. Cedar Creek SP
11. Burnsville Lake WMA
12. Holly River SP
13. Elk River WMA
14. Kanawha SF
15. Beech Fork SP
16. Cabwaylingo SF
17. Chief Logan SP
18. Panther SF
19. Berwind Lake WMA

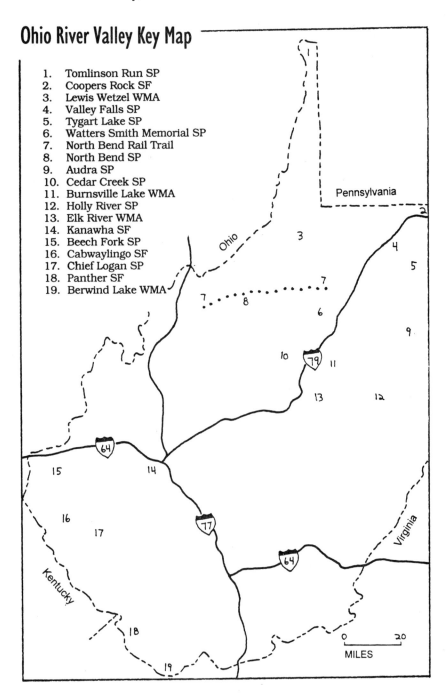

Weather & Climate Readings at Charleston

Month	Avg High F°	Avg Low F°	Precipitation (Inches)	Snowfall (Inches)
Jan	41	23	2.9	12.2
Feb	45	26	3.1	10.5
Mar	57	35	3.6	4.6
Apr	67	43	3.3	1.0
May	76	52	3.9	0
Jun	83	60	3.6	0
Jul	85	64	5.0	0
Aug	84	63	4.0	0
Sep	78	57	3.2	0
Oct	68	44	2.9	0.2
Nov	57	36	3.6	1.6
Dec	46	28	3.4	6.1

Introduction

Except for the Eastern Panhandle and a small area in the Alleghenies east of the Allegheny Front, all rain that falls in West Virginia drains into the Ohio River. From there it flows to the Mississippi before eventually emptying into the Gulf of Mexico. Rain that falls in the mountains travels more than 2,000 miles before finally finding an outlet in the sea. The Ohio River forms most of West Virginia's western border, separating it from Ohio. The river itself has a relatively narrow eastern floodplain, due to West Virginia's mountainous topography. The area covered in this section, however, encompasses a full fifty percent of the state's land.

This is a diverse region that is typically broken up into several different areas in state geographies or other guide books. At the region's eastern edge are the western slopes of the Alleghenies, with a topography that differs from the mountain region only in that the elevations are more modest. The southwest corner of the state is coal country, dotted with mining towns such as Matewan, Logan, Bluefield, and dozens of others. The topography here is dominated by a three-dimensional jigsaw puzzle of scrambled ridges and hollows. Rivers follow tortuous courses through the maze, often with a railroad line clinging to their banks. For years the railroad was the only way to get the coal out and the men who mined it in. North of there is Charleston, the state capital and West Virginia's most cosmopolitan city. To the west is Huntington, a major natural gas and chemical products center. In the Northern Panhandle is Wheeling, another coal capital with a reputation today for its beautiful Victorian architecture.

So why is such a diverse region encompassed in a single chapter in this guide? Because despite its size, the opportunities it offers for backcountry travel are limited and dispersed. There are several reasons for this. The first is topography. Because the terrain here is generally the least mountainous in the state, it was most hospitable to agriculture, road-building, and development. Of course West Virginia is still West Virginia; you won't find any hundred-mile stretches of straight highway (or ten-mile stretches for that matter). The second is geography. With broad, navigable rivers such as the Ohio and Kanawha, transporting goods was easier here than elsewhere in the state, and so the state's major cities grew up beside the rivers. And the third is the natural resources that lay below the ground and on top of it. Early on the region's wealth of timber and coal was exploited with little regard for conservation or sustainability.

In short, a higher percentage of the land is privately owned than elsewhere in the state. And much of the public land is wildlife management areas known best by hunters. Since with one or two exceptions the region lacks dramatic scenic areas such as the New River Gorge, Dolly Sods, or Seneca Rocks, it is often overlooked by the visitors who flock to those areas in the tens of thousands.

Despite its more modest reputation and offerings, the region provides some real gems for outdoor travelers willing to venture off the beaten path. Like the 60-mile *North Bend Rail Trail*, a part of the cross-country *American Discovery Trail*. Or Coopers Rock State Forest, a rock climbing, hiking, and mountain biking mecca that overlooks the magnificent Cheat River Gorge, all just 10 minutes from downtown Morgantown. Or Holly River State Park, an often overlooked backcountry area at the edge of the Alleghenies where you can mountain bike or hike through lush forests, or fly fish for trout in a pair of mountain creeks. Or one of the large recreational lakes tucked up against the Alleghenies in the part of the state often referred to as the "Mountain Lakes Area," where you can paddle for miles against the lakes' forested shores Or the several state parks and forests in the southwest corner of the state. Here you can drive along roads that wind through the mountains and mining towns, taking you back in time to a fascinating epoch in American history. And when you head into the backcountry it won't be with a crowd of other likewise-minded adventurers. Outside the major cities, this part of the state retains its rural character. Once you're off the main highway and driving on twisting country roads, getting to some of these remote areas is half the fun.

The climate here is warmer than elsewhere in the state. Spring and fall are still the best seasons for outdoor recreation. Spring blossoms and autumn foliage add color and drama to woodlands and meadows. Summer days can be hot and muggy, and insects are a bother. Winter is still cold, but snowfall accumulations are considerably smaller than in the mountains.

Tomlinson Run State Park

Located northwest of Pittsburgh near the tip of the northern panhandle, Tomlinson Run is the northernmost park in West Virginia. Its latitude is not far south of New York City's. The park occupies 1,401 acres of short, steep hills, rolling terrain, and overhanging cliffs of sandstone and shale. The park takes its name from the drainage that flows from a small lake in the park's western half to the Ohio River, which is just minutes away. Recreation at the park is divided between facilities such as an outdoor swimming pool, miniature golf, and pedalboat rentals on the lake, and backcountry pursuits such as hiking and mountain biking on the park's trails. Fishing on the lake or at 4 small ponds is also popular. And a developed car campground can accommodate overnight stays.

New Cumberland (SW) is the closest town.

contact: Superintendent, Tomlinson Run State Park, P.O. Box 97, New Manchester, WV 26056; 304/564-3651; wvweb.com/www/tomlinson_run.html.

getting there: From downtown New Cumberland, turn N onto WV-2 and go 0.8 mi to WV-8. Turn R and go 3.3 mi to the park entrance, L.

topography: Tomlinson Run flows W through rolling countryside before emptying into the Ohio River a short distance from the park. The river and a small impoundment are the park's major geographical features. Large areas of the park have been cleared and landscaped, though a few large parcels of forested land remain. Elevations are between 800 ft on the creek and 1,200 ft in the uplands. **maps:** USGS East Liverpool South.

starting out: Trail maps and park brochures are available at the park office and campground store. A pay phone is at the latter. Water and rest rooms can be found at several locations around the park.

Alcohol is prohibited.

activities: Hiking, Camping, Mountain Biking, Fishing.

hiking: 6 trails wind through forested uplands, along the lakeshore, and past the fishing ponds. Sandstone and shale cliffs provide scenic views. Combined the trails cover 8 mi. The trails don't all intersect, but by hiking along short stretches of road and a bit of backtracking, they can all be connected. Making trail connections via other trails is necessary for the *Laurel Trail* and *White Oak Trail*. The trails follow blazed paths from signed trailheads. Hiking is easy to moderate. Trailheads are located at several different locations.

camping: Overnight stays are in a large, 50-site campground that has 2 separate loops. The sites are large and spread out across a forested area that provides outstanding privacy. Each site has a picnic table and grill. Facilities include modern rest rooms with showers, a camp store, and pay phone. In a forested area that offers excellent privacy. Sites cost $11/night, $14 with hook-up. Some of the sites can be reserved. The campground is open Apr 15–Oct 31.

mountain   biking: All park trails are open to mountain bikes. Although the terrain is hilly, none of the trails is very technical. Riding is easy to moderate. See above under hiking for access and other info.

fishing: Angling for bass, trout, bluegill, and catfish is popular on 5 different impoundments—29-acre Tomlinson Run Lake and 4 1-acre fishing ponds. Fishing is possible from shore on all 5 impoundments; on the lake it's also possible to rent a boat.

lodging: Ogelbay Park (800/624-6988) in Wheeling is the state's premiere municipal park. Although its lack of a backcountry disqualifies it from inclusion in this guide, a visit by any outdoor enthusiast is well rewarded. Among the many facilities at the 1,500-acre resort style park are a lodge and 33 cabins, each one named after a local species of flora.

The cabins come in configurations that sleep from 8–26 people. Each of the modern, furnished cabins includes heat and a/c, a fireplace, kitchen, and bathroom with shower. Rates begin at $150/night for a small standard cabin (sleeps 9). Weekend and weekly rates are also available.

Coopers Rock State Forest

This sprawling 5,300 forest and recreation area occupies the northern rim and semi-mountainous plateau of the Cheat River Gorge. Located 5 miles east of the university town of Morgantown, the forest is a favorite outdoor destination. Recreational opportunities are exceptionally diverse. The Conoquonessing sandstone that forms the canyons walls and substrata is a magnet for area rock climbers. At the bottom of those walls rumbles the Cheat River, one of the most challenging and popular whitewater runs in West Virginia. A large network of more than 40 miles of multi-use trails are open to hiking, mountain biking, and cross-country skiing. Recreational facilities include a car campground; a large and scenic picnic area with rustic stone shelters, tables, and grills; and a small trout-stocked lake. Recreation is concentrated in the southern half of the forest; the northern half is used primarily as a research laboratory by West Virginia University. Adjacent to the picnic area is a protected overlook that provides sweeping views of the gorge and surrounding countryside.

Morgantown (W) is the closest city.

contact: Superintendent, Coopers Rock State Forest, Route 1, Box 270, Bruceton Mills, WV 26525; 304/594-1561.

getting there: From I-68, take exit 15 (CO-73/12). The forest is on either side of the highway. Follow signs the short distance to the HQ or to the overlook, campground, and main parking areas.

topography: The Cheat River flows NW through a deep, spectacular gorge. The park includes the precipitous N slope, though most of the acreage encompasses the milder terrain of the upland plateau. Large sandstone formations are a geologic centerpiece. A forest of broadleaf and conifer species covers most of the SF. Elevations range from 870 ft on Lake Lynn to 2,600 ft on Chestnut Ridge. Elevation at the river put-in in Albright is 1,200 ft. **maps:** USGS Lake Lynn, Masontown, Bruceton Mills, Valley Point.

starting out: Pick up a trail map and other park info at the office. Water, rest rooms, picnic facilities, and a concession stand are located near the main parking lot.

Alcohol is not allowed in the forest.

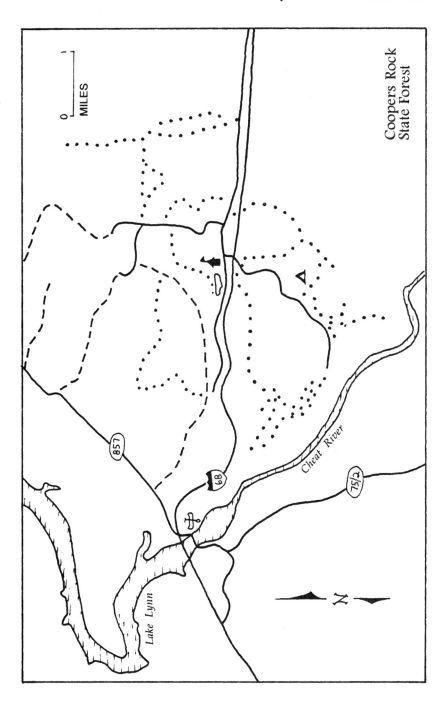

Coopers Rock
State Forest

activities: Hiking, Mountain Biking, Rock Climbing, Kayaking/Canoeing, Camping, Cross-country Skiing.

hiking: The forest's vast trail network extends into almost all of its furthers reaches, taking in highlights that include extraordinary views, sandstone formations, and cool, deep forest that is a haven for wildlife. The 16 multi-use trails cover a total distance of 42 miles. The trails follow a combination of single-track footpaths and old roads and roadbeds. Many of the trails intersect with one another, allowing for hikes of many different lengths and numerous loop possibilities. The interstate effectively divides the forest in half, however. About half of the trails are blazed, but all are easy to follow. Most trailheads are signed; they're located throughout the park. Hiking is easy to moderate. Traffic is moderate to heavy.

mountain biking: All trails in the forest are open to mountain bikes. All are ridable too. The terrain and trails are well suited to bikes; riding on the roads is mostly easy and even the single-tracks are relatively wide and obstruction-free. Riding is mostly moderate, with some steep sections. See above under *hiking* for more info.

rock climbing: Rock climbing is one of the most popular activities in the forest, and the 4 sandstone formations offer the best and most climbing routes in this part of the state. The freestanding monoliths have verticals of about 30–50 ft. 35 different routes have been mapped, ranging in difficulty from 5.5 to 5.11. Access is via a short hiking trail that begins in the SE corner of the main parking area. Climbers must register at the forest office before taking to the crags. While there, ask for the route map that was done by Adventure's Edge outfitters in Morgantown.

kayaking/canoeing: Just N of Albright, the Cheat River enters a 20-mile-long canyon that runs all the way to Cheat Lake. Along the route the river runs beneath steep mountain slopes and sandstone cliffs that rise as much as 1,000 ft from the water. The river itself drops 330 ft from put-in to take-out. Along with the Gauley and the New, the Cheat is one of the marquis whitewater rivers in WV. Rapids reach class V, with most falling in the class III-IV range. This is not a river for novices. If you don't have a lot of whitewater experience but would still like to paddle the river, contact one of the rafting outfitters listed in the back of this book. The river can be run for most of the spring; in summer the water is usually too low, except following a period of rain. A gauge is located on the bridge in

Albright. The authors of *Wildwater West Virginia* recommend a minimum reading of 1 ft.

The put-in is on the E end of the bridge in Albright. To reach the take-out: From I-68 take exit 10. Turn E and go 0.3 mi to CO-857. Turn L and go 0.9 mi to the low bridge across the lake. There's a little room roadside to park on either side; if not, try asking for permission to use one of the marinas just up the road.

camping: Camping in the forest is at a 25-site car campground. The campground is laid out in a large loop in an area that has been unfortunately cleared of most of its forest cover. As a result the sites offer almost no privacy. And on weekends, you can expect the campground to be full. Each site has a picnic table, grill, and lantern post. A rest room and showers facility with hot water is near the entrance. Some of the sites can be reserved in advance. Sites cost $14/night. The campground is open from Apr 15 to Dec 15. If there are no available sites in the campground, cross over to the other side of the forest and camp at Chestnut Ridge Park. Sites always seem to be available there, and it's right on the edge of the forest.

cross-country skiing: All trails are open to cross-country skiing, and with few exceptions, all are suitable. 2 trails that cover 5 mi are designated specifically as cross-country trails. But with half a foot of snow on the ground, the forest's roads and footpaths are equally inviting. The season runs from Dec to Mar, with most of the snow coming in Jan and Feb. See above under *hiking* for more trail info.

Lewis Wetzel Wildlife Management Area

Covering 12,448 acres of steep mountain ridges and remote hollows, this large, primitive backcountry area is known mostly to hunters. White-tailed deer, wild turkey, red fox, mink, and ruffed grouse are among the wildlife species that flourish in this remote woodland setting. Apart from the hunters who come every fall and winter, the WMA is visited by only a small handful of outdoor enthusiasts each year. It's too bad, since the rugged terrain and lush forest offer such a prize destination for naturalists and hikers. The WMA exists in an almost entirely undeveloped state. The only signs of human intrusiveness in the backcountry are a network of roads in various stages of disrepair. These are used by both hikers

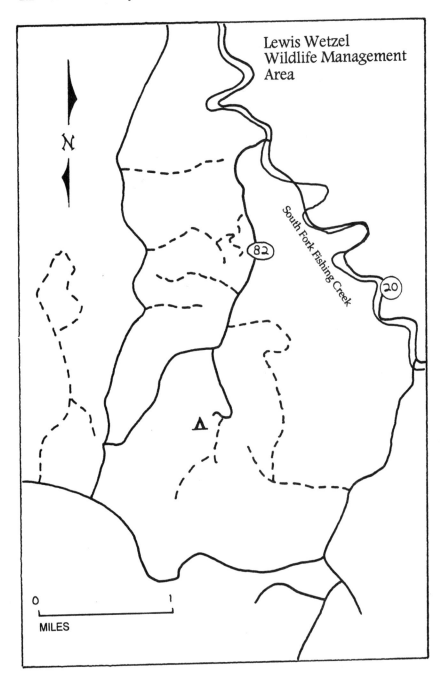

Lewis Wetzel
Wildlife Management
Area

N

South Fork Fishing Creek

82

20

0   1

MILES

and hunters, and comprise the entire trail network. A small primitive campground accommodates those wishing to visit for more than a day.

Jacksonburg (N) is the closest town.

contact: Refuge Manager, Lewis Wetzel Wildlife Management Area, 1304 Goose Run Rd, Fairmont, WV 26554; 304/367-2720.

getting there: From WV-20 in Jacksonburg, turn S onto CO-82 at the steel bridge. Drive 3.2 mi to the WMA office and camping registration board.

topography: Despite its location in the Ohio River Valley, the WMA terrain is relatively mountainous. Elevations reach 1,500 in the uplands, with a low point of 770 ft on Buffalo Run. The landform resembles a series of steep hills and folds. Forest cover is dense and covers most of the acreage; hardwoods and hemlocks are the major types. **maps:** USGS Pine Grove, Center Point, Folsom.

starting out: The WMA is primarily a primitive backcountry area—facilities are limited. You can pick up a trail map at the self-registration station. The WMA office is next door, but it doesn't really operate as a visitor center. A hand water pump and pit toilets are in the camping area.

activities: Hiking, Camping.

hiking: The WMA features a large network of primitive trails that are actually old roadbeds—most closed or unsuitable to automobiles, some open to vehicles during hunting season. In all, there are more than 30 miles of hikable trail. Highlights are deep hardwood forests, an abundance of wildlife, and the remote setting. The trails aren't blazed, but most are easy to follow as they are quite wide. Hiking on the trails is moderate to strenuous. A trail map is necessary to locate most of the trails. CO-82 provides the main access, since most of the roads intersect with it within a mi or 2 of the WMA office.

camping: Camping on the WMA is at one of the most attractive small primitive campgrounds in the state. The large camping area is situated in a small valley between steep forested ridges. The grassy valley has been cleared and is mowed. Each of the 6 very large sites has a picnic table and grill. Pit toilets and a hand water pump are the only facilities. Sites cost $5/night. The campground is open year round.

Valley Falls State Park

The 1,145 acres that this park encompasses rise from the north bank of the Tygart Valley River. The park was once the site of a grist mill, remnants of which can still be seen. Recreation focuses on both the river and the densely forested uplands. Kayakers come from all over to paddle the mouth-watering series of drops and falls that begin in the park and continue for more than a mile downstream. Anglers cast the same waters for bass and walleye. On land, hiking trails wind through the hardwood forest that covers the park's ridges and hollows. Facilities in the park are presently limited to a large riverside picnic area with shelters, tables, and grills. Future plans, however, call for a swimming pool, campground, cabins, and tennis courts. large picnic area down by the river with tables, grills, and several shelters.

Grafton (SE) and Fairmont (NW) are the closest towns.

contact: Superintendent, Valley Falls State Park, Route 6, Box 244, Fairmont, WV 26554; 304/367-2719.

getting there: From I-99 take exit 137. Turn S onto WV-310 and go 7.6 mi to Rock Lake/Valley Falls Rd (CO-31/14). Turn R and go 0.8 mi to a fork. Bear L and go 1.6 mi to the park entrance. From US-50 in Grafton, turn N onto WV-310 and go 6 mi to the park entrance.

topography: The Tygart Valley River—and the series of river-wide falls—are the major geographical features in the park. The river forms most of the park's S and W boundary. From there, the terrain rises in minor ridges of less than 100 ft. Elevations are between 300 ft on the river and 500 ft. Most of the park is forested, although a long stretch along the river has been cleared. **maps:** USGS Fairmont East.

starting out: A trail map and park brochure are available at the park office. Water, rest rooms, and a pay phone are located in the picnic area.

Swimming or wading is not permitted in the park.

activities: Hiking, Kayaking, Fishing, Mountain Biking.

hiking: The park's compact network of 8 trails covers almost 11 mi. Although the trails are short, they interconnect so that loops of various lengths can be formed. Most of the trails wind through the forested ridges and hollows that comprise park uplands.. A couple trails also parallel the river and provide access for kayakers or anglers. Trails follow both single-track and old road beds. Hiking is mostly easy and moderate, but a few steep sections do exist. Trailheads are signed along the main park road. Since parking is limited except at the riverside picnic area, that's the best place to start.

kayaking: The Tygart Valley River, whose water levels are controlled by dam releases in Grafton, runs through the park. The run here is a very popular 1.5-mi stretch that takes in a series of drops and falls as high as 15 ft. The string of class III-V rapids is for experts only. Rapids in the park are both spectacular and easy to access. Put-in is in the park. There's about a 200 yd easy carry from the parking lot. Scouting the first series of rapids is easy from here, as you can easily observe the river from the massive sandstone boulders that line its R bank. This is advisable, since water levels vary considerably, depending on the dam release schedule. To reach the take-out: Leave the park and retrace your route to WV-310. Turn L and go 2.7 mi to Hammond Rd (CO-86). Turn L and go 1.5 mi (at 0.8 mi the pavement ends and the road gradually becomes extremely rugged) to a small parking area, R (beyond here the road is basically impassable). From the parking area is about a 5 min portage down the yellow brick road to the river. Kayakers should register at the park office before heading out onto the river.

fishing: Fishing on the Tygart Valley River here is for smallmouth and largemouth bass and walleye. Anglers can either fish the long flat section behind the first falls, or hike down below the falls and wade the more turbulent waters. The flat section can be fished from a canoe, which will allow you to cover a good section of the river. Below the falls you'll need to keep an eye out for paddlers, since this is a pretty popular whitewater run. Access is from the picnic area.

mountain biking: A couple of park trails are open to mountain bikes. These include the *Rhododendron Trail* and *Deer Trail*, which follow an old RR grade for part of their route. Some section follow single-track trails. Riding is easy to moderate. Access is from the main parking area.

Tygart Lake State Park

This popular park occupies 2,134 acres on the northern shore of Tygart Lake. Located in Grafton, Tygart Lake and the park are very popular outdoor recreation destinations. On summer weekends, the park is full of folks sunbathing, swimming, picnicking, fishing, and boating. To accommodate their interests, the park is rather heavily developed. In addition to a lodge and cabins, there are several large picnic areas, a marina, four boat ramps, and a campground. If you're looking for wilderness solitude, this probably isn't the place for you. If, on the other hand, you simply want to get out in the sun for a couple of hours and don't mind the company of a lot of other like-minded souls, Tygart Lake isn't a bad place to stop.

Grafton is the closest town.

contact: Superintendent, Tygart Lake State Park, Route 1, Box 260, Grafton, WV 26354; 304/265-3383; wvweb.com/www/tygart_lake.html

getting there: From the jct of CO-310 and US-50 in Grafton, turn W onto US-50 and go 0.4 mi to Yates Ave. Turn L and go 1.9 mi to Beech St. Turn R and go 0.1 mi to Walnut St. Turn L and go 0.2 mi to Grand St. Turn R and go 1.9 mi to Scab Hollow Rd. Turn L and go 0.5 mi to the Corps of Engineers HQ and dam visitor center, R. The main SP entrance is another 2.9 mi up the road, R.

topography: Elevation on the lake is 333 ft. The surrounding terrain rises in moderate hills and folds. The highest elevations in the park do not exceed 500 ft. A hardwood forest covers much of the park, though large areas have been at least partially cleared to accommodate the rec facilities. **maps:** USGS Grafton, Thorton.

starting out: Trail maps and park info is available from the dam visitor center or the park office. The former is open weekdays only. Water and rest rooms are located at the visitor center and in several places in the park.

hiking: There are nearly 5 mi of trails in the park. The 4 main trails are spread out along the lakeshore. Their main purpose seems to be to connect the different rec areas and centers of activity. The *Tygart Dam Trail*, for instance, leads from the lodge to the dam visitor center. Another trail leads from Picnic Area #1 to the park office and Picnic Area #3. Trailheads are signed along the main park road. Hiking on the trails is generally easy, and the treadways are clearly defined and easy to follow.

camping: A 40-site car campground can accommodate overnight stays. The campground is located in a sparsely wooded area that is not especially attractive. Privacy at the sites is minimal to adequate. Each site has a picnic table and grill. Rest room/shower facilities with hot water are available. The sites cost $11/night, $14 with hookup. The campground is open from Apr 15 to Oct 31.

fishing: Tygart Lake supports populations of many of the species of game fish caught in West Virginia. The reason is the various temperature ranges that exist at different levels on the lake. In summer, when the temperature near the surface rises, cold water species such as trout are able to retreat to the cooler depths. Among the species that anglers most ardently pursue are largemouth and smallmouth bass, muskellunge, catfish, crappie, walleye, and trout. Most fishing on the lake is done from boats, though there are also places from which to cast on shore.

canoeing/kayaking: As a paddling destination, Tygart Lake leaves much to be desired. Although the lake is attractive when the water is at flood pool, when it's not, the shoreline is an unsightly band of brown earth. Also the lake is most popular with motor boats and jet skis, so the whine of engines is an almost constant presence. Maybe the best thing about the lake is the easy access from the park boat ramps. Unless you're using a canoe to fish the lake, you're better off looking for a more serene and attractive spot for paddling.

lodging: If you want to stay more than a day but aren't interested in camping, you can overnight in the lodge (304/265-2320) or one of the cabins. Although the lodge's architecture is the definition of drab, the rooms themselves aren't bad, with wood-paneled walls. Rates begin at $44/night for a double in the spring or fall season. The lodge is open from Apr 15 to Oct 31.

The 10 wood-frame cabins (304/265-3383) provide lodging for 2–6 people. The cabins are heated and furnished, with kitchens, baths, and fireplaces. rates start at $80/night for a small cabin during the spring/fall season. Cabins are open from Apr 15–Oct 31.

Watters Smith Memorial State Park

As its name suggests, this 532-acre park is dedicated to the memory of Watters Smith, a pioneer who settled in the area in 1796. The park was left to the state by one of Smith's descendants in 1949. The main attraction is the group of farm buildings that date from the 19th century. These include a horse and cattle barn, blacksmith shop, smokehouse, and farm barn. Inside the buildings are many of the implements that were used during the four generations the farm was operational. A museum is located in the farm house, built in 1876. In addition to the park's historical attractions are limited opportunities for outdoor recreation. Hiking trails wind through the woodlands and connect the several rec areas. A picnic table with shelter, tables, and grills is available for outdoor gatherings. And a pool is open daily from 11 AM.

Clarksburg (NE) is the closest city.

contact: Superintendent, Watters Smith Memorial State Park, PO Box 296, Lost Creek, WV 26385; 304/745-3081.

getting there: From I-79 take exit 110. Turn W onto WV-270 and go 4.1 mi to Duck Creek Rd (CO-25/6). Turn L and go 1.8 mi to the park.

topography: Rolling uplands characterize most of the park. Forested areas and landscaped and mowed areas are both present. **maps:** USGS

starting out: You can pick up a trail map and other park info at the office. The swimming pool is the center of activity in the park. Water, rest rooms, and a pay phone are all there. The museum is open daily except M and Tu.

Alcohol is not allowed.

activities: Hiking.

hiking: Several trails wind through the forested regions of the park. Combined the trails cover about 4 mi. They follow narrow dirt footpaths over the park's mild ridges. The trails are not blazed, but are nevertheless easy to follow. Hiking is easy to moderate. Most trailheads are signed. Access is from the back of the picnic area and on Duck Creek Rd.

North Bend Rail Trail

In the years just prior to the Civil War, the Baltimore & Ohio Railroad cleared a corridor and laid down tracks between Clarksburg and Parkersburg. The route passed through terrain that was rolling and mountainous, and to get through ridges and over creeks and hollows, the construction of 12 tunnels and 32 bridges. Although the railroad tracks are gone, the bridges and tunnels still remain, providing a reminder of the days before West Virginia existed as a state. In the early 90s conversion of the rail corridor into a multi-use trail was begun. That process still continues, though the large majority of the trail that will run between Clarksburg and Parkersburg is now complete. The current termini are at Walker (W) and Wolf Summit (E). Between these small communities, the trail passes through rolling farmland, forested ridges, and a handful of other small towns. The trail is part of the 5,500-mi, coast-to-coast *American Discovery Trail*, which is also a work in progress. The North Bend Trail is open to bikers, hikers, equestrians, and cross-country skiers. Although the trail is operated as a state park, you won't find any of the amenities associated with other parks along its route—except at North Bend SP, covered separately below.

contact: Superintendent, North Bend State Park, Route 1, Box 221, Cairo, WV 26337; 304/643-2931; wvweb.com/www/north_ bend.html.

getting there: There are numerous access points to the trail, including North Bend State Park (see below). To reach the E terminus: From the jct of WV-20 and US-50, turn W onto US-50 and go 5.7 mi to Wolf Summit Rd (CO-11). Turn R and go 0.3 to the first RR crossing. Turn L just after the tracks and go 0.2 mi to the trailhead and parking area. • To reach the W terminus: From I-77 take exit 174 and turn S onto WV-47. Go 6.9 mi to Walker Rd (CO-7). Turn L

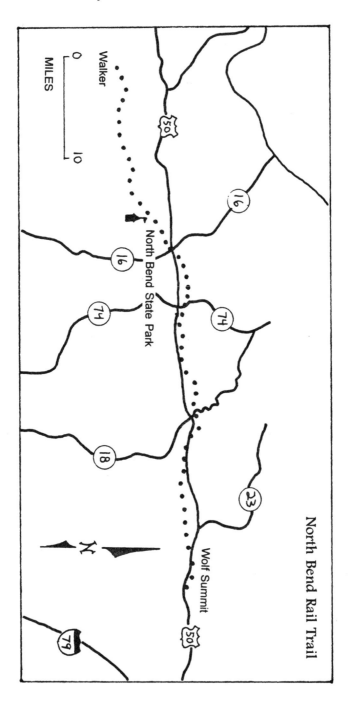

North Bend Rail Trail

and go 2.9 mi to the rail trail and a small parking area.

topography: The trail passes through the rolling countryside typical of the Ohio River Valley. Farms, small communities, and forested areas are all encountered. Elevations are between 700 ft (Walker) and 1,100 ft (Wolf Summit). **maps:** USGS (W to E) Petroleum, Cairo, Harrisville, Ellenboro, Pennsboro, West Union, Smithburg, Salem, Wolf Summit.

starting out: Facilities along the trail are limited. Your best bet for water and rest rooms is to stop in one of the small towns along the route, or in North Bend SP. There are no recreation developments along the trail itself.

activities: Mountain Biking, Hiking, Cross-country Skiing.

mountain biking: Although it's nominally a multi-use trail and is open to hikers, equestrians, and cross-country skiers, the North Bend Trail was designed with mountain bikers in mind. The treadway of crushed gravel and cinders is most easily ridden on fat-tire bikes, and the mild grade makes riding in either direction. And with a little effort (OK, a lot of effort), it's possible to ride the entire trail in a single day. Shorter rides are the norm, however, and the numerous access points that let you ride almost any section of the trail you want. Riding is easier from W to E, since the trail drops approximately 400 ft over the 60 mi.

hiking: After mountain bikers, hikers are the most consistent users of the trail. Although you won't be able to cover as much of it in a single day as on a bike, the same mild grade and scenic surroundings that are it main appeals apply to hikers. And since the trail is wide, level, and well maintained, variations on hiking such as trail running are possible. Access to the trail is at numerous points, all via US-50, which parallels the trail for its entire length.

cross-country skiing: When there's snow on the ground, the trail becomes the ideal linear nordic track. Skiing is easy along the entire trail, so it's a great place to learn. And when snow blankets the rolling farmland and small communities along the route, the trail becomes as photogenic as any place in the state. See above for additional trail info.

North Bend State Park

Located amidst the rolling farmland of the mid-Ohio River Valley, this 1,405-acre park is adjacent to the Hughes River and the *North Bend Rail Trail*. The park incorporates both a forested backcountry and numerous recreational facilities. Among the latter are an outdoor swimming pool, miniature golf, tennis courts, picnic areas, 2 campgrounds, cabins, and a lodge. Hikers and mountain bikers can explore the forested slopes and hollows via a system of multi-use trails. Wildlife that inhabits the less developed parts of the park includes white-tailed deer, red fox, wild turkey, opossum, and raccoon.

Harrisville (E) is the closest town.

contact: North Bend State Park, Route 1, Box 221, Cairo, WV 26337; 304/643-2931; wvweb.com/www/north_bend.html.

getting there: From US-50 exit at Ellensboro. Turn S onto WV-16 and go 4.9 mi to a jct with WV-31. Continue straight onto W Main St and go 3.2 mi to the park entrance.

topography: The park occupies the rolling terrain common to most of the Ohio River Valley. The North Fork Hughes River is the major drainage. Most areas of the park are covered with a broadleaf forest, though some areas have been cleared to accommodate rec facilities. Elevations range from 680 ft on the river to 1,136 ft in the uplands. **maps:** USGS Harrisville, Cairo.

starting out: If you need a trail map or other info, you can get them in the lodge. Also there are water, rest rooms, and a pay phone.

activities: Hiking, Mountain Biking, Camping

hiking: In addition to the *North Bend Rail Trail*, which skirts the park's NW edge, 11 other trails in the park cover 15.5 mi. The trails mostly wind in and around the popular rec areas, which makes the isolation the rail trail a welcome relief for those in search of backcountry solitude. Only the 4.5-mi *Nature Trail* winds through the park's undeveloped regions. The trails mostly follow narrow footpaths, though some routes are over RR grades and unimproved roads. Trails are blazed and easy to follow. Hiking is easy to moderate in most places. Trailheads are signed in various locations. Access to the *North Bend Rail Trail* is from the picnic area across from the River Run campground.

mountain biking: The main biking route in the area is the 60-mi North Bend Rail Trail, which passes by the park's NW perimeter on its way from Parkersburg to Clarksburg (see separate entry for details). In the park itself, however, most trails are open to bikes. Only the *Extra Mile Trail* is closed to riding. Other trails follow single-tracks, old RR grades, and unimproved roads. Most trails can't really compare with the rail-trail, though they do offer more technical riding conditions. Riding is easy to moderate.

camping: Camping in the park is at either of 2 developed car campgrounds. The River Run campground has 49 sites in a large open area next tot he Hughes River. The lack of forest cover and the small size of the sites minimizes privacy. When the campground is full, it's a rather unappealing place to spend a night. Each site has a picnic table and a grill. A bathhouse with hot water is centrally located. Sites cost $11/night, $14 with hook-up. The campground is open from Apr 15 to Oct 31.

The Jug Handle campground has 29 sites, most of which are also beside the Hughes River. The sites here are larger and the setting is a little more rustic. Privacy is adequate. Each site has a picnic table and grill. A bathhouse is located in the middle of the area. Sites cost $11/night. The campground is open from Apr 15 to Oct 31.

lodging: In addition to camping, overnight options in the park include a lodge and cabins. The lodge has 29 rooms that offer hotel-style accommodations in a somewhat homier setting. A restaurant is also in the lodge. Rates range from $44 to $59/night for a double.

8 heated cabins—2 or 3 bedroom layouts are available—offer more room. Each of the cedar-sided, furnished cabins has a kitchen, bathroom with shower, and fireplace. Rates begin at $78/night for a small cabin. The cabins and lodge are open all year.

Audra State Park

This small park covers 355 acres on the banks of the scenic Middle Fork River. Recreation in the park is limited, with a picnic area, car campground, and two hiking trails providing the main activities. A concrete slab beach on the river provides a place to sunbathe or swim in the river. The park was once the site of a grist mill, traces of which can still be seen.

Buckhannon (SW) and Philippi (NE) are the closest towns.

contact: Superintendent, Audra State Park, Route 4, Box 564, Buckhannon, WV 26201; 304/457-1162; wvweb.com/www/audra.html.

getting there: From downtown Bellington, turn W onto Brown Ave. Go 8.7 mi to the park entrance. • From the jct of WV-20 and US-33 just N of Buckhannon, drive E on US-33 3.4 mi to CO-9. Turn L and go 10 mi to the park.

topography: The Middle Fork River, which flows through the center of the park, is the major geographical feature. A lush forest of hardwoods, rhododendron, and hemlocks cling to the slopes that rise and fall on either bank. **maps:** USGS Audra.

starting out: The park's center of activity is a concrete "beach" on the N bank of the river. Nearby is the park office, where you can pick up a trail map and other info. Water and rest rooms are in the picnic area.

activities: Camping, Hiking.

camping: This small state park is home to one of the most attractive car campgrounds in the state. In a lush setting of rhododendron, hemlocks, and hardwoods, 67 sites are spread out in a sprawling, heavily forested area beside the river. The sites are only moderate in size, but they're very well spaced. Privacy is outstanding. Each site has a picnic table and grill. Modern rest rooms with showers are centrally located. Sites cost $11/night. The campground is open from Apr 15 to Oct 31.

hiking: A pair of hiking trails in the park covers 3 mi. Highlights are the scenic forest setting, views of the river, and Alum Cave, which can be seen from a boardwalk spur. The trails follow a combined paved path and narrow footpath. Hiking is moderate. Trailheads are in the picnic area and at the campground entrance.

Cedar Creek State Park

Located in Gilmer County, Cedar Creek State Park covers 2,483 acres of forested hills and developed recreation areas. The hardwood forest is a haven for wildlife. White-tailed deer, red fox, raccoon, opossum, wild turkey, and Canada geese are all present. Popular recreation facilities include an outdoor swimming pool, large picnic area, tennis courts, miniature golf, softball field, car campground, and fishing ponds. The area's historical heritage is represented by a one-room schoolhouse and a restored log cabin, which serves as the campground store. Backcountry travel is possible on the network of hiking trails.

Glenville (NE) is the closest town.

contact: Superintendent, Cedar Creek State Park, Route 1, Box 9, Glenville, WV 26351; 304/462-7158;

getting there: From the jct of WV-5 and US-19 in Glenville, turn S onto US-19 and go 4.5 mi to Cedar Creek Rd. Turn L and go 2.9 mi to the park.

topography: Park terrain is characterized by a jumble of short ridges and narrow valleys. The elevation change isn't great—from a low of 750 on the creek to 1,448—but some of the slopes are relatively steep. A forest of hardwoods blankets most of the acreage. USGS Glenville, Tanner, Cedarville, Normantown.

starting out: You can get park info and a trail map at the campground store or park office. Water, rest rooms, and other facilities are at the pool, picnic area, and campground. A small selection of camping supplies is available in the campground store.

activities: Hiking, Camping, Fishing.

hiking: 5 trails cover 8.5 mi of park terrain. The trails are arranged in 2 main loops—one follows the ridges and creeks above the campground, the other follows Cedar Creek and then climbs into the uplands that overlook it. The trails can be connected in several different combinations to allow hikes of various lengths. Highlights are scenic views, the forest setting, and the opportunity to see wildlife, especially white-tailed deer. Trails follow blazed single-track footpaths that are easy to follow. Trailheads are signed and located near the campground and fishing ponds. Hiking is easy to moderate.

camping: Camping in the park is at a 35-site developed car campground. The sites are laid out in a long, narrow corridor that has been mostly cleared of trees and landscaped. The area is attractive, but the lack of forest cover minimizes privacy at the sites. Each site has a picnic table and grill. Sites cost $11/night, $14 with hook-up. A bathhouse with hot water is in the campground. The campground is open from Apr 15 to Oct 31.

fishing: 3 stocked fishing ponds are the most popular spot int he park among anglers. Although backcountry aficionados will find nothing here to challenge them, the ponds do offer easy access for families and those not wanting to undertake an arduous trek. Trout are taken from the ponds in late winter and early spring. Bass and catfish are caught year round. Fishing is from the ponds' banks, which are grassy and mowed to facilitate casting. Wading in the pools is not permitted.

Nearby Cedar Creek offers another fishing destination. Its slow-moving waters support a population of muskellunge. The medium-sized creek can be fished from the shore or waded. Access is via the Fishermen's Trail, which follows it for a mile.

Burnsville Lake Wildlife Management Area

Burnsville Lake is a US Army Corps of Engineer project that encompasses 968 acres of water surrounded by 13,224 acres of publicly owned land. The lake was created when a dam was constructed across the Little Kanawha River 125 miles above its mouth at the Ohio River. Outdoor recreation is available both on the lake and in the forested uplands that surround it. Boating and fishing are the most popular activities. A pair of developed rec areas—Riffle Run and Bulltown—provides boat ramps, as well as developed campgrounds and picnic areas. The vast backcountry that surrounds the lake is a haven for wildlife. White-tailed deer, red fox, raccoon, wild turkey, and ruffed grouse are just some of the species present. Most of the land is managed by the DNR as a WMA open to hunting in fall and winter. At other times of year hikers, mountain bikers, naturalists, and others can explore the backcountry via a trail that connects the rec areas. Next to the Bulltown rec area is the Bulltown Historical Area. A collection of 19th century buildings were moved from the flood zone when the lake was created. Also here was the Weston and Gauley Turnpike, an important transportation route during the Civil War. Converting it to a trail is proposed.

Burnsville (NW) is the closest town.

contact: Resource Manager, Burnsville Lake, HC 10, Box 24, Burnsville, WV 26335; 304/853-2371.

getting there: To reach the lake HQ and the Riffle Run Rec Area: From I-79 take exit 79. Turn E onto WV-5 and go 0.3 mi to Main St. Turn R and go 2.5 mi to the main office, R. The rec area is 0.2 mi further down the road. • To reach the Bulltown Rec Area: From I-79, take exit 67. Turn E onto US-19 and go 11 mi to Millstone Run Rd (CO-19/12). Turn L and go 0.9 mi to the rec area entrance, L.

topography: Narrow ridges and relatively deep folds characterize the land around the lake. The lake itself is long and narrow, squeezed between the steep upland slopes. Elevations are between 800 on the lake and 1,500 on the highest ridges. Flora includes broadleaf forest and wildlife openings. **maps:** USGS Orlando (predates lake).

starting out: Info and maps are available at the Army Corps of Engineers office near the Riffle Run Rec Area. It's open weekdays from 8 AM to 4 PM. Water and rest rooms are located at both the Bulltown and Riffle Run rec areas. A pay phone is located in the Riffle Run campground.

activities: Canoeing/Kayaking, Fishing, Camping, Hiking, Mountain Biking.

canoeing/kayaking: With an area of almost 1,000 acres and a shoreline of 30 mi, Burnsville Lake offers paddlers plenty of room to roam. The lakeshore, which is almost entirely undeveloped, offers one of the most scenic settings on a large lake in WV. Rolling hills and modest ridges alternate between hardwood forest cover and pastures belonging to small farms. The contrast is appealing and the atmosphere is generally one of bucolic isolation. Perhaps the only sour note is the presence of power boats on the lake. While they're unavoidable, the lake's long profile and numerous feeder creeks provide a measure of refuge. Access to the lake is at boat ramps at both rec areas. A launch fee of $2 is charged.

fishing: Fishing is one of the most popular activities on the lake. Game fish regularly caught on the lake include largemouth and smallmouth bass, crappie, muskellunge, channel catfish, and bluegill. Although there are places to fish from the shore in both rec areas, you'll have more luck and be able to escape into more remote regions if you fish from a canoe or other boat.

Another option, particularly for fly fishermen, is the tail race of the Burnsville Dam. The cold lake water released from the dam supports populations of trout. Access is from the dam picnic area. Follow directions above to the Riffle Run rec area.

camping: Camping around the lake is at either of 2 developed car campgrounds. Riffle Run has both a developed campground and a small primitive camping area. The large campground has 54 sites arranged in an area that has been cleared and landscaped. The sites are moderately sized and fairly close to one another. Privacy at the sites is minimal. Each site has a picnic table, grill, and lantern post. Shower/rest room facilities are centrally located. Sites cost $14/night. The 6 primitive sites are arranged in a row in an open area above the picnic grounds. Each site has a picnic table, grill and lantern post. The sites are small and right on top of each other. Forget privacy unless you have the area to yourself (not unusual). Sites in the primitive campground cost $5/night. The campgrounds are open Apr 25 to Dec 7.

The Bulltown camping area covers a vast expanse on the lakeshore. 194 sites are spread out among sparse forest cover. Sites are small and only moderately spaced. Privacy is adequate, but if the campground is crowded, you'll definitely feel it. Each of the sites has a picnic table, grill, and lantern post. Bathhouses are centrally located. Sites cost $14/night. Canoe camping is possible at some of the sites, which are lakeside. The campground is open Apr 25 to Dec 7. Reservations are accepted for the period May 16 to Aug 31. Call 304/452-8006.

hiking: Although the trail map shows a large network of potential hiking trails, in practice only one is maintained. It follows old road beds for 11 mi through the rolling uplands between the 2 rec areas. Conditions on the trail depend on when you hike it. If it's recently been mowed (this happens 3 times per year), it's easy to hike. At other times it can become so overgrown that bushwhacking is almost necessary. Both trailheads are signed, and although the trail isn't blazed, it isn't difficult to follow. Access is from either of the camping areas.

mountain biking: The trail described above is open to mountain bikes. Keep in mind that the trail can be even more difficult to ride than to hike when it is allowed to become overgrown.

lodging: Just a short drive E of the lake in Orlando is the Kilmarnock Farm (800/452-8319), a working 300-acre sheep and angora goat farm. The farmhouse has 2 rooms that are open to guests. Although visitors can entertain themselves at the area attractions, they may also choose to join in farm activities such as farming or gardening. Hunting packages are available too. Rates are $49/night for 2 people. Breakfast and dinner are both available.

Holly River State Park

The second largest state park in West Virginia, Holly River encompasses 8,292 acres of forested mountain ridges and deep, shady coves. The park features a diversity of outdoor recreation and a wide array of facilities. An exceptional trail network provides access to all corners of the park, including highlights such as scenic falls and overlooks. A secondary network of RR grades and old road beds provides challenging terrain for mountain bikers. Campers can stay at the large car campground or venture into the backcountry and overnight at a primitive camping area. 9 rustic cabins provide an additional option for those wanting to stay more than a day. Among the recreational facilities are an outdoor swimming pool, picnic areas, tennis courts, an archery range, various game courts, and a softball field. Somehow none of these amenities interfere with the park's main attribute, which is the sheer physical beauty of the area. The deep forest is a haven for all sorts of wildlife, and any trip into the backcountry is almost guaranteed to produce a sighting of a white-tailed deer or two. The

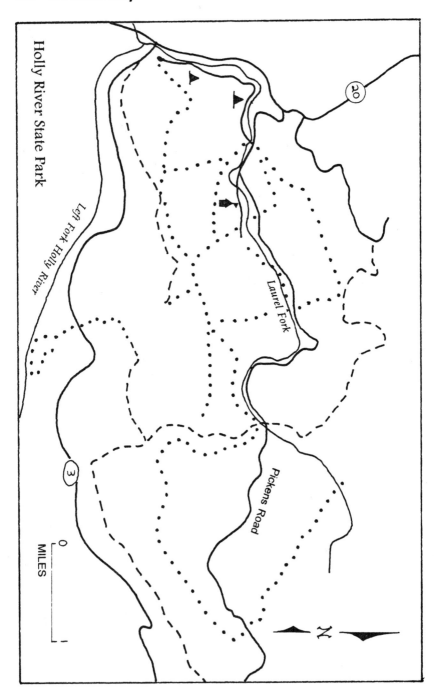

Holly River State Park

Left Fork Holly River

Laurel Fork

Pickens Road

MILES

park is an ideal destination for daytrips or as a basecamp for multi-day visits to the region.

Webster Springs (S) is the closest town.

contact: Superintendent, Holly River State Park, PO Box 70, Hacker Valley, WV 26222; 304/493-6353;

getting there: From the jct of WV-4 and WV-20 near the State Wildlife Center, turn S onto WV-20 and go 17.9 mi to the park entrance, L.

topography: A lush forest of hardwoods, hemlocks, rhododendron, mosses, and ferns covers most of the park backcountry. The landform is comprised of steep slopes and narrow valleys. Several small creeks flow W and drain the area. Elevations are between 1,500 ft on Laurel Fork and 2,800 ft. **maps:** USGS Goshen, Hacker Valley.

starting out: Stop by the park office for a trail map and other info before heading into the backcountry. Water, rest rooms, a pay phone, restaurant, and picnic area are all there.

Alcohol is not allowed in the park.

activities: Hiking, Mountain Biking, Camping, Fishing.

hiking: Holly River's extensive network of trails covers 33 mi of single-track footpaths, railroad grades, and gated roadbeds. The layout of the trails encourages connections and loops of various lengths. Highlights are the magnificent forest, several scenic falls, wildlife, and trout creeks. The trails are blazed and easy to follow. Trailheads are signed and located in several different places around the park. No matter where you start, it's possible to connect ultimately with just about any other trail. Hiking is easy to strenuous, with most of the trails in the moderate range. To reach the *Potato Knob Trail*, leave the park and turn L onto WV-20. Go 1.3 mi to CO-3. Turn L and go 3.1 mi to the signed trailhead and small parking area, R.

mountain biking: Although mountain bikes are not allowed on any of the hiking trails, there are enough roads—both gated and open to vehicles—to make Holly River a favorite riding destination. With good reason. Even the open roads pass through some of the prettiest forest scenery outside the Monongahela NF. And the gated roads provide isolation and the challenge of riding on very primitive surfaces. In all there's about 12 mi of roads suitable to biking. Riding in the park is moderate to strenuous, due both to topography and the rugged condition of some of the trails. A couple of different loops can be formed. The park office is a good starting point for either.

camping: Camping in the park is either at a primitive backcountry camping area or a developed car campground. The primitive camping area can only be reached on foot or by bike. The hike is less than a mi from Pickens Rd; The bike route is about 4 mi. The camping area has a picnic table, stone grill, and pit toilet. There's no water, so be sure to bring enough.

The 88-site developed car campground sprawls across a huge area that's forested with hemlocks and hardwoods. The campground is arranged into small groups of sites, which minimizes any sense of crowding. Each of the sites has a picnic table and grill. Privacy ranges from minimal at the sites that are mostly in the open to excellent at the sites tucked into pockets of forest. Bathhouses with hot water are spaced around the campground. Sites cost $14/night. Some sites can be reserved. The campground is open from Apr 15 to Dec 1.

fishing: Fishing in the park is on the 2 forks of Holly River, Left Fork and Laurel Fork. The tributaries are similar. Both are small trout creeks that flow through lush forests where hemlock and rhododendron are prominent. Their beds and rocky, with flows that rumble over and around ledges and other rock formations, creating very good pooling. Gradients are mild to average. Access to Laurel Fork is from the main park road. Access to Left Fork is from the *Potato Knob Trail* described above under *hiking*. Both creeks are stocked.

lodging: Overnight visitors can stay at any of 9 cabins in the park. Construction of the rustic cabins is either stone or log. The furnished cabins each have a kitchen, bathroom with shower, and wood-burning fireplace. The cabins can accommodate 2 or 4 people. Rates for 2 people start at $65/night during spring and fall. Summer rates are higher; rates for longer stays are lower. The cabins are open from Apr 15 to Dec 1.

Elk River Wildlife Management Area

At the center of the Elk River WMA is Sutton Lake, created when the river was impounded by a US Army Corps of Engineers dam at the town of Sutton. Occupying a long, narrow basin amidst mountain ridges, the lake's profile is similar to the river's. The lake is very scenic, with sandstone bluffs rising from the water and a heavy forest of predominantly hardwoods covering the numerous ridges and hollows that radiate from the shoreline. The lake is 14 mi long, covers 1,440 acres, and has a shoreline of 40 miles. 18,225 acres if land around the lake are managed by the state as a Wildlife Management Area. The primary objectives are to preserve wildlife habitat and to provide for low-impact outdoor recreation. Common wildlife species in the area include white-tailed deer, wild turkey, and ruffed grouse. Outdoor recreation is focused mostly on the lake, with boating and fishing the most popular activities. In fall and winter, hunting is the main activity. A trio of car campgrounds around the lake provide facilities for multi-day visits.

Sutton (W) is the closest town.

contact: Resource Manager, Sutton Lake, P.O. Box 426, Sutton, WV 26601; 304/765-2816 • Elk River Wildlife Management Area, Division of Natural Resources, Box 38, French Creek, WV 26218; 304/924-6211.

getting there: From I-79 take exit 62. Turn N onto WV-4 and go 2.2 mi through the town of Sutton and cross the bridge over the Elk River. Turn L and go 1 mi to the dam and resource manager's office. • To reach Baker's Run and Mill Creek camping areas: From the bridge across the Elk River, turn R onto CO-19/40 and go 3.8 mi to Wolf Creek Centralia Rd (CO-17). Turn L and go 9.9 mi to the rec area entrance, L. • To reach the Bee Run Rec Area: from downtown Sutton, drive N on WV-4 for 3.1 mi to WV-15. Turn R and go 1.1 mi to the rec area entrance, R.

topography: Elevation on the lake is 922 ft during summer. The surrounding terrain is hilly, with some semi-mountainous ridges. Most of the land is covered with a hardwood/pine forest. **maps:** USGS Sutton, Newville.

starting out: You can pick up maps of the lake and rec areas at the resource manager's office near the dam. Water and rest rooms are located at both rec areas. Unless you're camping, you have to pay the $2 entrance fee at Baker's Run Rec Area.

Alcohol is not allowed in the rec areas.

activities: Canoeing/Kayaking, Fishing, Hiking, Camping.

canoeing/kayaking: Sutton Lake's long, narrow profile—14 mi long, 1,440 acres, 40-mi shoreline—means that there's plenty of paddling room for canoeists and kayakers. And the lack of development along the forested shoreline means that the surroundings are quite scenic. About the only drawback to the lake is the presence of powerboats, which can be a nuisance, with their wakes and engines' incessant whine. Fortunately, the lake's shape keeps them pretty well dispersed. Access is at either of the campgrounds. The boat launch fee at Bee Run is $2.

fishing: Sutton Lake supports populations of most of the warm-water sport fish commonly found in WV. Among these are largemouth,smallmouth, and spotted bass; walleye; crappie; bluegill; and channel catfish. Anglers have most luck fishing from boats, as the lake's size demands that you be able to cover a lot of water. It's possible to fish from the shore at open areas in either of the rec areas.

Another popular angling option is to fish for the trout that are stocked in the dam's tailrace. The cold water flowing through the dam from the bottom of the lake provides the perfect habitat for these fish. Access is from the picnic area just below the dam.

hiking: Primitive conditions prevail throughout the WMA, where hiking is primarily on old roadbeds and hunter's trails. In all, there are more than 30 miles of trails to follow. These pass through the deep hardwood forest and skirt the lake's perimeter. Except during hunting season, the trail's are virtually deserted. A topo map and compass should be considered essential here to navigate the vast backcountry. The largest concentration of trails is accessible from CO-17. Hiking is moderate to strenuous.

camping: Camping around the lake is only permitted at 3 developed car campgrounds. The 2 located on the Elk River portion of the impoundment are described below.

The Baker's Run Campground has 124 sites arranged in a landscaped area not far from the dam. The sites are large and well spaced, but the lack of forest cover minimizes privacy. The campground is more popular with RV and trailer campers than with tenters. Since many of the sites are along the lakeshore, canoe or kayak camping would be possible. Each site has a picnic table and grill. Bathhouses with hot water are centrally located. The sites cost $12/night, $14 with hook-up.

Bee Run is a primitive car campground. 12 Sites are laid out in 2 rows in a small clearing. The sites are small and closely spaced; they provide no privacy at all. Each site has a picnic table and grill. Sites cost $5/night. Pit toilets and a hand water pump are the only facilities. The campground is open all year.

Kanawha State Forest

Located just south of Charleston, this 9,302-acre forest provides urban dwellers with a natural oasis and great opportunities for outdoor recreation. The chief draw in the forest is the seemingly endless network of multi-use trails. A total of more than 50 miles of pathways wind through the forest of hardwoods and hemlocks that blankets most of the backcountry. Hikers, mountain bikers, and cross-country skiers all make use of the trails. Backpacking or bikepacking are possible at either of two primitive backcountry sites. A scenic car campground is also located in the forest. Other recreational facilities include an outdoor swimming pool, archery range, and picnic area. In the backcountry, remnants of the coal-mining industry that once flourished here can still be seen. Anheuser Busch operated the mine at the end of the 19th century. Today the woodlands are quiet except for the sounds of songbirds and small gurgling creeks. White-tailed deer are frequently seen.

Charleston (N) is the closest city.

contact: Superintendent, Kanawha State Forest, Route 2, Box 285, Charleston, WV 25314; 304/558-3500.

getting there: From I-64 take exit 58A. Turn S onto US-119. Go 0.6 mi and bear R, continuing on US-119. Go 1.4 mi to Oakwood Rd. Turn L and go 1 mi to Bridge Rd. Turn R and go 0.6 mi to Connell Rd. Turn R and go 2.1 mi to Kanawha Forest Dr (SR-21). Turn L and go 2.4 mi to the SF entrance.

topography: The ridges and hollows of the SF lie at elevations between 704 ft and 1,500 ft. The terrain is steep in a few spots, but for the

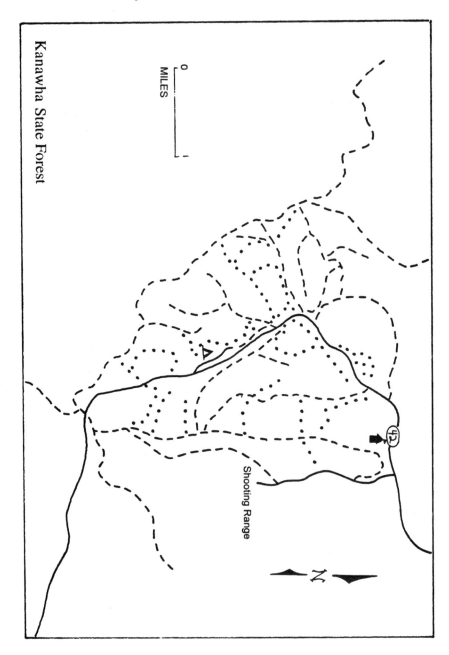

Kanawha State Forest

MILES

Shooting Range

most part it's only moderately rugged. The forest cover is comprised mostly of hardwoods, with some hemlocks also present. **maps:** USGS Charleston West, Racine.

starting out: You can pick up a trail map and other brochures in the main office. A pay phone is also there. Water, rest rooms, and other facilities are located in the picnic areas and swimming pool.
Alcohol is not allowed. Pets must be kept on a leash.

activities: Hiking, Mountain Biking, Camping, Cross-country Skiing.

hiking: There are just over 20 mi of hiking trails in the forest. Trails are laid out in a large network that covers most of the forest's acreage. In addition, 30 mi of old logging roads and rail grades augment the hiking opportunities. Hikes of almost any length are possible, and dozens of different loops can be formed by combining 2 or more trails. Highlights include the dense forest setting, wildlife, and remnants of the area's coal-mining history. Hiking trails follow narrow footpaths that are signed and blazed. Gated roads and rail grades are not blazed, but are easy to follow. Access to the trail network is from several points along the main forest road. Trail improvements include interpretive signs, shelters, and footbridges. Some creek crossings are unimproved. Hiking on the trails is easy to moderate, with just a few steep sections. Trail use is heavy.

mountain biking: Bikers can ride on 6 mi of hiking trails open to bikes or on the vast network of dirt and gravel roads—both gated and open to motor vehicles—that lace the forest's backcountry. Single-track is fairly limited in the forest, but many of the roads are little more than double-track ruts—that just happen to pass through some beautiful forest scenery. Rides of almost any length and difficulty can be put together by riding the trails and roads in combination. Riding is most technical and strenuous on the single-track trails; on the roads, it tends to be easy to moderate.

camping: Primitive backcountry camping is permitted in a couple of designated areas. There are no improvements to these areas. The hike in is about 1 mi to the Goose Pen Camp, 4 mi to the Mossy Rock Camp. Access is on a trail that begins behind the pool and group camping area. Permits, available from the forest office, are required before camping in these areas.
An attractive 46-site car campground is set in a narrow hollow below the main forest road and beside a small creek. The sites are

large and well-spaced, and a canopy of hemlocks and hardwoods provides shade. Each site comes with a picnic table and grill. The only drawback to the area is its proximity to the road. A shower /rest room building is centrally located. Rustic sites cost $11/night. Sites with hookups cost $14/night. The campground is open from Apr 15 to Oct 31.

cross-country skiing: In winter, some of the trails and all of the backcountry roads can be used as nordic ski tracks. The same trail map that's used for hiking and biking can be used to plot routes and locate trailheads. Skiing on the trails is mostly moderate. See above under *hiking* and *mountain biking* for more trail info.

Beech Fork State Park

Located south of Huntington, this 2,100-acre park occupies the slopes that rise from Beech Fork Lake. The lake itself is a US Army Corps of Engineers project that covers 720 acres. It was created in 1978 when a dam was built across Beech Fork. The park's main purpose is as the site of a vast car campground that provides overnight accommodations on the lake. It's designed primarily to appeal to RV campers—backcountry enthusiasts will find it a bit overwhelmingly large and crowded. The lake itself is extremely popular too, and days when there are only a handful of boats on the water are rare. A restriction against engines over 10 hp at least keeps things relatively quiet. The lake is stocked with several species of warm-water fish, and angling is one of the lake's major attractions. A handful of hiking trails in the state park round out the list of recreational opportunities.

Huntington (N) and Wayne (SW) are the closest towns.

contact: Superintendent, Beech Fork State Park, 5601 Long Branch Rd, Barboursville, WV 25504; 304/522-0303.

getting there: From I-64 in Huntington take exit 11. Turn E onto WV-10 and go 1.9 mi to Hughes Branch Rd (SR-43). Turn R and go 7.6 mi to the park entrance.

topography: The large lake is surround by rolling countryside. Elevation on the lake is 580 ft. The majority of the upper slopes are forested with hardwoods and pines. Areas around the lake have been cleared and landscaped. None of the hills rises to more than 1,000 ft. **maps:** USGS Lavalette, Winslow.

starting out: Trail maps and other info are available in the park office. Rest rooms and water are located inside.

activities: Camping, Fishing, Canoeing/Kayaking, Hiking.

camping: Camping is the main attraction in the SP. The vast car campground sprawls across 4 different areas, all on the lakeshore. Since the campground caters primarily to RVs and trailers, most of the forest cover has been removed. The result is a campground that offers little in the way of atmosphere or privacy. There are 270 sites in all. The sites are generally large and well spaced. Each site has a picnic table and grill. Rest rooms and separate shower facilities are at the center of each campground loop. Sites cost $14/night. Part of the campground is open year round.

canoeing/kayaking: The 720-acre lake is set amidst scenic surroundings of modest mountain swells covered in a forest of hardwoods and pines. There are 2 main branches, each with several small coves ideal for exploration from a canoe. Since boat engines are limited to 10 hp, the whine of powerboat engines so common on large recreational lakes isn't a concern here. It's actually possible to paddle in relative serenity, though the lake is popular and you certainly won't be alone. Boat ramps are located in the state park and at several other sites around the lake.

fishing: After boating, fishing is the most popular activity on the lake. Although fishing from shore is possible, you'll be happier if you can move around the lake more freely in a canoe. The main catches are largemouth bass, walleye, crappie, and channel catfish, all of which are stocked.

hiking: 3 trails cover 7 mi in the SP. The trails wind through the wooded uplands that rise from the lake's shoreline, providing a nice retreat from the often hectic goings-on in the campgrounds. Highlights are the lake views and the chance to observe some of the wildlife that inhabit the area. Trailheads are signed and the trails themselves are blazed. Hiking is easy to moderate. Access is from the main park road and the Moxley Branch Camping Area.

Cabwaylingo State Forest

8,123-acre Cabwaylingo State Forest is located in remote Wayne County only a short distance from the Ohio River. The unusual name is derived from the beginnings of the names of four regional counties: CABell, WAYne, LINcoln, and MinGO. Its main appeal is the lush, deep forest that clings to the mountain slopes and riots in the damp, cool coves. The forest is managed for timber production, oil extraction, wildlife habitat, and outdoor recreation. Facilities for the last are limited and fairly low-key. There's an outdoor swimming pool, picnic area, car campground, and rustic log cabins. Access to the backcountry is via 12 miles of hiking trails. Wildlife that inhabits the forest includes white-tailed deer, wild turkey, red fox, and ruffed grouse.

Wayne (N) and Logan (SE) are the closest towns.

contact: Superintendent, Cabwaylingo State Forest, Route 1, Box 85, Dunlow, WV 25511; 304/385-4255.

getting there: The SF entrance is located on Twelvepole Creek Rd (CO-35). Take WV-152 S from Dunlow to the forest entrance, L.

topography: W Fork Twelvepole Creek flows through the forest, draining the short, steep ridges. Forest cover is general, and consists of hardwoods, pines, and hemlocks. Elevations are between 700 ft and 1,500 ft. **maps:** USGS Wilsondale, Kiahsville, Webb.

starting out: You can pick up a trail map and other info about the forest at the main office. Water and rest rooms are located in the picnic area.

Alcohol is not permitted.

activities: Hiking, Fishing, Camping.

hiking: A network of 7 trails provides access to the backcountry of forested ridges and coves. Trails cover a total distance of 12.5 mi. Almost all of the trails are one-way dead ends that begin from the main road. Backtracking is necessary along most trails and loop options are few. The main attractions along the trails are the lush, remote forest setting, wildlife, and ridgetop views. The footpaths are well worn, blazed, and easy to follow. Trailheads are signed. Hiking is easy to moderate.

fishing: Twelvepole Creek is a small stocked trout creek that flows through the forest from one end to the other. Although the forest road follows it for this entire stretch, it is nevertheless quite attractive. Its gradient is mild and it flows over a very rocky bed. Cover is good in most places, despite large open areas on the bank closest to the road. Access is from the road.

camping: Camping in the forest is at a 34-site campground that's located on a wooded hilltop. Hardwoods and pines shade the large sites, and the whole area is very scenic. Privacy at the sites is excellent. Each site has a picnic table and fireplace. Rest room /shower facilities are centrally located. Sites cost $7/night. The campground is open all year.

lodging: Overnight visitors to the forest can stay at any of 13 rustic cabins. The furnished cabins can accommodate from 2 to 6 guests. Each cabin has a kitchen, bathroom with shower, and fireplace. Rates for 2 people start at $35/night in spring and fall. Rates are slightly higher in summer, slightly lower for stays of more than a night. The cabins are available from mid-Apr to Oct 31.

Chief Logan State Park

Situated on the western bank of the Guyandotte River, this park occupies 3,303 acres in the coal fields of the state's southwestern corner. A restored C&O steam locomotive is a reminder of the central, symbiotic role coal and the railroad played in the development of the region in the late eighteenth and early nineteenth centuries. The park encompasses a large forested backcountry as well as numerous recreational facilities. Among these are a car campground, riding stables, large picnic areas, amphitheater, outdoor swimming pool, miniature golf course, and tennis courts. A new wildlife center houses native species that are rarely seen in the wild. Backcountry recreation centers on the hiking trails, which wind through the forest and connect many of the park facilities.

Logan (SE) is the closest town.

contact: Superintendent, Chief Logan State Park, Logan, WV 25601; 304/792-7125; wvweb.com/www/chief_logan.html.

getting there: From downtown Logan, take WV-10 N 3.5 mi to the park entrance, L.

topography: The steep, rugged slopes of the region are more character-istic of a mountain region than a river valley. The ridges are short and jumbled, however, with none of the long, straight landforms common in the Alleghenies. Elevations are between 650 ft and 1,883 ft. Most of the park is forested, though large areas have been cleared and landscaped along the main park road. **maps:** USGS Chapmanville, Henlawson, Holden.

starting out: Trail maps and other park info are available in the park office. A pay phone is there as well. Water and rest rooms are available in the park.
  Alcohol is not allowed.

activities: Hiking, Camping.

hiking: 8 park trails cover a distance of 13 mi. Trails range from a short nature interpretive trail to a 3-mi ridgetop trail. Longer hikes are possible by stringing together 2 or more trails. Most of the trails don't stray very far from the park roads and centers of activity. Highlights are ridgetop views, remnants of old coal mines, and wildlife. The trails follow narrow footpaths that are blazed and easy to follow. Hiking is easy to moderate. Trail use is heavy. Trailheads are signed and located at the main centers of activity.

camping: Camping in the park is at a developed car campground that's located at the end of the park road. 24 sites are arranged on either side of the road and around the cul de sac. The setting at the end of a narrow valley is very scenic. The sites are large and well spaced, but the lack of any forest cover reduces privacy to a minimum. Each site has a picnic table and a grill. A bathhouse has showers and modern toilets. Sites cost $14/night. The campground is open from Apr 15 to Oct 31.

Panther State Forest

Panther State Forest covers 7,810 acres of forested ridges and coves in the rugged mountains of West Virginia's coal country. The forest is located in McDowell County, close to the borders of both Virginia and Kentucky. The forest remains in a largely primitive condition, with an extensive backcountry served by a small network of trails. Recreational facilities include an outdoor swimming pool, scenic picnic areas, and a small primitive car campground. The hardwood forest that blankets most of the acreage is a main attraction, with wild flowers, mosses, and ferns all abundant on the forest floor. An observation tower at the forest's highest point provides panoramic views of WV, KY, and VA.

Welch (E) is the closest town.

contact: Superintendent, Panther State Forest, Box 287, Panther, WV 24872; 304/938-2252.

getting there: From the jct of CO-1 and CO-3 in Panther, turn S onto CO-3 and go 0.4 mi to CO-1. Turn L and go. 4.5 mi to the forest entrance.

topography: The rugged terrain of short steep ridges and narrow hollows that characterizes this part of the state is present within the forest's borders. Forest cover grows dense on these steep slopes; hardwoods, hemlocks, and rhododendron are most prominent. Elevations are between 990 ft and 2,132 ft. **maps:** USGS Panther, Iaeger.

starting out: The forest is open daily from 6 AM to 10 PM. Begin your trip with a stop at the forest office, where you can pick up a trail map and guide. A hand water pump is located in the last picnic area.

Alcohol is not permitted.

activities: Hiking, Fishing, Camping.

hiking: There are 6 miles of trails in the forest. All are short, covering between 0.5 mi and 1.5 mi. Trails can be linked, however, to create longer hikes. Highlights along the trails are scenic overlooks, a fire tower, wildlife, and the dense forest. Most trails follow narrow footpaths; one trail follows the route of an old road bed. *Crane Branch Trail* is a self-guided interpretive trail with pamphlets available at the trailhead. Trails aren't blazed, but are easy to follow nevertheless. Trailheads are signed and are located along the main forest road. Hiking is moderate.

fishing: Panther Creek is a stocked trout stream that flows through the forest. It's a small to medium creek that descends on a mild to average gradient. Although the forest road follows it through the SF, it is nevertheless an attractive creek with good cover on both banks. Access is from pullouts along the road.

camping: A small primitive camping area with 6 sites is located beside the main forest road and Panther Creek. Sites are large and fairly well spaced. Scattered hardwoods and hemlocks provide shade, but privacy is minimal. Each site has a picnic table and a grill. Pit toilets and a hand water pump are located in the area. Sites cost $7/night.

Berwind Lake Wildlife Management Area

Berwind Lake WMA encompasses 18,000 acres in McDowell County. On the border with Virginia, it is the southernmost outdoor recreation area in West Virginia. It is one of the most remote as well, and few visitors to the WMA are from outside of the immediate vicinity. The centerpiece of the WMA and recreational focal point is a scenic 20-acre lake for fishing and boating. Picnic shelters, tables, and grills are located along its landscaped shoreline. A swimming pool and concession area offer additional family recreation. Hunting on the WMA is popular in the forested backcountry. Wildlife species present include white-tailed deer and wild turkey.

contact: Division of Natural Resources, 2006 Robert C. Byrd Dr, Beckley, WV 25801; 304/256-6947.

getting there: From downtown War, turn S onto Warrior Mine Rd (SR 12/4) and go 3.5 mi to the WMA entrance.

topography: The modest mountain ridges and hollows of the WMA are heavily forested by a mixed deciduous forest. Pines are present at the edges of woodland areas. Dry Fork flows through the WMA and drains the slopes to the E and W. **maps:** USGS War.

starting out: Facilities (water, rest rooms) are available at the pool and concession stand. There's no on-site information center in the WMA.

activities: Fishing, Canoeing.

fishing: Anglers fish on the 20-acre lake for both warm-water species and trout. There's plenty of room to cast from shoreline, most of which is open. Or you can launch a canoe and cover more water. Trout are stocked in the lake monthly. Boats with gasoline engines are not allowed on the lake.

canoeing: Although you wouldn't want to make a special trip just to paddle the small lake, it's an attractive setting for a short float. Especially if you bring a rod and reel and cast for some of the lake's fish.

Outfitters & Guides

The following businesses sell gear or offer services for the outdoor activities covered in this book. These stores are arranged here geographically, by city, following the general pattern of the book. Within a given city, listings are alphabetical. Fishing supply stores have not been included, as they are common throughout the state wherever fishing is popular. An alphabetical list of whitewater guides follows the geographical listings.

Key to some terms used below: camping=tents, backpacks, sleeping bags & clothes; paddling=canoes, kayaks & accessories; topos=USGS 7.5 minute topographic maps.

The Eastern Panhandle & Potomac Highlands

Harpers Ferry

Blue Ridge Outfitters—US-340; 304/725-3444
Daily: 8 AM–6 PM
Sells: paddling, fly fishing, topos; Rents: paddling, fly fishing, biking; Trips: paddling, fly fishing, biking

Seneca Rocks

The Gendarme—behind Harpers Store; 304/567-2600
M–F: 8:30 AM–5:00 PM, Sa: 8:30 AM– 9 PM, Su 8:30 AM–6 PM
Sells: camping,climbing, topos; Rents: climbing; Guides: climbing

Seneca Rocks Mountain Guides—across from Harpers Store; 800/451-5108
Daily: 8 AM–9 PM
Guides: climbing

Petersburg

Eagle's Nest Outfitters—Route 220; 304/257-2393
M–F: 8 AM–6 PM, Sa & Su: 7 AM–8 PM
Sells: camping, paddling, fly fishing, topos; Rents: camping, paddling, fly fishing; Trips: paddling, fly fishing

Davis

Blackwater Bikes—William Ave; 304/259-5286
M–Th: 10 AM–6 PM, F: 10 AM–8 PM, Sa: 9 AM–5 PM, Su: 10 AM–4 PM
Sells: camping, biking, topos; Rents: biking; Trips: biking

Timberline Mountain Bike Ctr—488 Timberline Rd; 304/866-4312
M–Th: 9 AM–7 PM, F–Su: 8 AM–8 PM
Sells: biking; Rents: biking; Trips: biking; Shuttles

St George

Blackwater Outdoor Center—Route 1 Box 239; 800/328-4798
Daily: 9 AM–5 PM
Sells: camping, climbing, paddling, biking, cross-country skiing, topos; Rents: paddling, biking, cross-country skiing; Trips: climbing, paddling, biking, cross-country skiing

Franklin

CMI Extreme Sports—1 Mill Rd; 304/358-7211
M–F: 9 AM–5 PM, Sa: 11 AM–5 PM
Sells: camping, climbing, biking, topos; Rents: climbing, biking; Trips: climbing, biking

Mill Creek

Appalachian Adventures—Route 219; 304/335-6221
M–F: 6 PM–9 PM, Sa & Su: 9 AM–9 PM
Sells: camping, climbing, fly fishing, topos; Rents: camping, climbing, canoes, fly fishing, biking; Trips: climbing, paddling, fly fishing, biking

Snowshoe

Snowshoe Mtn Biking Ctr—Snowshoe Mtn Resort; 304/572-1000
M–Sa: 9 AM–6 PM Su: 9 AM–6 PM (May–Nov)
Sells: biking; Rents: biking; Trips: biking

Slatyfork

Elk Mountain Outfitters—jct of US-219 & WV-66; 304/572-3000
M–Th: 10 AM–6 PM; F & Sa: 9 AM–7 PM; Su: 9 AM–5 PM
Sells: camping, fly fishing, biking, topos; Rents: fly fishing, biking
Trips: fly fishing

Elk River Touring Center–Route 219; 304/572-3771
Daily: 9 AM–6 PM
Sells: biking; Rents: biking, cross-country skiing; Trips: biking, cross-country skiing

Marlinton

Appalachian Sport—106 8th St; 304/799-4050
M–Sa: 9 AM–5 PM, Su: 12 PM–4 PM
Sells: camping, paddling, fly fishing, biking, topos; Rents: paddling, biking

Greenbrier River & New River Valleys

Fayetteville

Blue Ridge Outdoors—101 E Wiseman Ave; 304/574-2425
Daily: 8 AM–8 PM
Sells: camping, climbing, cross-country skiing, topos; Trips: climbing

Mountain State Kayak & Canoe—233 1/2 N Court St; 800/84KAYAK, 304/574-3120
Su, M, W & Th: 9 AM–6 PM; F & Sa: 9 AM–8 PM
Sells: paddling; Rents: paddling; Trips: paddling

Ridge Rider Mountain Bikes—103 Keller Ave; 304/574-BIKE
Daily: 9 AM–7 PM
Sells: biking, topos; Rents: biking, paddling; Trips: biking

Thurmond

Thurmond Supply—1 Main St; 304/469-2380
Daily: 9 AM–5 PM
Sells: biking; Rents: biking

Lewisburg

Free Spirit Adventures—104 Foster St; 304/645-2093
M–F: 9 AM–5 PM, Sa: 8:30 AM–12:30 PM, Su: by appointment
Sells: biking; Rents: biking; Trips: biking; Shuttles: *Greenbrier River Trail*

Outdoor Passage—Route 219 S in Quarry Rd Village; 304/645-6380
M: 12 PM–5 PM, Tu–Sa: 10 AM–5:30 PM
Sells: camping

Woods Water & Wheels—200 W Washington St; 304/645-5200
M–F: 10 AM–6 PM, Sa: 9:30 AM–4:30 PM
Sells: camping, climbing, paddling, biking; Rents: paddling, biking;
Trips: paddling, biking

Beckley

Bicycle Store—112 Marshall Ave; 304/253-5202
Daily: 8 AM–5 PM
Sells: biking

Bluefield

Backwoods Bike Shop—2009 Stadium Dr; 304/327-5797
M–F: 10 AM–6 PM, Sa: 9 AM–4 PM
Sells: biking

Ohio River Valley

Wheeling

The Outdoors Store—1065 Main St; 304/233-1080
M & F: 9 AM–7 PM, Tu–Th & Sa: 9 AM–5 PM
Sells: camping, climbing

Triadelphia

Wheelcraft Bicycles—RD 2, Box 375; 888/547-0202
M & F: 10 AM–7 PM, Tu–Th: 10 AM–5 PM, Sa: 10 AM–4 PM
Sells: biking

Morgantown

Adventure's Edge—131 Morgantown Rd; 304/296-9007
M: 9 AM–7 PM, Tu–F: 9 AM–6 PM, Sa: 9 AM–5 PM
Sells: camping, climbing, cross-country skiing, topos; Rents:
climbing

The Pathfinder—235 High St; 304/296-0076
M–F: 10 AM–6 PM, Sa: 10 AM–5 PM
Sells: camping, climbing, paddling, biking, cross-country skiing,
topos

Wamsley Cycles–345 Spruce St; 304/296-2447
M–F: 9:30 AM–7:30 PM, Sa: 9:30 AM–5:30 PM, Su: 9:30 AM–5 PM
Sells: biking

Whitetail Bicycles—206 High St; 304/291-2270
M: 10 AM–8 PM, Tu–F: 10 AM–6 PM, Sa: 10 AM–4 PM
Sells: biking; Rents: biking

Clarksburg
Holy Moses Bike Shop—645 W Pike St; 304/622-7235
M–F: 10 AM–5 PM, Sa: 10 AM–3 PM, by appointment
Sells: biking; Rents: biking

Bristol
RJ Cycles—Route 50 at Raccoon Rd Exit; 304/782-1144
Tu–Su: 10 AM–6 PM
Sells: biking; Rents: biking; Shuttles: North Bend Rail Trail

Vienna
Vienna Bicycle Shop—2910 Grand Central Avenue; 304/295-5469
M–F: 10 AM–6 PM, Sa: 10 AM–5 PM
Sells: camping, biking

Parkersburg
Bob's Bicycle Shop—2207 Camden Ave; 304/424-6317
M–F: 10 AM–6 PM, Sa: 10 AM–3 PM
Sells: biking

Pedals & Paddles—1100 Murdoch Ave; 304/422-2453
M–F: 10 AM–6 PM; Sa: 10 AM–3 PM
Sells: paddling, biking; Rents: paddling, biking; Shuttles

Uncle Bob's Outdoors—2311 Ohio Ave; 304/485-0014
M–Sa: 10 AM–8 PM; Su: 12 PM–6 PM
Sells: camping,climbing

Gassaway
Elk River Outfitters—298 S State St; 304/364-8253
Sa & Su: 8 AM–5 PM
Sells: paddling; Rents: paddling; Guides: paddling

Charleston

Charleston Bicycle Center—409 53rd St; 304/925-8348
Tu–F: 10 AM–6 PM, Sa: 9 AM–4 PM
Sells: biking

Mountain State Outfitters—4112 MacCorkle Av SE; 800/690-2234
M: 10 AM–8 PM, Tu–F: 10 AM–6 PM; Sa: 10 AM–5 PM
Sells: camping, climbing, paddling, fly fishing; Trips: fly fishing

Nitro

Currey's Bike Shop—107 21st St; 304/755-8794
M–F: 10 AM–6 PM, Sa: 9 AM–4 PM
Sells: biking, topos; Rents: biking

Hurricane

Mountain State Bicycles—107 Liberty Sq; 304/757-0308
M–F: 10 AM–8 PM, Sa: 10 AM–6 PM, Su: 11 AM–4 PM
Sells: biking

Barboursville

Pedal Power—2981 Cyrus Creek, US-60; 304/736-4902
M–Sa: 9 AM–8 PM
Sells: biking; Trips: biking

Huntington

Huntington Bicycle Center—623 16th St;304/525-5312
M–Sa: 10 AM–6 PM
Sells: biking

Jeff's Bike Shop—901 3rd Ave; 304/522-2453
M: 10 AM–8 PM, Tu–F: 10 AM–6 PM, Sa: 10 AM–5 PM
Sells: biking

Whitewater Guides

ACE Whitewater—800/SURFWVA
Rafting: Gauley, New

Blackwater Outdoor Center—800/328-4798
Rafting: Blackwater Canyon, Cheat, Dry Fork, Laurel Fork, Glady
Fork, Shavers Fork; Canoeing: Cheat

Cheat Mountain Outfitting—304/456-4023
Canoeing: Greenbrier, Tygart

Class VI River Runners—800/CLASSVI
Rafting: Gauley, New

Extreme Expeditions—888/GOEXTREME
Rafting: New

Greenbrier River Company—800/775-2203
Canoeing: Greenbrier River

Mountain River Tours—800/822-1386
Rafting: New, Gauley

New & Gauley River Adventures
Rafting: Gauley, New

New River Scenic Whitewater Tours—800/292-0880
Rafting: New

Rivermen—800/545-RAFT
Rafting: Gauley, New

Rivers—800/TRYRIVERS
Rafting: Cheat, Gauley, New; Canoeing

Songer Whitewater—800/356-RAFT
Rafting: Gauley, New

Wildwater—800/WVA-RAFT
Rafting: Gauley, New

Environmental Organizations

The organizations listed below are working to preserve the natural resources of West Virginia. Many of the national organizations have local chapters in which you're automatically enrolled when you join.

American Bass Association, Inc
2810 Trotters Trail
Wetumpka, AL 36092
205/567-6035

American Cetacean Society
PO Box 2639
San Pedro, CA 90731
310/548-6279

American Fisheries Society
5410 Grosvenor Ln
Suite 110
Bethesda, MD 20814
301/897-8616

American Hiking Society
P.O. Box 20160
Washington, DC 20041-2160
703/255-9304
www.outdoorlink.com

American Rivers
801 Pennsylvania Ave, SE
Suite 400
Washington, DC 20003
202/547-6900
gopher.igc.apc.org:70/11/orgs
/amrivers

American Trails
1400 16th St, NW
Washington, DC 20036
202/483-5611

Appalachian Trail Conference
P.O. Box 807
Harper's Ferry, WV 25425
304/535-6331

Bat Conservation International
PO Box 162603
Austin, TX 78716
512/327-9721
www.batcon.org

Boy Scouts of America
PO Box 152079
1325 W. Walnut Hill Ln
Irving, TX 75015
214/580-2000
www.scouting.org

Center for Marine Conservation
1725 DeSales St., NW
Suite 500
Washington, DC 20036
202/429-5609

The Cousteau Society, Inc
870 Greenbrier Circle
Suite 402
Chesapeake, VA 23320
804/523-9335

Defenders of Wildlife
1101 Fourteenth St, NW
Suite 1400
Washington, DC 20077
202/682-9400
www.defenders.org

Ducks Unlimited, Inc
One Waterfowl Way
Memphis, TN 38120
901/758-3825

Earth Island Institute
300 Broadway
Suite 28
San Francisco, CA 94133
415/788-3666
www.earthisland.org

Earthwatch
PO Box 403N
Mt Auburn St
Watertown, MA 02272
800/776-0188
gaia.earthwatch.org

Environmental Defense Fund
275 Park Ave S
New York, NY 10010
212/505-2100
www.edf.org

Federation of Fly Fishers
502 South 19th St
Suite 1
Bozeman, MT 59771
406/585-7592

Girl Scouts of America
420 Fifth Ave
New York, NY 10018
212/852-8000

Greenpeace, Inc
1436 U St, NW
Washington, DC 20009
202/462-1177
www.greenpeace.org

The Humane Society
2100 L St, NW
Washington, DC 20037
202/452-1100

International Game Fish Assoc
1301 E. Atlantic Blvd
Pompano Beach, FL 33060
305/941-3474

The Izaak Walton League
707 Conservation Ln
Gaithersburg, MD 20878
800/453-5463
www.iwla.org

League of Conservation Voters
1707 L St, NW
Washington, DC 20036
202/785-8683
www.lcv.org

League of Women Voters
1730 M St, NW
Washington, DC 20036
202/429-1965
www.electriciti.com/~lwvus

National Audubon Society
700 Broadway
New York, NY 10003
212/979-3000
www.audubon.org

National Geographic Society
17th & M Sts, NW
Washington, DC 20036
202/857-7000
www.nationalgeographic.com

National Organization for River
Sports
314 N 20th St
PO Box 6847
Colorado Springs, CO 80934
719/473-2466

National Parks & Conservation
Association
1776 Massachusetts Ave, NW
Washington, DC 20036
202/223-6722
www.npca.org

National Recreation & Park
Association
2775 S. Quincy St
Suite 300
Arlington, VA 22206

National Wild Turkey
Federation
P.O Box 530
Edgefield, SC 29824
803/637-3106

National Wildlife Federation
1400 16th St, NW
Washington, DC 20036
202/797-6800
www.nwf.com

Natural Resources Defense
Council
40 W 20th St
New York, NY 10011
212/727-2700
www.nrdc.org

The Nature Conservancy
1815 N Lynn St
Arlington, VA 22209
703/841-5300
www.tnc.org

Rails-to-Trails Conservancy
1400 Sixteenth St, NW
Suite 300
Washington, DC 20036
202/797-5400

The Sierra Club
730 Polk St
San Francisco, CA 94109
415/776-2211
www.sierraclub.org

Southern Environmental Law
Center
201 W Main St
Suite 14
Charlottesville, VA 22902
804/977-4090

Trout Unlimited
1500 Wilson Blvd
Suite 310
Arlington, VA 22209
703/522-0200
xenon.proxima.com

The Wilderness Society
900 Seventeenth St, NW
Washington, DC 20006
202/833-2300
www.wilderness.org

World Wildlife Fund
1250 24th St, NW
Washington, DC 20037
202/293-4800

Index

Order Form

Return to:
Out There Press
P.O. Box 1173
Asheville, NC 28802

Name: _____

Address: _____

City/State/Zip: _____

QTY	Guides to Backcountry Travel & Adventure	Price	Total
	North Carolina	$16	
	Virginia	$16	
	South Carolina	$15	
	West Virginia	$15	
	Other Titles		
	Sea Kayaking the Carolinas	$15	
	NC Residents add 6% sales tax		
	Shipping		$3
	Order Total		

Please enclose a check or money order for the total amount and return to the above address. Allow 2 weeks for delivery.